CHICAGO CUBS
Firsts

ALSO AVAILABLE FROM LYONS PRESS

Boston Red Sox Firsts
New York Mets Firsts
New York Yankees Firsts

CHICAGO
Cubs Firsts

The PLAYERS, MOMENTS, and RECORDS That Were FIRST in TEAM HISTORY

AL YELLON

FOREWORD BY PAT HUGHES

LP

LYONS
PRESS

Essex, Connecticut

An imprint of Globe Pequot, the trade division of
The Rowman & Littlefield Publishing Group, Inc.
4501 Forbes Blvd., Ste. 200
Lanham, MD 20706
www.rowman.com

Distributed by NATIONAL BOOK NETWORK

British Library Cataloguing in Publication Information available

Library of Congress Cataloging-in-Publication Data

Names: Yellon, Al, author.
Title: Chicago Cubs firsts : the players, moments, and records that were first in team history / Al
  Yellon.
Description: Essex, Connecticut : Lyons Press, [2024] | Series: Sports team firsts
Identifiers: LCCN 2023057261 (print) | LCCN 2023057262 (ebook) | ISBN 9781493074518
  (trade paperback) | ISBN 9781493074525 (epub)
Subjects: LCSH: Chicago Cubs (Baseball team)--History.
Classification: LCC GV875.C6 Y44 2024 (print) | LCC GV875.C6 (ebook) | DDC
  796.357/640977311--dc23
LC record available at https://lccn.loc.gov/2023057261
LC ebook record available at https://lccn.loc.gov/2023057262

∞™ The paper used in this publication meets the minimum requirements of American National
Standard for Information Sciences—Permanence of Paper for Printed Library Materials, ANSI/
NISO Z39.48-1992.

CONTENTS

FOREWORD

BASEBALL IS FULL OF FIRSTS! THE FIRST AFRICAN AMERICAN PLAYER. The first perfect game. The first triple play. And then there are firsts exclusive to the Cubs: The first night game at Wrigley Field. Their first no-hitter. The first Cubs game broadcast on radio and television. If you watch enough Cubs games, you're bound to see things you've never seen before, including more firsts, some of which are exclusive to Wrigley Field. Many stories like these, about firsts for the Cubs, are within the pages of this enjoyable read by Al Yellon.

I remember the first Cubs game I broadcast on Opening Day 1996 with Cubs legend and my good friend Ron Santo. Ronnie was the first known diabetic on the Cubs. I also remember the first broadcast I did with my current radio partner Ron Coomer in 2014. And I'll never forget the Cubs' World Series win in 2016, when I became the first person to say, "The Chicago Cubs win the World Series!" on the radio. I've called the first Cubs games for many managers over the years on Cubs radio, including Joe Maddon, David Ross, and now Craig Counsell.

The Cubs were not always named the Cubs. Their first moniker was White Stockings, and they had other nicknames before "Cubs" stuck. Did you ever wonder how that came to be and when they were first called by that now-famous name? That story is in these pages.

Have you ever wondered when the first triple play was turned by the Cubs? How about when the Cubs played their first spring training game in Mesa, Arizona? Who was the first player drafted by the Cubs to be elected to the Baseball Hall of Fame in Cooperstown? This book will examine many other firsts you might not have thought of. Among them: The first Cubs pinch-hitter to hit a grand slam and the first time the Cubs won a game by forfeit. You'll find those stories within the pages of this fun book and, for the first time, learn the exact date when the iconic "W" flag first flew atop the Wrigley Field scoreboard.

Even in 2023, 147 years after the Chicago National League franchise was founded, firsts for the team keep on coming. Something happened to the Cubs last year that had never before occurred. It was the first time three Cubs players won Gold Gloves—Ian Happ (left field), Dansby Swanson (shortstop), and Nico Hoerner (second base). For Nico, it was his first Gold Glove.

Baseball and the Cubs have a rich history, but there are many firsts still to come. Let's explore many of the firsts that have happened and the stories behind them, shall we? And away we go . . .

Pat Hughes
June 2024

Pat Hughes has been the radio play-by-play announcer for the Cubs since 1996 and was honored by the National Baseball Hall of Fame with the 2023 Ford Frick Award for excellence in baseball braodcasting.

INTRODUCTION

THE CHICAGO CUBS ARE LITERALLY THE VERY FIRST FRANCHISE OF what we now know as "Major League Baseball," so there's the first "first" we'll cover in these pages.

Now that statement comes with a few caveats. The Cubs as we know them today began in 1876 (and were commonly referred to with the name "White Stockings") upon the creation of the National League, although the franchise's history technically goes back to the predecessor National Association's creation in 1871. With the Great Chicago Fire happening later that year, that franchise went on hiatus for a while, and professional baseball's organization and schedule was rather chaotic until the NL's formation five years later.

The Cubs are the only Major League Baseball team that has existed from 1876 to 2024 in its current city, though with a few name changes along the line (and you'll find out more about that later!). Thus, if I were to present a book of "firsts" for what was long known to WGN-TV viewers as "The Chicago National League Ball Club," they would almost all be from before 1900.

So I'm not going to do Cubs "firsts" exclusively that way in these pages, although we will ride the baseball time machine into the 19th-century version of the sport from time to time. Back then, baseball was a game that would be mostly recognizable to you as a modern fan. But the game also had some significant differences from what we know in the 21st century, and we'll examine some of those as we go along. I'll also cover players from across the grand sweep of Cubs history over nearly the past 150 years because those men from decades and even over a century ago represented the same franchise you root for today, and they should not be forgotten.

In these pages, then, we'll look at various events, people, and places in Cubs history that were the first to occur in relation to a specific question about Cubs history. Did you ever wonder who was the very first Cub to record an official save? Retroactively, baseball historians have credited "saves" going back to the very beginning of the professional sport, so if we were to acknowledge that, we'd have to credit one of the three men given a "save" for the 1876 Cubs—Cal McVey, or two position players who were given one, Deacon White or John Peters.

But that's not what is being asked in the question posed. The question asks for the name of the pitcher who recorded the first *official* save for the Cubs. The save became an official baseball rule in 1969, so the answer to the question as posed is Ted Abernathy, who posted a save in a 7–4 win over the Pirates Tuesday, April 15, 1969, at Wrigley Field. (More on this later.)

It's a shame the Cubs didn't give Abernathy more save chances in 1969. Perhaps that would have helped that star-crossed team get some further wins down the stretch when Phil Regan ran out of gas.

Anyway, those are the types of firsts you'll learn about in this book, along with some stories about the players involved in creating them. (There will be more on Abernathy, in particular, a bit later.)

I hope you enjoy learning about little morsels of Cubs history that were the first of their kind. Let's begin at the very beginning, shall we?

THE 19TH-CENTURY CUBS

Okay, so the Cubs are one of the original National League franchises and the only one to remain in the same location since the league's creation in 1876.

Just who was the very first player to get a hit for the Cubs (then known as "White Stockings")?

Before we discuss this and I reveal the name of the first safe hit by a Chicago National League player, it's important to understand that the game as it was played nearly 150 years ago wasn't anything near the way baseball is played in the 21st century.

Yes, there were nine fielders and nine hitters, and there were nine innings and three outs per inning. The team with the most runs at the end of those nine innings (or extra innings if needed—with no placed runner!) was the winner.

You wouldn't, however, have recognized how a pitcher delivered the ball to the hitter in 1876. Today, a pitcher stands on a raised mound 60 feet, six inches from home plate and has to keep one foot on a slab called the "rubber" while throwing a pitch overhand (or, occasionally, sidearm, or, more rarely, underhand).

In 1876, pitchers threw on flat ground from a "box" located 50 feet from the plate, and the pitcher could get a running start into that box before delivering the pitch. Also, the batter was permitted to call for a "high" pitch (above the waist but below the shoulders) or a "low" pitch (below the waist but above the knees).

Pitchers also had to throw underhand. Sidearm, three-quarters, and overhand deliveries weren't legalized in the National League until 1884.

Last, it took nine balls, rather than the current four, to draw a walk.

Having said all that, the Chicago National League club that would eventually become the Cubs as we know them first took the field in a league game at Louisville on Tuesday, April 25, 1876. The *Chicago Tribune* reported that, rather than automatically have the home team bat last as is the rule today, a coin toss was held, and the Chicago team won, so they chose to bat last. Home teams occasionally batted first, for presumed strategic reasons, as late as the first decade of the 20th century, and this practice was not outlawed by rule until 1950.

In that first game for the Chicago NL franchise, neither team scored in the first, and Louisville went down scoreless in the second. Outfielder Paul Hines then led off the bottom of the second inning. From the *Tribune*: "He hit hard at the first one, and sent it to Carbine so briskly that he couldn't hold it, giving Hines a life."

That "life" was the first hit in franchise history. Hines advanced to third on a single by pitcher/manager Al Spalding and two outs later scored the first run of the game on a ground ball that was fielded by Louisville first baseman Joe Gerhardt, but it was thrown away for an error.

Thus, Paul Hines not only had the very first hit in Cubs franchise history but also scored the very first run. Chicago defeated Louisville that day 4–0. The Chicago NL franchise won the league pennant with a 52–14 record, six games ahead of Hartford and St. Louis, who tied for second.

A week after Hines recorded the first hit in proto-Cubs history, Ross Barnes hit the first home run for the franchise. It came in the team's fourth game, a 15–9 win at Cincinnati. On what the *Tribune* called "a cold and disagreeable day," Barnes "made the finest hit of the game, straight down the left field to the carriages, for a clean home run." It gave Chicago a 9–4 lead. Barnes went 3-for-6 that afternoon, scoring four runs.

Had there been Most Valuable Player voting in 1876 as we understand it today, Barnes would certainly have been the runaway winner in the National League. He had won two previous batting titles in the National Association, the NL's predecessor, and by any measure he would have been considered among the league's first "superstars."

2

While Hines batted .331 that season, the best Chicago NL hitter was Barnes, who led the league with a .429 batting average (and also led the league in runs, hits, doubles, triples, walks, on-base percentage, and slugging percentage). Barnes did that by taking advantage of something else you wouldn't recognize today, commonly called the "fair-foul rule."

That rule stated that if a ball first hit in fair territory, it was in play no matter where it went after that, even if it landed in foul territory. Barnes became quite adept at hitting balls that would bounce fair, then go foul out of reach of any fielder, and thus reached first base more often than any other 1876 NL hitter. His batting average of .429 was 63 points higher than any other batter, and his .462 on-base percentage was nearly 80 points better than anyone else's. He walked 20 times; pitchers must have been afraid to throw strikes to him. No other NL hitter that year walked more than 15 times.

The fair-foul hit was soon banned, and Barnes' performance dropped off the following year. He hit just .272 in 22 games, but the rule change might not have been the only reason for Barnes' decline. He also suffered from a mysterious illness that sapped his energy. After the 1877 season the proto-Cubs let him go, but he wasn't quite done with the Chicago National League club. In 1878, he sued them for not paying his salary when he was ill the previous year, becoming the first professional player to sue his employer. A Cook County, Illinois, judge dismissed the suit later that year, according to Barnes' SABR biography.

After his playing career, Barnes settled in Chicago and was at various times reported to have had a membership in the Chicago Board of Trade, working in the hotel business, and also as an accountant. He died May 5, 1915, at the age of 64.

The Cubs played six doubleheaders in 2022, three of them due to games rescheduled after the owners' lockout.

When was the first time the Cubs played two games in one day?

Doubleheaders were fairly uncommon in the early days of baseball, largely because team owners didn't feel as if they could afford to give away their product—two for the price of one. When games were postponed by rain in the early days of the National League, clubs would simply reschedule them for a convenient off day, at times even changing the location of a makeup game, as happened in September 1877 when the Chicago NL franchise was rained out at Hartford. The field at Hartford was unplayable, so the game was played at New Haven, about 40 miles away.

This wasn't uncommon in the early days of the National League, including swapping games between cities. In August 1878, for example, a Chicago-Providence game was rained out in Providence. It was made up in Chicago on September 4.

Two years later, a similar rainout happened in Chicago for a game between the then–White Stockings and the Troy Trojans on September 1. The *Chicago Tribune* reported that due to "the rain of Wednesday, and the inability of Troy to remain over another day on account of home engagements," the teams agreed to play two games on Thursday, September 2, 1880, which is the date of the very first doubleheader for the Chicago NL franchise now known as the Cubs.

Like many doubleheaders today, these games were played with separate admissions at Lake Front Park, today the site of Millennium Park at the corner of Michigan and Randolph in downtown Chicago.

The *Tribune* reported that the game of "the forenoon, beginning at 11 o'clock," was won by Chicago 1–0. Abner Dalrymple singled, went to third on a double by George Gore, and scored on an infield out in the first inning, and that was the only scoring of the game. Proto-Cubs hurler Larry Corcoran, who had thrown a no-hitter two weeks earlier and would later throw two more for the ballclub, scattered seven Troy hits. The game was "witnessed by less than 100 people," according to the *Tribune*.

Bad Chicago weather nearly caused another postponement of the afternoon affair, but it was completed in front of about 500 people, this time with a Troy victory by a 5–1 score. As was common in those days, Corcoran made the start again—he would start 63 of the 86 games in 1880 and throw 536 1/3 innings—and held Troy without a hit through five innings. The Trojans scored a run in the first inning and another in the fifth due to White Stockings errors, and after Chicago closed the gap to 2–1 in the top of the sixth—remember, home teams didn't always bat last back then—Troy scored three off Corcoran in the bottom of the inning and cruised to victory.

The White Stockings got the last laugh in 1880, though, finishing with a 67–17 record and winning the National League pennant by 15 games over Providence.

The Cubs wouldn't play "split" doubleheaders again until 1927, when they would play holiday twin bills with a morning game at 10:30 a.m. and an afternoon game at 3 p.m. This scheme lasted five seasons, through 1931, then Wrigley Field doubleheaders returned to single-admission status. For the rest of the 1930s, doubleheaders remained popular, largely due to the Depression, as teams used "two for the price of one" to incentivize fans to come to games in years where they had little money. This continued in the World War II years due to travel restrictions and gasoline rationing and stuck around for a while in the years immediately following the war. The doubleheader mania came to a peak in 1944, when the Cubs played 39 of them—accounting for just about half (78) of the 157 games played (three ties included). That year also saw the most doubleheaders in a season at Wrigley Field, 20 in all. Twelve of those twin bills fell after September 1, seven of them forced by bad weather. The 1944 Cubs wound up playing 35 games in the 31 days from September 1 through October 1, with a good 21–14 record, perhaps presaging the 1945 pennant-winning Cubs team.

In late August 1967, bad weather in New York forced the postponement of an entire three-game series between the Cubs and the Mets. Because the teams didn't have any more games scheduled in New York, the entire three-game set was moved to Wrigley Field the following week. Between those three makeup games and another Wrigley rainout from June that had been rescheduled, the teams played a seven-game series with doubleheaders on three consecutive days, September 1, 2, and 3. Then the Cubs played a *scheduled* Labor Day doubleheader against the Dodgers on September 4. The Cubs won five of the eight doubleheader games, but perhaps foreshadowing his overuse of Randy Hundley in 1969, manager Leo Durocher made Hundley catch every inning of seven of those eight games, one of them 11 innings, and brought him in for defense for the last three innings of the other game. Durocher did this to Hundley again in 1968, when the Cubs played three doubleheaders in four days from July 4 to 7. Hundley caught every inning of six of those seven games, getting a break only in the second game on July 4, one of six games all season he didn't start. That was followed by the All-Star break, after which Hundley again caught every inning of both games of a doubleheader on July 11. Hundley wound up starting 156 games at catcher, catching every inning of 147 of them, and catching in 160 of the Cubs' 162 games, playing 1,385 1/3 (95.3 percent) of the team's 1,453 1/3 innings in 1968.

Over time, doubleheaders faded away as game times lengthened, fans didn't want to stay that long at the ballpark, teams didn't want to give away "two for the price of one," and abuse of players such as what Durocher did to Hundley took a toll on players' health.

The last scheduled single-admission doubleheader at Wrigley Field was played on Monday, July 4, 1983, against the Montreal Expos. The Cubs were swept in that one, and the most recent single-admission doubleheader of any kind at Wrigley happened on Thursday, August 3, 2006, against the Arizona Diamondbacks, played in the afternoon. That occurred because a game against the D-Backs the previous night was rained out and there was no other way to reschedule the postponement. The Cubs and Arizona split that pair, the Cubs losing the opener 10–2 and winning the nightcap 7–3.

Split doubleheaders returned to Wrigley Field after the Cubs received permission from the city of Chicago, in a revised night game ordinance, to play such double dips beginning in 2002, commensurate with an increase in the allowed number of night games from 18 to 30. The first such split doubleheader was played on Monday, September 2, 2002, against the Milwaukee Brewers, and the Cubs split it, losing the opener 4–2, winning the nightcap 17–4.

Three doubleheaders were played at Wrigley Field in the 2020 pandemic season with only a 45-minute gap between games, but those can't really be considered "single-admission" because no fans were permitted to attend.

Twenty-eight different Cubs have hit three home runs in a game. Sammy Sosa has the most three-homer games as a Cub with six, which is tied for the MLB record with Johnny Mize and Mookie Betts, through the end of the 2023 season.

Who was the first Cub to hit three home runs in a game?

This question has a simple answer, but it comes with so many caveats we might as well put a baseball-sized asterisk on it.

The answer is Ed Williamson (sometimes also referred to during his playing career as "Ned" Williamson), who accomplished this feat on Friday, May 30, 1884, when the Cubs were still known as the Chicago White Stockings. He did it against the Detroit Wolverines at Lake Front Park in downtown Chicago, and that park is the singular reason for Williamson's accomplishment. Before I tell you about Williamson's achievement, which was also the first three-homer game by any National League player, a bit of ballpark history is required.

The Chicago National League Ball Club had moved into that park in 1883, a renovation and enlargement of their previous ballpark on the same site. The location was what is now the northwest corner of Millennium Park in downtown Chicago, the infield and stands located just north of where Cloud Gate (popularly called "The Bean") now stands. The left-field corner of the park was where the southeast corner of Michigan Avenue and Randolph Street is now located.

Because there were then railroad tracks running to the east of this park, it took a very elongated form, with the wall in the left-field corner only 180 feet from the plate and the same in the right-field corner just 196 feet away, the shortest-ever corner dimensions for any MLB park.

As a result, in 1883 balls that went over those walls were ruled to be ground-rule doubles. And, in fact, that year the Chicago NL team hit a *lot* of doubles—277, to be exact, in 98 games. The next-most was 209, by Boston.

Cap Anson's men had won three straight pennants from 1880 to 1882 and four titles in the seven-year history of the NL through 1882. But in 1883 a 59–39 record, not terrible, was good only for a second-place finish, four games behind pennant-winning Boston.

Something had to be done, thought Anson, and so it was decreed that in 1884, those ground-rule doubles over the walls at Lake Front Park would be declared home runs.

What could possibly go wrong?

Well, a lot could, and did. And, in fact, one could argue it went right for the White Stockings. In 112 games they smashed 142 home runs—103 more than second-place Buffalo. Four Chicago NL players (Williamson, 27; Fred Pfeffer, 25; Abner Dalrymple, 22; and Anson, 21) hit more than 20—two *teams* (Cleveland, 16; and Philadelphia, 14) didn't hit 20 home runs in 1884. The most hit by any non-Chicago player was 14, by Buffalo's Dan Brouthers. Twenty-five of Williamson's league-leading 27 dingers were hit at the home sweet home of Lake Front Park.

Anyway, you can probably see where this is going. While all those home runs helped the proto-Cubs to 842 runs, the most in the league by 134, the tiny dimensions also wreaked havoc with the pitching staff, which allowed a league-leading 83 home runs (no one else served up more than 46) and 646 runs allowed, the latter somewhat surprisingly only fourth worst in the eight-team league. The result was a 62–50 record and a fifth-place finish.

Williamson's three-homer game happened with the team entering that Friday afternoon's doubleheader with a poor 7–14 record. Chicago defeated Detroit 11–10 in the first game, and the *Tribune* reported about Williamson's performance in the nightcap: "It was a great day for Williamson, who for his five times at bat had the great record of three home runs and one two-base hit, besides catching without a flaw."

Errors were a big part of the game back then—the White Stockings made six in that game—so a note about an errorless game was certainly worth making. Chicago NL completed the doubleheader sweep by winning 12–2. Incidentally, Williamson served as catcher in his three-homer game, though he was primarily a third baseman.

Clearly, the dimensions of the park were beyond ridiculous and the rule allowing a 180-foot blast—just twice the distance from home plate to third base—to be a home run was absurd. After 1884, the National League required minimum outfield wall distances of 210 feet, but it didn't matter for Anson's ballclub, as they were forced out of Lake Front Park in 1885 when the land the park sat on was given to the federal government and mandated for noncommercial use. The team moved to the West Side of Chicago in 1885, and they would play most of their time in that part of town for the following 30 years. In their first year on the West Side, they again became NL pennant winners with an 87–25 record. They led the league in home runs again—but with 54, just twice as many as Williamson alone had hit in 1884.

As for Williamson, he never hit more than nine home runs in any season after 1884, and he died in 1894 of complications from tuberculosis, aged just 36.

No one would hit more than 27 home runs in a major-league season after 1884 until someone hit 29 in 1919. You might have heard of him—some guy named Babe Ruth.

In the post-1900 modern era of baseball, no Cub hit three home runs in a game until Hack Wilson did it in the offensive-explosion 1930 season. It happened on Saturday, July 26, 1930, at Philadelphia, and the Phillies were on their way to allowing a league-leading 142 home runs. Wilson smashed a two-run homer in the first inning, matched it with another two-run shot in a seven-run second, and added a solo shot in the top of the eighth, also drawing a walk and scoring four times in a 16–2 Cubs win. The *Chicago Tribune* called him "charmed" by a pregame

The 1885 Chicago White Stockings. Ed Williamson is second from left in the front row.

performance by a band on the field, saying he was "marching jauntily" and perhaps inspired to his three-homer afternoon. The homers were the 30th, 31st, and 32nd of what would become a team- and league-record 56-homer season.

The Cubs have made many trades in their history, some great (Ryne Sandberg and Larry Bowa for Ivan de Jesus), some awful (Lou Brock for Ernie Broglio), and trading players between teams is an accepted part of the game.

When did the Cubs make their first trade, and who were the players involved?

While trading players is now an accepted part of professional baseball, things weren't always that way. For about the first decade after the formation of the National League in 1876, players who went from one team to another were generally exchanged for some amount of cash. In large part, this was because certain owners got into financial trouble and figured the cash would be worth more to them than the players' future services.

Further, while the reserve clause binding players to teams had been instituted in 1879, it didn't have that effect in its early years, unlike the standard practice for many decades basically renewing player contracts for perpetuity. That, of course, eventually led to player strikes and collective bargaining and the free agent system we have today.

Thus, a player would have had to approve going from one team to another, and any player coming back in return would have to give the same approval. Baseball also wasn't the big money business in the 19th century that it is now. Men often felt they could make better livings doing something else, so they had that as possible leverage over playing for one team or another.

It's in that context that the swap that is generally recognized as the first between major-league teams happened on November 15, 1886. On that date, the Cincinnati Red Stockings of the American Association sent catcher Jack Boyle and $400 (roughly $13,000 in 2024) to the St. Louis Browns in exchange for outfielder Hugh Nicol.

This deal unleashed a flurry of small trades that offseason, and the Cubs—then, of course, known as the White Stockings—made a swap on April 21, 1887, about 10 days before that season opened. In that trade, they sent right-handed pitcher Jim McCormick to the Pittsburgh Alleghenys for left-handed pitcher/outfielder George Van Haltren and $2,000 (roughly $64,000 in 2024). This is the first recognized trade in the history of the Cubs franchise.

This trade did not get completed without some controversy. Van Haltren, born in St. Louis, moved with his family to the Bay Area in California as a child, and as he grew up, he became a good baseball player, good enough that he began to attract the attention of local scouts in the San Francisco area. The Pittsburgh club acquired his rights in February 1887, but per Van Haltren's SABR biography, he did not want to report to Pittsburgh because his mother was seriously ill. Instead he remained in California playing for the local team.

That prompted the Alleghenys to arrange the trade with the Chicago NL club. The SABR biography noted:

> *Unintimidated by threats to have him blacklisted issued by Chicago club owner A.G. Spalding, Van Haltren remained close to home until his mother died in late May 1887. Only then did Van Haltren report to Chicago and sign the $1,400-a-season contract that awaited him.*

That was pretty good money for a 21-year-old in 1887, equivalent to about $45,000 in 2024.

Van Haltren pitched in 20 games (11 starts) for the White Stockings in 1887, posting a 3.86 ERA, and did about the same the following year, with 30 appearances (24 starts) and a 3.52 ERA. Also serving as an outfielder for those two years as well as 1889 (with no pitching appearances that year), Van Haltren batted .290/.367/.415 with 16 home runs in 260 games, pretty good power numbers for those days.

But that ended Van Haltren's tenure in Chicago. As did quite a number of players, he "jumped" to the short-lived Players' League in 1890, a league founded by John Montgomery Ward in an attempt to give players more control over their fates. It lasted just one year, and Van

Haltren switched teams again, this time to Baltimore of the American Association. When that league folded after 1891, the Baltimore franchise was given a spot in the National League, but Van Haltren didn't even play a full 1892 season there; instead, he was reacquired by the same Pittsburgh franchise that had traded him to Chicago five years earlier. Following the 1893 season Van Haltren was purchased by the New York Giants, and he played the rest of his career there, batting .321/.384/.414 in 1,227 games over 10 seasons in New York.

Leaving the major leagues then at age 37, Van Haltren returned to the West Coast and played 1,046 games for Seattle and Oakland in the Pacific Coast League from 1904 to 1909, batting .255 with nine home runs before retiring at age 45. He also managed the Oakland team for much of his tenure there from 1905 to 1909 and later scouted for the Pirates. He passed away in his home in Oakland on September 29, 1945, aged 79.

Through the end of the 2023 season, a major-league cycle (a single, double, triple, and home run) has been accomplished 344 times.
Who was the first Cub to hit for the cycle?
A Cub went cycling before the team was even called "Cubs."

Jimmy Ryan of the then–Chicago White Stockings hit for the cycle on Saturday, July 28, 1888, against the Detroit Wolverines at West Side Park, the first of two parks for the Chicago National League franchise located on the West Side of Chicago. About 10,000 "yelled themselves hoarse," according to the *Chicago Tribune*.

Ryan had first come to the major leagues in Chicago in 1885, and 1888 was his second full season as a White Stockings outfielder, though at times in his career he also played shortstop and pitched.

In this 1888 game, Ryan singled in the first inning and stole second and third. In the second, he tripled, the ball eventually landing "among the benches near the Congress Street wall," and he followed that with a solo home run in the fourth. He tripled for a second time in the fifth inning and hit a double, completing the cycle and a 5-for-5 afternoon in a game won by Chicago by a modern-day football score, 21–17. Ryan also reached base on a two-base error in this slugfest, in which he also pitched.

He is the only player in major-league history to record a pitching win and hit for the cycle in the same game—though Shohei Ohtani came close to doing that in 2023 and might match that feat someday.

Ryan had what was probably his best season in 1888. He hit .332/.377/.515 in 129 games and led the National League in hits (182), doubles (33), home runs (16), slugging percentage, and total bases (283), and had there been an MVP Award back then, he certainly would have won it.

Ryan bolted for the new Players' League in 1890, but when that circuit folded after just one year, he returned to the Chicago NL franchise and played there for another decade, producing well but never quite matching his 1888 performance, though he would hit for the cycle again on July 1, 1891, against the Cleveland Spiders, going 4-for-5 with three runs scored in a 9–3 win. The *Chicago Tribune* described that day as "one continual and lovely picnic for Jimmy Ryan," in so doing becoming the first (and still only) Cubs player to hit for the cycle more than once.

Later in his career, Ryan became a hero at a baseball game in another and much more important way. A fire broke out in the grandstand at West Side Grounds on August 5, 1894, and Ryan's quick action, along with his teammate Walt Wilmot, in knocking down a wire fence with their bats, is credited with saving hundreds of lives in what otherwise might have been a terrible disaster.

While Ryan is not in the Hall of Fame, he retired after 1903 with stellar numbers: .308/.375/.444 with 2,513 hits, 118 home runs, and 419 stolen bases. The hits total is the ninth-largest of anyone who retired before 1911. He also had a reputation as a stellar defensive outfielder and remains to this day the National League's career leader in outfield assists with 375. He is arguably the best 19th-century player not enshrined in Cooperstown and does have a plaque in the Cubs Hall of Fame, recently installed in the concourse underneath the left-field bleachers at Wrigley Field.

Ryan continued to play baseball in the minor leagues until age 45, then settled in Chicago, where he died of a heart attack in 1923. His grave was unmarked for decades until a cooperation between the Cubs and the Society for American Baseball Research had a headstone made and installed at Calvary Cemetery in Evanston, Illinois. A ceremony was held there on November 30, 2022, a fine remembrance for a player who should not be forgotten.

Here are all the other Cubs who have hit for the cycle:

Hack Wilson, vs. Philadelphia Phillies at Wrigley Field, June 23, 1930

Babe Herman, vs. Cardinals at St. Louis, September 30, 1933

Roy Smalley, vs. Cardinals at Wrigley Field, June 28, 1950

Lee Walls, vs. Cincinnati Reds at Wrigley Field, July 2, 1957

Billy Williams, vs. Cardinals at St. Louis, July 17, 1966 (second game)

Randy Hundley, vs. Houston Astros at Wrigley Field, August 11, 1966 (first game)

Ivan de Jesus, vs. St. Louis Cardinals at Wrigley Field, April 22, 1980

Andre Dawson, vs. San Francisco Giants at Wrigley Field, April 29, 1987

Mark Grace, vs. San Diego Padres at Wrigley Field, May 9, 1993

In modern baseball, forfeited games are rare. There have been just three in the past 50 seasons, the last one in 1995.

When was the first time the Cubs won a game by forfeit?

While teams generally don't win or lose by forfeit anymore, these sorts of things used to be commonplace in the early days of baseball, largely because of disputes over umpire decisions or teams simply refusing to do what umpires said they must do by the rules.

Going into the game of Friday, September 25, 1891, the Cubs, then generally known by the nickname "Colts," were leading the National League by two games and hosting the Pittsburgh (then usually spelled "Pittsburg") Pirates at the first iteration of West Side Grounds.

The score was 4–2 Pirates going into the bottom of the eighth inning. Colts player/manager Cap Anson led off the inning with a home run (it "negotiated the left wall," per the *Chicago Tribune* recap of the game) to make the score 4–3.

After the next hitter, Cliff Carroll, made the first out of the inning, Colts third baseman Tom Burns hit a ball that went off the shin of Pirates pitcher James "Pud" Galvin. Burns made it to second base with a double.

Fred Pfeffer was the next hitter and, according to the *Tribune*, fouled off a number of pitches before Burns took off for third. At that point, Pfeffer hit a ground ball to Pirates second baseman Lou Bierbauer. Burns did not hesitate and rounded third and tried to score. Burns, on a head-first slide, avoided the tag of Pirates catcher George "Doggie" Miller and was called safe by umpire James McQuade.

This caused a tremendous "row," wrote the *Tribune* in the terminology of the time, but McQuade did not change his call. The game was tied.

Miller then "grew abusive," said the *Tribune* article, and was ejected from the game. However, Pirates manager Bill McGunnigle didn't agree with this decision and told Miller to go back into the game. Miller stayed on the field as McQuade "called for a watch," meaning a timepiece and, having acquired one, told Miller, "If you are not on the bench in one minute, I will give the game to Chicago."

Miller stayed on the field and, true to his word, McQuade then awarded the game to the Colts by forfeit, the first such win in Chicago NL franchise history. The Pirates protested the game, claiming Rule 26 of baseball at the time gave such players "five minutes" to obey such an umpire's order. But another section of the rules said that games could be forfeited if "one side fails to resume playing one minute after the umpire calls 'Play.'"

The forfeit stood and the Colts had a 9–0 victory, by the custom that a forfeited game has such a score. The statistics stood as played, and the game is listed with its 4–4 score at baseball-reference.com.

However, even though the Colts led the league by two games after the forfeit win, they collapsed immediately thereafter. A game between the same two teams the following day ended in a 6–6 tie due to darkness, and after that the Colts lost five of their final six games, while the Cincinnati Reds went 6–0. The Colts finished second, 3 1/2 games out of first place.

The Chicago NL franchise had two previous forfeits, both losses. The first happened in 1876 to St. Louis (left the field in protest of a call) and the other in 1884 to Buffalo (refused to continue after protesting an out call). They also lost two other pre-1900 forfeits after that 1891 forfeit victory: in 1892 to Pittsburgh, stalling for a hoped rainout and in 1894, refusing to play at Louisville because they didn't like the baseballs provided by the home team.

In the modern era, here are the forfeited games in which the Cubs have been involved:

August 7, 1906: The Cubs were awarded a game by forfeit over the Giants in New York. The previous day, an umpiring call went against the home team and the umpire, Jim Johnstone, had to have a police escort out of the park. The next day Johnstone didn't show up, and the other umpire, Bob Emslie, also refused to take the field. When the Giants appointed a player as an umpire—the custom at the time—the Cubs refused to take the field and the game was forfeited to New York. But it was learned that police had asked that the umpires not show up for fear of a riot, and NL President Harry Pulliam reversed the decision and forfeited the game to the Cubs.

October 5, 1907: Several Cubs angrily protested a call in the fourth inning of this game against the Cardinals in St. Louis, and manager Frank Chance and three other players were ejected. Johnny Evers had been ejected in the previous inning. Umpire Cy Rigler told Chance to put nine players on the field and he did, but several of them were pitchers. The game, which the Cubs led 2–0 at the time, was forfeited to St. Louis. It was the first game of a doubleheader on the second-to-last day of the season, and the Cubs had clinched the pennant long before. The second game was played without incident.

July 6, 1913: The Cubs and Cardinals had agreed beforehand that a doubleheader on this date would end by 5 p.m. so the Cubs could catch a train for their next series in New York. The second game began at 3:45, and with the Cubs trailing 5–1 by the second inning, they began to stall in an attempt to have 5:00 come before the game could be made official. At one point, manager Johnny Evers called on a pinch-hitter for pitcher Orval Overall, but the player was in the clubhouse. At-bats were taken slowly, and as if there were a modern-day pitch timer used, umpire Mal Eason began calling strikes when the hitter further stalled. In the third inning, Ivey Wingo of the Cardinals bunted. Cubs pitcher Ed Reulbach threw wildly to first base, and as Wingo began running around the bases, Cubs fielders made no attempts to put the runner out. At that point, umpire Eason called the game, awarded to St. Louis by forfeit, with fans "jeering" the home team, per the *Chicago Tribune*, and as Eason left the field, hundreds "patted him on the back" and "cheered him for his action."

July 18, 1916: This game at Weeghman Park against Brooklyn (then known as "Robins" after their manager, Wilbert Robinson) was tied 4–4 in the top of the 10th. The visitors had runners on first and third with nobody out and again a "pitch timer" type of violation was called when umpire William "Lord" Byron thought Cubs pitcher Hippo Vaughn took too long to throw a pitch. Cubs manager Joe Tinker came to the field to argue, claiming Brooklyn was "stealing signs" and Vaughn simply wanted to tell his catcher about that. Tinker refused to leave the field, even when police were summoned, so Byron forfeited the game to the Robins. This is the most recent forfeited game the Cubs franchise has been involved in.

INDIVIDUAL CUBS ACHIEVEMENTS

In all of major-league history, there have been just 15 unassisted triple plays.

Who was the first Cub to turn an unassisted triple play?

This feat was accomplished by Cubs shortstop Jimmy Cooney against the Pittsburgh Pirates in the bottom of the fourth inning of the first game of a doubleheader at Pittsburgh on Monday, May 30, 1927. Two future Hall of Famers were involved!

The Pirates were leading 5–4 entering that inning. Lloyd Waner led off with a single, and Clyde Barnhart walked. Lloyd's brother Paul came to bat. Waner hit a line drive past pitcher Tony Kaufmann's head, but Cooney was positioned close to second base and, per the *Chicago Tribune*, was "standing on the sack when the singing pill plunked into his mitt." That created both the first and second outs, and Barnhart, who had left first base on the hit, was easily tagged out by Cooney running back toward first.

The Cubs rallied and won the game 7–6 but lost the nightcap to the Pirates 6–5.

Cooney's unassisted feat directly led to another one the following day. According to a *Sports Illustrated* article written four decades after the event, Detroit players had been in their clubhouse reading about Cooney's triple play and Tigers first baseman Johnny Neun said, "I wonder how long it will be before anybody makes another one." Then, reportedly, he began studying the newspaper accounts of the play and brainstorming how he might do this if the opportunity presented itself.

It would happen in that very day's game on Tuesday, May 31, 1927, and in a manner that won the game for Detroit. Leading 1–0 in the top of the ninth, Tigers pitcher Rip Collins was hanging on to a 1–0 lead over Cleveland, whose first two hitters, Glenn Myatt and Charlie Jamieson, reached to begin the ninth inning. Homer Summa smacked a line drive right at Neun, who caught it for the first out. Jamieson, who had taken off for second, was quickly tagged for out number two, and Neun, instead of tossing to second to complete the triple play, ran toward the bag and tagged it to put out Myatt, who had taken off for third thinking the ball was a hit. Neun later said he had made a dash for glory. It was the first game-ending unassisted triple play in major-league history. Cooney's and Neun's feats are the only such plays made on consecutive days, and it would be many years before they were repeated. Ron Hansen of the Washington Senators made the next unassisted triple play, 41 years later, against Cleveland, on Tuesday, July 30, 1968. It would not be accomplished again in the National League for 64 years, when Mickey Morandini of the Philadelphia Phillies turned one against the Pittsburgh Pirates on Sunday, September 20, 1992.

Jimmy Cooney played in just three more games for the Cubs after that doubleheader in 1927. He and Kaufmann were traded to the Phillies on July 7 for Hal Carlson, who wound up in the rotation and pitching in the World Series for the Cubs in 1929. Cooney is also the only player to participate in two unassisted triple plays, having been one of the outs on the bases when Glenn Wright turned one for the Pirates against the Cardinals on Thursday, May 7, 1925.

Cooney left the major leagues after 1928 and returned to his native Cranston, Rhode Island, where he worked for many years for a printing company. He passed away in Rhode Island in 1991, aged 96. He remains the only Cubs player to turn an unassisted triple play.

In recent years, Cubs fans have been thrilled by seeing Willson Contreras and Christopher Morel hit home runs at Wrigley Field in their first major-league at-bats.

Who was the first Cub to hit a home run in his first major-league at-bat, and what other home run distinction does he hold?

Paul Gillespie, a catcher who had been acquired by the Cubs in 1942, was the first Cubs player to homer in his first MLB at-bat. Originally signed by the Dodgers, Gillespie made his way to the Cleveland organization and then to Tulsa, then a top Cubs farm club, in early August 1942. On August 11, the Cubs purchased his contract, but he sat on the big-league bench for a month before he played, starting behind the plate in a meaningless game between the Cubs and Giants at the Polo Grounds on September 11. The Cubs, in sixth place, and the Giants, in third, had both been mathematically eliminated from the pennant race by then by the high-flying Dodgers, though the Cardinals would eventually surpass Brooklyn and win the 1942 NL pennant.

Just 1,704 attended the Friday, September 11, 1942, Cubs vs. Giants game in New York and witnessed Gillespie come to bat in the top of the second inning, oddly enough, right after one of the great home run hitters in major-league history, Jimmie Foxx, had struck out.

Gillespie hit a solo home run off Giants right-hander Harry Feldman to give the Cubs a 1–0 lead. The *Chicago Tribune* reported:

> *There was nothing gradual about Gillespie's debut. A big, rangy fellow, he found himself in the majors right up to his ears at the start with three Giants reaching base in the first inning, but he helped [Hiram] Bithorn through safely. A left hand batter, Gillespie knocked a home run into the right field lower deck in the second inning.*

The *Tribune* article doesn't mention where Gillespie's home run landed, but the Polo Grounds had short fences in both left and right field due to its odd, oval-shaped configuration. It's possible that Gillespie's home run went only about 260 feet.

Gillespie later drove in another run with a single, but the Cubs lost the game 4–3 when Bithorn issued a bases-loaded walk to the Giants in the bottom of the ninth. Gillespie would homer again in his second major-league game two days later against the Boston Braves, but the Cubs lost that one too. He spent all of the 1943 season and most of 1944 in the military, serving in the US Coast Guard. Receiving a medical discharge in early September 1944, Gillespie joined the Cubs and played in nine more games, homering once.

Gillespie and Mickey Livingston split most of the catching duty for the pennant-winning 1945 Cubs, and Gillespie hit pretty well: .288/.366/.360 in 75 games, homering three times. During the 1945 World Series, though, Livingston took on most of the duty, starting six of the seven games behind the plate. Gillespie played in only three games, starting just one and going 0-for-6 overall.

With the return of World War II veterans, Gillespie found himself on the outside looking in as longtime veteran Clyde McCullough returned to take over catching duties. Gillespie played four more seasons in the Cubs minor-league system, retiring after 1949.

That retirement gave the home run he hit in the second game of a doubleheader against the Pirates on Saturday, September 29, 1945, great significance. The Cubs had clinched the NL pennant by winning the first game, so the nightcap had no meaning toward the pennant race. Gillespie hit a two-run homer in what became a five-run fourth inning of that second game, which the Cubs won 5–0 in a rain-shortened seven innings. Gillespie left the game after that homer, replaced by Len Rice.

Despite a decent hitting line of .283/.358/.405 and six home runs in 205 at-bats (and just 12 strikeouts), Gillespie never played in the majors again after 1945. He thus became the first player in major-league history to homer in his first and last at-bats.

That feat has been accomplished by just one other player since then. John Miller homered on Sunday, September 11, 1966, in his first major-league at-bat with the Yankees—oddly enough, exactly 22 years to the day after Gillespie did the same. Three years later, on Tuesday, September 23, 1969, Miller homered as a Dodger, and he never batted in the majors again.

Here are the details of the eight other Cubs to homer in their first major-league at-bats:

Frank Ernaga vs. Milwaukee Braves, off Warren Spahn at Wrigley Field, May 24, 1957

Cuno Barragan vs. San Francisco Giants, off Dick LeMay at Wrigley Field, September 1, 1961 (the only home run of his career)

Carmelo Martinez vs. Cincinnati Reds, off Frank Pastore at Wrigley Field, August 22, 1983

Jim Bullinger vs. St. Louis Cardinals, off Rheal Cormier at St. Louis, June 8, 1992

Starlin Castro vs. Cincinnati Reds, off Homer Bailey at Cincinnati, May 7, 2010

Jorge Soler vs. Cincinnati Reds, off Mat Latos at Cincinnati, August 27, 2014

Willson Contreras vs. Pittsburgh Pirates, off A. J. Schugel at Wrigley Field, June 19, 2016

Christopher Morel vs. Pittsburgh Pirates, off Chase De Jong at Wrigley Field, May 17, 2022

Since the color barrier was broken in Major League Baseball, the Cubs have had many great and popular Black players, including Billy Williams, Fergie Jenkins, Andre Dawson, and, more recently, Dexter Fowler.

Who was the first Black Cubs player?

It's Mr. Cub, Ernie Banks, but that distinction comes with a tiny bit of an asterisk, and here's the reason for said asterisk.

Before 1953, six MLB teams had debuted a Black player:

Dodgers, Jackie Robinson, 1947

Indians, Larry Doby, 1947

Browns, Hank Thompson, 1947

Giants, Monte Irvin, 1949 (also Thompson, debuting for the Giants on the same day as Irvin)

Braves, Sam Jethroe, 1950

White Sox, Minnie Minoso, 1951

Though the Cubs were beginning to sign Black players for their minor-league system, it would take two years after Minoso with the White Sox for a Black player to join the Cubs' major-league roster.

The first Black player to be added to the Cubs' major-league roster was Gene Baker, who the team placed on their active roster on September 1, 1953. Baker had been in the Cubs organization since 1950, and in 1953 he batted .284/.367/.445 with 20 home runs and 20 stolen bases for their then-top minor-league affiliate Los Angeles Angels.

Banks' contract with the Kansas City Monarchs of the Negro Leagues was purchased six days later, on September 7. He was the first player signed to the Cubs by Buck O'Neil, who the team had just hired as a scout.

Both Baker and Banks reported to the Cubs on September 14, but neither played in a game for nearly a week. Banks made his debut as the starting shortstop on Thursday, September 17, 1953, against the Phillies at Wrigley Field for a Cubs team that entered that day's game 61–83 and 37 games out of first place. Just 2,793 diehard fans witnessed the debut of a man whose 19-year career with the Cubs sent him to a first-ballot Hall of Fame election in 1977. Of the debut, the *Chicago Tribune* noted that Banks was among four rookies to play on "Rookie Day," including pitchers Don Elston and Bill Moisan and outfielder Bob Talbot. Acknowledging Banks' status as the first Cubs Black (then called "Negro") player, Edward Prell of the *Tribune* simply wrote of Banks that he "was unimpressive in the field, making an error and failing to hit in three at-bats." Banks did draw a walk, but it was the team's pitching that failed that day, with the Cubs crushed by Philadelphia 16–4. Banks would get his first major-league hit two days later against the Cardinals at St. Louis, a single off Vinegar Bend Mizell, and the next day hit the first of his 512 home runs in St. Louis against Cardinals right-hander Gerry Staley.

While Baker was technically the first Black player on the Cubs' roster, his debut was delayed by a minor injury and he became the second Black Cubs player the following day, entering the game on Sunday, September 20, at St. Louis in the top of the seventh as a pinch-hitter for Elston with the Cubs trailing 11–4. He struck out. Baker would record his first MLB hit two nights later in Cincinnati off Reds right-hander Bob Kelly but would not play at Wrigley Field until he started and played the entire game at second base on Friday, September 25, against the Cardinals, another crushing loss, 11–2. Baker singled twice and scored one of the two runs that afternoon.

Ernie Banks, the Cubs' first Black player, at the Polo Grounds in New York in 1957. JAY PUBLISHING VIA TRADINGCARDDB.COM, PUBLIC DOMAIN, VIA WIKIMEDIA COMMONS.

Baker had been a very good shortstop in the Cubs system, but as he was considered to be someone who could adjust better to a position change, Baker was the one moved to second base. And because you already likely know much about Ernie Banks' career, in which he made 14 All-Star teams and hit 512 home runs for the Cubs, here's more about Baker, who actually was a solid everyday player until injuries ruined his career.

Baker and Banks made a very good double-play combination for the Cubs for the next three seasons. In 1955, both Baker and Banks made the National League All-Star team, and while Banks finished third in MVP voting, Baker also got some MVP votes and finished 21st while batting .268/.323/.392 with 29 doubles, seven triples, and 11 home runs. Baker and Banks tied for the 1955 team lead in stolen bases—with nine. (It was not a running era in baseball; the MLB leaders, Jim Rivera and Bill Bruton, had just 25.) Banks, in fact, played in 424 consecutive games from the start of his career, which remains the National League record for such things.

Baker had a good year again in 1956, but as he was six years older than Banks, the Cubs began looking elsewhere for a double-play partner for Ernie. Just a few weeks into the 1957 season, the Cubs traded Baker to the Pirates for Dale Long and Lee Walls and installed Bobby Morgan at second base. This was likely yet another 1950s-era Cubs mistake, as Morgan didn't hit much, and the Cubs moved on to Tony Taylor at second base in 1958. That might very well have worked out if . . . the Cubs hadn't traded Taylor to the Phillies, where he was a solid performer for more than a decade.

Meanwhile, Baker played well for the Pirates in 1957, but in July 1958 he suffered a serious knee injury that kept him out the rest of that year and all of 1959. He returned to the Pirates in 1960 but didn't play much, used mostly as a pinch-hitter and pinch-runner. Retiring from playing in 1961, Baker was named player-manager at Batavia in the New York-Penn League, thus becoming the first Black manager in Organized Baseball in the United States. Later he was promoted to the Pirates as a coach, the second Black coach in MLB after O'Neil, and he technically was the first Black manager in the major leagues, for a day, when he took over the Pirates for part of their game on September 21, 1963, after manager Danny Murtaugh and coach Frank Oceak were both ejected.

Later, the Pirates hired him as a scout, and he worked for them in that capacity for more than 25 years. He passed away in his hometown of Davenport, Iowa, in 1999, aged 74.

Baker might not have had the career or the fame Banks had with the Cubs, but he did get something in his playing career that Ernie never did—a World Series ring, won with the 1960 Pirates. Baker played in three games of that World Series, all as a pinch-hitter, going 0-for-3.

The men became great friends, a friendship that lasted a lifetime. When Banks was elected to the Hall of Fame, the first person he called to tell the good news was Baker.

In September 1953, Ernie Banks became the Cubs' first Black player. Who was the Cubs' first Black pitcher, and what pitching firsts did he accomplish in his first year with the team?

By 1953, when Banks and Gene Baker became the Cubs' first two Black players, there had been several successful Black pitchers in the major leagues. Perhaps the best of those was Don Newcombe, who had three All-Star seasons for the Brooklyn Dodgers from 1949 to 1951 before spending the next two years in military service.

Just days after the 1954 season ended, the Cubs acquired Sam Jones from Cleveland, along with a player to be named later, in exchange for . . . a player to be named later. In November 1954, Ralph Kiner was sent to Cleveland, and Gale Wade (and $60,000, a not insignificant sum at the time) came to the Cubs to complete the deal.

Jones would become the Cubs' first Black pitcher when he made his debut for the team with a five-inning relief appearance against the Cincinnati Reds on April 11, 1955. Those five innings of relief (for starter Bob Rush) helped the Cubs win that game 7–5, and Jones was placed into the starting rotation.

Jones' first six starts for the team produced mediocre results: a 5.49 ERA, largely due to 35 walks issued in 39 1/3 innings. Jones actually held opponents to a .186 BA in those six outings, but all the walks led to far too many runs allowed.

It was with that record that Jones took the mound at Wrigley Field to face the Pittsburgh Pirates on Thursday, May 12, 1955, in front of a sad little crowd of just 2,918. The Cubs were just a game under .500 at 13–14 but already 10 games out of first place because the Dodgers had got off to an otherworldly 22–3 start.

The Cubs scored single runs in the first, second, fifth, and seventh innings on that overcast afternoon. That included a home run by Ted Tappe (no relation to future Cubs College of Coaches member El Tappe), one of just five he would hit in a brief MLB career.

The Pirates were gifted multiple baserunners by Jones, all on walks, but could not score. The Cubs defense helped out by turning two double plays.

And so it was that this game entered the ninth with Jones having allowed no hits. At the time, Hippo Vaughn's nine no-hit innings against the Reds on May 2, 1917, was considered the Cubs' most recent no-hitter, in a game that became known as the "double no-hit game" because Fred Toney of the Reds completed a no-hitter while Vaughn gave up a hit in the 10th and took the loss, so at the time, it was thought to have been a few days more than 38 years since a Cub had thrown a no-hit game.

Jones set about making his task as difficult as possible. He walked Gene Freese leading off the ninth, then sent him to second on a wild pitch. Two more walks loaded the bases, bringing the tying run to the plate in the person of Dick Groat, a future MVP then playing in his first full year. Jones struck him out on three curveballs. Roberto Clemente, another future Hall of Famer then in his rookie year, was the next hitter. Jones threw two strikes past Clemente, who fouled off the next two offerings before striking out. One more hitter stood between Jones and immortality. That was Frank Thomas, who possessed prodigious power (and who would play for the Cubs five years later).

Jones struck Thomas out on three pitches, the last one his 136th of the game, and the no-hitter went into the books. After the game, the *Chicago Tribune* dutifully interviewed Vaughn, then 67, about his experience. Since then, Major League Baseball has removed Vaughn's feat from the list of official no-hitters, so the no-no on the Cubs' list previous to Jones' game is the one thrown by Jimmy Lavender against the Giants on August 31, 1915. Thus, officially, Jones is the first Cub to throw a no-hitter at Wrigley Field, as well as the first Black pitcher to throw a no-hitter.

Jones would go on to be named to the National League All-Star team in 1955 and lead the NL with 198 strikeouts, though he would also lead the league in walks (185) and losses (20). That was a 3.2 bWAR season, second to Bob Rush among Cubs pitchers.

Jones was popular among teammates and fans and was nicknamed "Toothpick Sam" for always having one in his mouth. Another sobriquet given Jones was "Sad Sam," after another pitcher named Sam Jones who pitched in the big leagues from 1914 to 1935 (and, oddly, also threw a no-hitter). The Sam Jones who pitched for the Cubs had a personality quite the opposite of "sad," cited as "amiable" in his SABR biography, which added: "He didn't talk much and mumbled when he did. He had quirks: He was afraid of airplanes and snorted like an old horse because of a sinus condition."

The 1956 season didn't prove quite as good for Jones, and the Cubs slumped from 72 wins to 60, so of course management felt another shakeup was needed. Thus, on December 11, 1956, the Cubs traded Jones, Jim Davis, Hobie Landrith, and Eddie Miksis to the St. Louis Cardinals for Wally Lammers, Jackie Collum, Ray Katt, and Tom Poholsky.

Those four men the Cubs acquired likely don't mean much to you, the Cubs fan. That's because none of them had any impact on the Cubs. Lammers never played in the major leagues. Collum pitched in only nine games for the Cubs, and not well, before being traded to the Dodgers for Don Elston. (Okay, *that* deal worked out all right.) Katt never played for the Cubs at all. In early 1957, he and Ray Jablonski were dealt to the Giants for Bob Lennon (nine games as a Cub) and Dick Littlefield (48 games, 5.35 ERA as a Cub). Poholsky pitched in 28 games for the Cubs in 1957, then was traded to the Giants for Freddy Rodriguez, who pitched in just seven games for the Cubs in 1958 before being traded to the Athletics for Dave Melton, who never played for the Cubs at all.

I mention all those names because they typify the flailing around the Cubs front office did for most of the 1950s, while often dealing away players who played well elsewhere. Sam Jones was one of those players. He had two good years for the Cardinals and then was swapped to the Giants before the 1959 season for Jablonski (that guy got around!) and Bill White, who became a solid performer for the Cardinals' World Series team in 1964 and later was a longtime broadcaster for the Yankees and also served as president of the National League.

As for Jones, he had a very good year for the Giants in 1959 when he led the National League in wins (21) and ERA (2.83) and finished second in Cy Young voting. There was only one Cy Young Award at the time for both leagues. Early Wynn of the White Sox won it. Jones would certainly have won the National League Award if there had been awards for each league back then.

The 1959 Cubs contended for a while; they were 4 1/2 games out of first place on July 28 with a 50–48 record. Ernie Banks won his second MVP Award, batting.304/.374/.596 with 45 home runs and leading the NL with a career-high 143 RBI.

Their pitching, though, was pretty mediocre—they gave 36 starts to pitchers who combined for a −1.9 bWAR. Swap those out for Jones' 5.7 bWAR in 1959 and the Cubs might have at least contended for the NL pennant. That was taken by the Dodgers with only 88 wins, and that was after winning a best-of-three playoff with the Braves. The Cubs finished just 12 games out of first place, the closest they had been to the top spot at the end of any season since their 1945 league title. They wouldn't finish that close to first place again until 1967.

Jones was still pitching in the major leagues in 1964 with the Baltimore Orioles, and after that he spent three years in the Pirates' organization in Triple-A with Columbus, putting up pretty good numbers but never getting a callup. He returned to his hometown in West Virginia and opened a successful car wash but passed away from cancer on November 5, 1971, aged just 45.

With Major League Baseball's early 1960s expansion to 10 teams in each league, the schedule was also expanded from 154 games to 162. Who was the first Cub to play *more* than 162 games in a season?

This is kind of an oddball feat because a player has to be (a) healthy all year and (b) either have the desire to play every day or a manager who doesn't think the player needs rest or (c) both, along with a curious combination of circumstances for a player to play more than the officially scheduled 162 games.

One way this can happen is if a player is traded during a season and the schedules of the two clubs he plays on are skewed to the point where the club he's traded to has more games remaining than the club he departed.

Or, in the case of the Chicago Cubs, it happened several times in the 1960s because of the lack of lights at Wrigley Field and games thus ending in ties due to darkness falling.

In 1965, that happened twice. Opening Day, April 12 vs. the St. Louis Cardinals, was played to a 10–10 tie before being stopped for lack of sunshine, and the second game of a doubleheader May 31 against the New York Mets was halted by darkness at 7:35 p.m., about 40 minutes before sunset that day, with the score tied 3–3.

Both Ron Santo and Billy Williams played in all 164 games for the Cubs in 1965. So who was the first to do that?

The honor goes to Williams, because the final game of that year was a road game played in Pittsburgh on Sunday, October 3. Williams batted third that day and Santo fourth, and thus Williams appeared in the game before Santo did.

At the time, Williams was in the middle of a consecutive-game streak that would reach 1,117 games before he ended it himself by asking out of the lineup on Thursday, September 3, 1970, at Wrigley Field. Interestingly, Williams had been held out of a game on Saturday, September 21, 1963, against a "tough lefty," Warren Spahn of the Milwaukee Braves. Williams had played in all 155 games before that date in 1963 as well as in the final 11 games of the 1962 season, so if he'd played in that game against Spahn, his consecutive-game streak would have been 1,284 games and he'd still hold the National League record.

On three other occasions, there have been Cubs player seasons of more than 162 games: Ernie Banks played in 163 games in that 1965 campaign and Williams played in 163 in both 1968 and 1969. Overall in MLB history, there have been 33 player seasons of 163 or more games. The Cubs have the most such seasons with five overall and are the only team to have more than one player to do it in a single season, with Banks, Santo, and Williams all accomplishing this "feat" in 1965.

With rest from fatigue becoming more important to baseball players and teams in the 21st century, only two players have played more than 162 games in a season since 1998—Hideki Matsui (163 for the New York Yankees in 2003, the result of the Yankees being involved in a tie game that year) and Justin Morneau (163 for the Minnesota Twins in 2008). Morneau's 163rd game was a divisional tiebreaker against the Chicago White Sox. With new rules making tie games nearly impossible today along with the end of divisional tiebreaker games, it seems likely we have seen the last major-league player to play in more than 162 games in a single season.

Catching is a demanding position, and most modern catchers will max out at a little more than 100 games caught per season. In the past, though, some catchers had very heavy workloads.

Who was the first Cubs catcher to be behind the plate for 160 games in a season?

This is the story of a manager and a catcher, with a front office either unwilling or unable to provide a suitable backup.

Randy Hundley was acquired by the Cubs, along with Bill Hands, from the Giants for Lindy McDaniel and Don Landrum. This deal happened on December 9, 1965, just a few weeks after Leo Durocher was named Cubs manager.

Hundley had played in a handful of games for the Giants in 1964 and 1965, but Durocher, not having many alternatives, installed Hundley as his starting catcher in 1966. The team lost a franchise-record 103 games, but Hundley hit .236/.285/.397 with 19 home runs in 149 games, pretty good numbers for that pitching-dominated era, and finished fourth in National League Rookie of the Year voting.

Of the 149 games Hundley played that year, 144 were as the Cubs' starting catcher, and he caught every inning of 137 games. Just two other Cubs catchers in the 90 years of the franchise up to that time had even caught 130 games—Johnny Kling (131 in 1903) and Gabby Hartnett (132 in 1930 and 138 in 1933).

But that wasn't enough for Durocher, who had a reputation of riding his starting players hard and rarely playing his reserves.

In 1967, Hundley started 147 of the Cubs' 162 games behind the plate and was there for every inning of all but one of those starts, plus he entered to play defense in three others. This included catching every inning in seven games over four straight days, when rainouts forced the Cubs to play doubleheaders every day from September 1 to 4. In the eighth of those games, Hundley entered in the seventh inning for defense. The Cubs carried just two other catchers all that year: Dick

Bertell, who caught in two games in April and was later released, and John Stephenson, who started 12 games behind the plate, mostly in August.

Durocher increased Hundley's workload even further in 1968, the year Randy set a major-league record by catching 160 games, 156 of them starts. He caught every inning of 17 of the Cubs' first 18 games then was given the ninth inning off in Game 19. Nine more games went by after that before Hundley got the last two innings off in Game 30. After that he caught every inning of every game through Game 53. Game 54, the second game of a doubleheader against the Braves, was started by John Boccabella, but Hundley entered in the seventh inning. Then Hundley caught every inning of the next 13 games before Boccabella again started the second game of a doubleheader against the Reds, but again Hundley entered the game, this time in the sixth inning.

That's when Durocher really cranked up Hundley's workload, and in the hottest months of the year. From June 24 through July 28, 1968, Hundley caught every inning of 33 of 34 games, sitting out only the second game of a July doubleheader against the Phillies, caught by Gene Oliver (Oliver's only game behind the plate for the 1968 Cubs). That also included catching every inning of four extra-inning games during that span.

Hundley was finally given a break in the late innings on July 29 and 30, but even so, he started the next 25 games, including catching every inning of a 13-inning game on August 4 at St. Louis and a 15-inning game at Cincinnati on August 11. Both of those were day games—just imagine doing that in the summer sun and heat.

At last, Hundley didn't start another doubleheader nightcap, August 21 vs. the Braves at Atlanta, the game started by Randy Bobb. Again, Hundley entered this game for defense in the sixth.

After that, Durocher put Hundley through another grind of 19 straight starts, including catching every inning of both games of doubleheaders on August 28, September 2, and September 4.

This brutal stretch ended on September 7 against the Phillies at Wrigley Field when Bobb started once again, only to see Hundley finish up the last couple of innings of a 4–2 loss.

Hundley must have been glad to see the season end after Durocher started him in each of the Cubs' final 17 games—and he'd likely have caught every inning of those 17 games, except he was ejected for arguing a call at the plate in the fourth inning of a game against the Mets in New York on September 17.

The 160 games caught and 156 games started at catcher by Hundley in 1968 are major-league records that will likely never be broken. Hundley caught 1,385 of the 1,453 1/3 innings played by the Cubs in 1968 (95.2 percent), and though his workload decreased a bit the following year, he still started 145 games behind the plate and played every inning of 136 of those.

It should be noted that in the pre-expansion era, two catchers—Frank Hayes (Philadelphia Athletics) and Ray Mueller (Cincinnati Reds)—both caught all their teams' games in 1944, 155 apiece. Mueller was the starting catcher in all of his. Both also were in the midst of still-standing records for consecutive games caught in their respective leagues. Hayes still holds the American League record for games caught in a season, of any length. Jim Sundberg is second to Hundley in games caught in a 162-game schedule, also 155, for the Texas Rangers in 1975.

Hundley is not only the first Cubs and MLB catcher to catch in 160 games in a season, he's the only one to ever do that, and probably for good reason. This extreme workload might have been a contributing factor to the serious knee injury Hundley suffered during a game against the St. Louis Cardinals at Wrigley Field on April 21, 1970. He missed three months and was never quite the same player after he returned. Another serious injury kept him out of all but nine games in 1971, and while he returned to the Cubs for two more seasons in 1972 and 1973, his offensive and defensive performance suffered. He was traded to the Twins for catcher George Mitterwald in December 1973 and played a year there in 1974 and one for the Padres in 1975 before returning to the Cubs in 1976 as a part-time player. The following year he was named Cubs bullpen coach, activated in September to play in two games as a farewell to his playing career.

The workload forced on Hundley by Durocher was really unconscionable; the physical demands on a catcher almost require a suitable backup. Whether the Cubs either could not or would not find someone like that during the late 1960s under Durocher is an unanswerable question to this day, but it very well could have led to Hundley not having the baseball career he might have had.

Hundley managed in the Cubs minor-league system from 1978 to 1981, and the following year created the concept of baseball fantasy camps, where fans over age 30 could play baseball with some of their favorites from years gone by. Hundley's camps operated through 2021 and were quite popular.

The save statistic was invented by Chicago newspaper columnist Jerome Holtzman, who was later MLB's first historian, in 1959. Ten years later it became an official MLB statistic.

Who was the first Cubs pitcher to record a save after the rule was made official?

Right-hander Ted Abernathy recorded the Cubs' first save after the save rule became official in a 7–4 win over the Pittsburgh Pirates on Tuesday, April 15, 1969. Just 4,362 witnessed this save, recorded on a cloudy, rainy, 55-degree afternoon at Wrigley Field. Abernathy threw the final 1 2/3 innings of that victory, allowing three hits but no runs, and got future Hall of Famer Bill Mazeroski to ground out to preserve the win.

Abernathy is a fascinating figure from the Cubs' almost-glory days of the late 1960s. The team acquired him twice, not giving up much either time to acquire him—then also tossed him away twice, not getting much in return.

He was best known for his "submarine" delivery, an underhanded pitching style where his hand nearly touched the ground while the ball got whipped toward the plate in a manner hitters were unaccustomed to seeing.

Originally a pitcher with a standard overhand throwing motion, Abernathy switched to a sidearm motion in high school after suffering a shoulder injury. When he began pitching in the major leagues, he was a starter with the original Washington Senators. The earlier injuries eventually led to shoulder surgery, and in an effort to remain in the big leagues, he changed to the underhanded delivery.

By then Abernathy had moved on to Cleveland, where he had just moderate success in 1963 and 1964, and so the Cubs were able to acquire him for cash considerations just before the 1965 season began—no players went to Cleveland in the deal.

Abernathy quickly became the team's choice to close out games, and he posted save after save, notable even though the stat was not yet official. The 1965 Cubs weren't very good, losing 90 games, but Abernathy posted 31 saves in 38 opportunities, becoming the first pitcher to record 30 or more saves in a season. He also set a Cubs team record that year with 84 appearances. That mark still stands, though it's been tied twice, by Dick Tidrow in 1980 and Bob Howry in 2006.

The next year, Abernathy, as did quite a number of Cubs, ran afoul of new manager Leo Durocher after a couple of poor outings early in the year. In late May he was traded to Atlanta for an outfielder named Lee Thomas, who hit .229 in 152 games for the Cubs in 1966 and 1967 and then was traded away for a pair of minor leaguers who never made it.

Meanwhile, after Abernathy had a middling year in Atlanta, the Braves moved him off their 40-man roster so they could protect younger players. By the rules of the time this made him eligible for the Rule 5 Draft, and he was selected by the Reds in November 1966. He went on to put together a spectacular year for the Reds in 1967, posting 28 saves and a minuscule 1.27 ERA. His 6.2 bWAR that year was the third best by any pitcher and led all relievers, garnering him some downballot MVP votes and a 20th-place finish in the award voting.

In 1968, Abernathy wasn't as good for Cincinnati, and the Cubs, perhaps realizing the mistake they made, reacquired him in exchange for Bill Plummer and Clarence Jones in January 1969.

Though Abernathy performed reasonably well for the Cubs in 1969, Durocher apparently still didn't trust him in closing situations. He posted only three saves the entire season, not even getting chances when closer Phil Regan was blowing games late in the year.

As he did in 1966, Durocher thought Abernathy was done and, having more influence on player transactions than managers do in modern times, helped engineer yet another deal, getting Abernathy swapped to the Cardinals in late May 1970 for an infielder named Phil

Gagliano. Gagliano went just 6-for-40 in 26 games for the Cubs before he was traded to Boston for Carmen Fanzone. The Cardinals didn't keep Abernathy very long either, as he appeared in only 11 games for St. Louis before they dealt him to the Royals a couple of months later.

At age 37, Abernathy was rejuvenated in Kansas City, posting 12 saves in half a season in 1970 and 23 more in 1971, then posting a 1.70 ERA in 45 appearances for the Royals in 1972 at age 39 before retiring.

The Cubs sure could have used some of that good pitching in those years. Despite the explosion of closers who have piled up saves over the five decades since Abernathy's retirement, his total of 149 career saves still ranks 92nd in MLB history, through the end of the 2023 season.

After his retirement, Abernathy returned to his home state of North Carolina and passed away in 2004, aged 71.

An "immaculate inning" is defined as a pitcher retiring three batters in an inning on nine pitches, all strikes, with no one reaching base; in other words, only the pitcher and catcher touch the baseball.

Who was the first Cubs pitcher to record an immaculate inning?

For the first few decades of major-league history, immaculate innings were pretty rare. Through 1989 there had been just 31 such innings.

With pitchers relying more and more on velocity in recent years and strikeout rates rising, there have been quite a few more over the last three-plus decades. There have been 114 immaculate innings thrown through the end of the 2023 season.

The first one thrown by a Cubs pitcher was the 24th in major-league history, thrown by Milt Pappas against the Philadelphia Phillies on Friday, September 24, 1971, at Wrigley Field in an otherwise unremarkable game the Cubs and Pappas lost 6–1. It happened in the top of the fourth inning with the Phillies leading 3–1. The batters were Greg Luzinski, Don Money, and Mike Anderson. Anderson, who was playing in just his 22nd major-league game, got the last laugh on the Cubs that day by hitting a home run off Phil Regan in the ninth inning.

Just 2,183 witnessed Pappas' feat, and the idea of an immaculate inning hadn't really caught on with baseball folks back then. Richard

Dozer's game recap in the *Chicago Tribune* didn't even mention it and instead focused more on the fact that by the loss, Pappas had lost his chance to be a 20-game winner, a plateau he never did reach. The following year, Pappas got his name in the record books again when he threw a no-hitter against the Padres at Wrigley Field on Saturday, September 2, 1972. That game came to within one strike of a perfect game when plate umpire Bruce Froemming called ball four on Larry Stahl on a borderline pitch.

Other Cubs pitchers to throw immaculate innings and the hitters they struck out:

Bruce Sutter, September 8, 1977, vs. Montreal Expos at Wrigley Field (Ellis Valentine, Gary Carter, and Larry Parrish)

Lynn McGlothen, August 25, 1979, vs. Giants at San Francisco (Larry Herndon, Joe Strain, and Jack Clark)

LaTroy Hawkins, September 11, 2004, vs. Florida Marlins at Wrigley Field (Jeff Conine, Juan Encarnacion, and Alex Gonzalez)

Hayden Wesneski, September 22, 2022, vs. Pittsburgh Pirates at Wrigley Field (Jack Suwinski, Zack Collins, and Jason Delay)

There has been just one immaculate inning thrown against the Cubs, by Jeff Robinson of the Pirates, on Monday, September 7, 1987, at Wrigley Field. The Cubs hitters were Leon Durham, Andre Dawson, and Rafael Palmeiro.

The 1972 players' strike was the first work stoppage by MLB players that actually cost games—each team played about seven fewer games than on the original schedule.

When players and owners finally came to an agreement, one of the new contract points was that players with 10 years of MLB service, the last five with the same team, could veto any trade.

Who was the first Cub to invoke his "10-and-5 rights"?

This contract provision was considered very important to players. At the time, they were still about three years away from arbitrator Peter Seitz's decision that led to free agency, so players were still bound by baseball's reserve clause.

For players with longtime service in the league who had become comfortable with one team and city, perhaps placing down roots and living there, this was a key to making the deal, as it allowed such players to stay where they were, or at least try to negotiate a better trade.

It was with this in mind that Ron Santo became the first Cubs player—in fact, the first MLB player—to invoke the new contract's 10-and-5 rights. It happened on Wednesday, December 5, 1973.

Santo had been a star with the Cubs for many years, though by 1973 his best years were behind him. He had been playing with juvenile diabetes for his entire career, though he had kept it private—only family and teammates knew—until he was honored with Ron Santo Day at Wrigley Field in August 1971. It was on that day that he revealed his disease, saying, "I didn't want anyone else to know about this originally. I'm a diabetic and had a full career in the major leagues and a darned good one. The reason I've done so well is I've accepted it and learned to live with it. I feel strongly we're going to find a cure for this." Santo devoted much of the rest of his life to raising funds for a juvenile diabetes cure, and at the time of his passing from complications from the disease in 2010, had raised more than $40 million.

Diabetes began to sap Santo's strength, and in 1973 he had his worst year since 1962. The team collapsed in the second half after being eight games ahead in the NL East at the season's midpoint, and so general manager John Holland decided to trade away the team's aging stars and start what we would now term a "rebuild."

First to go was ace Fergie Jenkins, traded to the Rangers on October 25, 1973, for Bill Madlock and Vic Harris. Two weeks later, second baseman Glenn Beckert was sent to the Padres for Jerry Morales.

But on December 5, when Holland had completed a trade of Santo to the Angels, Santo said, "No." He was raising his family in the Chicago suburbs and had multiple business interests that he didn't want to leave behind. Among players reported as possibly being part of that deal were Angels pitching prospects Andy Hassler and Bruce Heinbechner.

Holland told the *Chicago Tribune*, "More and more clubs were coming to us, and when I talked to Ron he said he would not accept assignment anywhere outside Chicago."

Santo added, "If I was 26 instead of 33, I might feel differently about moving. But I have only a couple of years left and I want to play them here. Of course I realize that decision may cut my career down even more."

That left only the White Sox as a possible destination, though *Tribune* writer Robert Markus suggested Santo consider Milwaukee, only about an hour's drive from his north suburban home. To help his case to stay in Chicago, Santo made a "personal plea" to Cubs owner P. K. Wrigley to get him traded to the White Sox, according to the *Tribune.*

It took just six days after Santo's rejection of the Angels for Holland to complete a deal sending Santo to the South Side of Chicago. In return, the Cubs received pitchers Steve Stone and Ken Frailing, catcher Steve Swisher, and a player to be named later. A week later the Sox sent pitcher Jim Kremmel to the North Side to complete the deal.

A bit of humor ensued when some writers, giving a nod to the holiday season, began to term 10-and-5 rights the "Santo Clause."

It was an awkward fit for Santo on the South Side because the Sox had an established third baseman in Bill Melton, a popular player who had set a White Sox team record and led the American League with 33 home runs in 1971 and hit 20—same as Santo—in 1973.

And so Sox manager Chuck Tanner installed Santo as the team's primary designated hitter, a position he disliked, with an occasional turn at third base. Santo wanted to get back in the field, so Tanner played him 39 times at second base, a position he'd played just three times in 14 years with the Cubs. Santo's numbers dropped precipitously in Comiskey Park, a pitcher's ballpark, and he hit just five home runs while batting .221. Both were career lows, and Santo retired as a player after the 1974 season.

At the time of his retirement, Santo was not viewed fondly by many Cubs fans, in part because of his performance decline and in part because of his outspokenness at a time when professional athletes didn't commonly do such things. It was only when Santo, who openly admitted he wanted the job to help his Hall of Fame chances, took a position as Cubs radio analyst on WGN radio, became beloved among Cubs fans for his unabashed rooting for the team on the air. He was elected to the

Future Hall of Famer Ron Santo, at Wrigley Field in 1973.
JEWEL FOODS VIA TRADINGCARDDB.COM, PUBLIC DOMAIN, VIA WIKIMEDIA COMMONS.

Hall in 2012, sadly posthumously after several iterations of Hall veterans committees failed to induct him. The Cubs retired his No. 10 on Sunday, September 28, 2003. At the Wrigley Field ceremony, Santo said, "This means more to me than the Hall of Fame—this is my Hall of Fame."

As for the players the Cubs received in the deal, Stone had three pretty good years for the Cubs before returning to the Sox as a free agent. Swisher also had some decent years on the North Side, even making the NL All-Star team in 1976. Kremmel pitched in 22 games for the Cubs in 1974 and in their system in 1975 and 1976 before leaving baseball, and Frailing pitched in 102 games for the Cubs from 1974 to 1976 with a 4.16 ERA. The Cubs got slightly more value than they gave up, as they got 3.1 bWAR combined among the four players, while Santo's bWAR in his lone Sox year was −1.6.

The deal the Cubs were going to make with the Angels would have brought them some value, though it also had a touch of tragedy. Andy Hassler wound up with 7.3 bWAR in a 14-year career pitching for six teams. Bruce Heinbechner, one of the Angels' better prospects in 1973, died in a car accident while driving to Angels spring training in Palm Springs in 1974.

Five sets of brothers have played for the Chicago National League Ball Club.
Who were the first Cubs brothers to combine on a shutout?
The first two sets of brothers to play for Chicago NL did so when the team was still generally known as "Colts," in the mid-1890s, and neither of those long-ago brother sets played for the team for very long.

In 1893, an infielder named Jiggs Parrott and his brother Tom, a pitcher, both played for the Colts, the first time brothers played for the same Chicago NL ballclub.

Tom, a right-hander, had been purchased from a minor-league team in Birmingham by the Cincinnati Reds in June 1893. But Tom Parrott claimed his deal with Birmingham permitted him to make his own major-league deal, so he signed a contract with the Colts—this in an era when such things happened, whether or not permissible. He did so largely because his brother Jiggs already was a member of the Colts.

Nic Young, then the president of the National League, resolved the dispute in favor of the Reds, but not before Tom Parrott pitched in four games for the Colts, posting a not-so-great 6.67 ERA.

Jiggs Parrott played 320 games for the Colts from 1892 to 1895 before they let him go; he played two years in the minor leagues before being diagnosed with tuberculosis. He died in 1898, aged just 26.

If you think "Jiggs" is an odd name (his real given name was Walter), wait until you hear the names of the next set of brothers to play for the Cubs.

Lew Camp, an infielder, was given the birth name Robert Plantagenet Llewellan Camp. His brother, known in his brief baseball career as "Kid," was born Winfield Scott Camp, named after the famed 19th-century general and presidential candidate. Names like this were often given to 19th-century men—and just as often, those men used much shorter versions in public. The brothers both played for the Colts in 1894, but Kid Camp died the following year, aged just 25.

Nearly three-quarters of a century would pass before another brother combination would play for the Cubs in the same year, Danny and Hal Breeden in 1971. On the same day, November 30, 1970, the Cubs traded for both Breedens. They first sent popular outfielder Willie Smith to the Reds for Danny. Hal was acquired from the Braves in exchange for future Hall of Famer Hoyt Wilhelm—who, yes, pitched in three games late in the year for the Cubs in 1970.

That brother combination lasted just about half a year, and the brothers played in the same game just four times. Both wound up back in the minor leagues after July 4 and never played for the Cubs again. Hal was traded to the Expos just before the 1972 season began for Dan McGinn. Danny, after playing all of 1972 in the Cubs minor leagues, went to the Padres in early 1973 for what baseball folks now call "cash considerations." He did have one moment to remember as a Cub—he was the catcher for Ken Holtzman's second no-hitter over the Reds in Cincinnati on June 3, 1971.

That leaves the next set of Cubs brothers, Rick and Paul Reuschel, as the answer to our question.

Rick Reuschel had burst onto the Cubs scene with a solid rookie season in 1972. By 1975, when brother Paul made his major-league debut, Rick was generally regarded as the best pitcher on the Cubs staff (though by 1975 that was largely by default, as that team's pitchers gave up 827 runs, most in the league by 88).

It was in that year, though, that the Reuschel brothers combined on a shutout. It happened at Wrigley Field on Thursday, August 21, 1975, a hastily rescheduled game from a rainout the previous day. Thus, just 8,377 saw this brother act. The Cubs rushed out to an early 5–0 lead thanks in part to a two-run homer by Rick Monday. While this was going on, Rick Reuschel was shutting down Dodgers hitters. He was removed with a runner on base and one out in the seventh, with brother Paul summoned from the bullpen. Paul Reuschel retired the first batter he faced, then hit Steve Yeager, but got out of the inning without allowing a run. Paul allowed two more baserunners, one reaching on an error in the eighth, another on a single in the ninth, but completed the combined six-hit shutout when he retired Yeager on a fly ball to right. The brothers had just one strikeout (by Paul) and one walk issued (by Rick) in this game, a 7–0 Cubs win. This remains the only shutout in MLB history thrown by brothers.

Since the Reuschels, there has been just one other set of brothers to play for the Cubs, Andrew and Austin Romine, who played for the team in 2021. Austin was a catcher and Andrew generally an infielder, but the Cubs gave them a chance for some brotherly togetherness in a game they were losing to the Milwaukee Brewers on August 12, 2021, when they sent Andrew to the mound in the ninth inning with Austin catching and the Cubs trailing 16–3. Andrew allowed a run to the Brewers in his mound stint, and when the Romines appeared in the game together, it was the first time brothers had played for the Cubs in the same game since the Reuschels both pitched in a 7–4 loss to the Expos in Montreal on Tuesday, May 30, 1978. Paul, who had not pitched well that year, was traded to Cleveland about four weeks later.

Rick Reuschel, meanwhile, had several more good years for the Cubs before being traded to the Yankees in 1981. After shoulder surgery, the Cubs re-signed him in 1984 but failed to put him on the postseason roster, an omission that likely hurt the team. General manager Dallas Green let Reuschel go to free agency, and he posted a very good year for the Pirates in 1985, a year the Cubs could have used him when all five rotation starters went down with injuries. They could have used Reuschel again in 1989 when, at age 40, he posted an All-Star season for the Giants and finished eighth in Cy Young Award voting. With 68.1 career bWAR, 214 wins, and 2,015 strikeouts, Rick Reuschel is one of the best pitchers of his era not in the Hall of Fame.

Famously, Willson Contreras homered on the first major-league pitch he saw in June 2016.
Who was the first Cub to hit a home run on the first major-league pitch thrown to him?
The first Cubs player to go yard on the first major-league pitch in his first at-bat is someone who couldn't do that now—right-handed pitcher Jim Bullinger, who accomplished this feat in the top of the sixth inning of the first game of a doubleheader on Monday, June 8, 1992, off Cardinals left-hander Rheal Cormier.

The homer broke up a scoreless game, which Bullinger had just entered in relief of Shawn Boskie in the previous inning. It was his fourth MLB game but first plate appearance, and he became the fifth Cub to homer in his first MLB at-bat, after Paul Gillespie (1942), Frank Ernaga (1957), Cuno Barragan (1961), and Carmelo Martinez (1983), but the first to do it on the very first pitch he saw. In the bottom of the inning, Bullinger celebrated his feat by recording his first MLB strikeout, fanning Milt Thompson.

The Cardinals tied the game up off Bullinger in the bottom of the sixth, and that's where the game stayed until the 13th inning, when the Cubs pushed across four runs that included RBI from Ryne Sandberg, Andre Dawson, and Mark Grace, and won the game 5–1.

This author attended that doubleheader in St. Louis. With the extra innings in Game 1, the second game didn't start until after 10:30 p.m. The Cubs swept the twin bill by winning the nightcap 6–4, and I vividly remember walking out of Busch Stadium at 1:50 a.m., the latest (or maybe earliest?) I've ever been at a baseball game.

As for Bullinger, he was selected by the Cubs out of the University of New Orleans in the ninth round of the draft in 1986—as an infielder. Over the next couple of seasons, it quickly became apparent that while

Bullinger was a decent fielder, he couldn't hit, batting just .222 in 621 minor-league games, so the Cubs tried him as a pitcher. Quickly taking to it, Bullinger posted a 3.99 ERA in 28 starts split between Double-A and Triple-A in 1991, and when he started 1992 with a 2.45 ERA and 14 saves at Triple-A Iowa, he was called up to the majors.

Bullinger's major-league numbers as a pitcher were up and down. Pitching mostly in relief in 1992 and 1993, he posted a 4.95 ERA but fared a bit better in 1994 and 1995 when used mostly as a starter (3.95 ERA in 57 games, 34 of which were starts). In 1996, though, Bullinger's ERA soared to 6.54 in 37 games (20 starts), and so he was allowed to depart via free agency. He signed with the Montreal Expos in 1997, pitched one year there, and finished up his MLB career with two outings for the Seattle Mariners in 1998, though he was still throwing in the minors and the Mexican League as recently as 2005.

Just six other pitchers in MLB history hit a home run on the first pitch they saw:

Billy Gumbert (1890 Pittsburgh Alleghenys)
Bill Duggleby (1898 Philadelphia Phillies—a grand slam!)
Clise Dudley (1929 Brooklyn Robins)
Bill LeFebvre (1938 Boston Red Sox)
Don Rose (1972 California Angels)
Esteban Yan (2000 Tampa Bay Devil Rays)

The Cubs franchise record for hits in a game is six. The first four times a Cub had six hits in a game, it happened in an extra-inning affair.

Who was the first Cub to collect six hits in a nine-inning game?

Frank Demaree (1937), Don Kessinger (1971), Bill Madlock (1975), and Jose Cardenal (1976) all had six hits for the Cubs in games that went to extra innings. The Cubs won three of those four games, losing only the Madlock game in 1975.

It wasn't until Friday, July 2, 1993, that a Cubs player had six hits in a regulation nine-inning game.

That player was Sammy Sosa, who went on to more fame hitting home runs, but at the time he was in just his second year with the ballclub.

On that evening against the Rockies in Mile High Stadium in Denver, Sosa was batting cleanup. In the first inning, he gave the Cubs a 2–0 lead by hitting a double after Mark Grace had also driven in a run with a double.

Sammy's next at-bat was in the third inning, with the Cubs now leading 3–0. He singled, advanced to second on a single by Candy Maldonado, and scored on a single by Steve Buechele. Buechele also later scored and the Cubs took a 5–0 lead.

But in the Rockies' original home, no lead was safe. The Rockies scored two in the bottom of the third, and 5–2 was the score when Sosa batted leading off the fifth. He singled for his third hit of the game and stole second. After a strikeout and intentional walk, Steve Lake singled Sosa in to make it 6–2.

Did I mention no lead was safe in Denver? The Rockies scored four times off Greg Hibbard and Jose Bautista in the fifth to tie the game, but the Cubs came right back and took the lead again in the top of the sixth. With one out and runners on first and third, Sosa hit an RBI single, hit number four, to give the Cubs a 7–6 lead. He then stole second for the second time in the game. Later in the inning, the Cubs plated another run and led 8–6.

The Cubs scored another pair in the seventh and led 10–6. In that inning, Sosa singled again for his fifth hit, but that did not figure in the scoring.

The Cubs and Rockies scored single runs in the bottom of the seventh, top of the eighth, and bottom of the eighth, and so when Sosa came to bat for the sixth time in the top of the ninth, the Cubs led 11–8. Sammy led off the ninth with a single and tried to steal his third base of the game. This time, he was thrown out. No further runs came home that night, and the Cubs won by that 11–8 score.

Despite its reputation as a paradise for hitters, this was the only six-hit game in the two years the Rockies played in Mile High Stadium (and only one player has had one in Coors Field in the 29 seasons the Rockies have called that ballpark home, Phil Ervin of the Reds in 2019). Sosa never repeated his six-hit performance; he had two other games in his career in which he had five hits, and oddly for a man who hit

609 career home runs, in this 1993 game in Denver Sosa had five singles and a double.

And no Cub has had a six-hit game in the more than 30 years since Sammy's, although since the end of the 2023 season there have been 26 by other players in nine-inning games.

After nearly 50 years as an American League–only rule, the designated hitter was made an MLB-wide rule beginning with the 2022 season.

But the Cubs had men previously serve as DH when interleague play began, when they played in American League ballparks. Who was the first Cub to serve as a designated hitter?

The Cubs' first interleague game was a crosstown matchup against the White Sox in what was then still called new Comiskey Park. It took place on Monday, June 16, 1997.

The Cubs had gotten off to a rough start that year, beginning the season by losing their first 14 games. That set a franchise and National League record that stands to this day. After that poor start, though, the Cubs had gone 28–26 over their next 54 games and entered the series against the Sox at 28–40. Meanwhile, the Sox, expected to be a contender in the AL Central, began the set with a 30–36 record, though in a weak division they stood just five games out of first place.

The first Cubs player to be entered into a lineup as a designated hitter in a regular season game, that afternoon on the South Side of Chicago, was Dave Clark, an outfielder who had signed with the North Siders before the 1997 season after having played previously for the Royals, Pirates, Dodgers, and Cleveland as well as an earlier stint with the Cubs in 1990. Sadly, Clark never wore No. 5 during his entire MLB career, apparently not wanting to make baseball fans glad all over.

The Cubs came out swinging the big bats in the first inning that 1997 afternoon against former Cub Jaime Navarro, who'd thrown well for the North Siders in 1996 and as a result received a free agent contract from the White Sox for four years and $20 million, big money in those days. Brian McRae led off the game with a single and scored on a triple by Brant Brown. Mark Grace's sacrifice fly scored Brown to make it 2–0 Cubs, and after Sammy Sosa flied to center, Clark came to bat and singled to left, the first at-bat and first hit ever by a Cubs designated hitter.

Clark went 1-for-4 in the game and was eventually replaced by Jose Hernandez, who struck out in his only plate appearance. The Cubs won the game 8–3.

This author attended that game and was amused by the response of a White Sox fan to the question, "When the Cubs play Cleveland, would you root for them?" I expected the answer "Yes," as the Sox and Cleveland were in competition for the AL Central title. Instead the Sox fan replied, "Oh no, we could never do that."

The Cubs wound up playing six games at AL parks in 1997, three on the South Side and three in Cleveland. In addition to Clark, Ryne Sandberg, Scott Servais, and Lance Johnson served as Cubs DHs in that first year of interleague play. Clark hit .385/.467/.615 (5-for-13) as a DH that year with two walks. He also became the first Cub to homer as a designated hitter when he went deep off Jeff Juden of Cleveland in Jacobs Field on Sunday, August 31, 1997. It wasn't enough, though, as the Cubs dropped that game 9–5.

The first designated hitter for the Cubs in a regular-season game at Wrigley Field was during the abbreviated 60-game 2020 season, in which the universal DH was used. That night, Friday, July 24, 2020, Victor Caratini served as the DH against the Brewers. His first DH at-bat for the Cubs was a ground out to third base, and Caratini went 1-for-3 in a 3–0 Cubs win.

The first Cubs DH after the universal DH rule was made permanent in 2022 was also against the Brewers, on Thursday, April 7, 2022, at Wrigley Field. Rafael Ortega was the DH that afternoon and led off the bottom of the first inning with a walk, going 0-for-2 with that base on balls. The Cubs won the game 5–4.

A few Cubs designated hitter records (through the end of the 2023 season):

Most games played, career: 64, Christopher Morel

Most home runs, career: 13, Christopher Morel

Most home runs in a season: 13, Christopher Morel, 2023

Highest OPS, minimum 10 games: 1.074, Alfonso Soriano

HOME RUN FIRSTS

In 1955, Ernie Banks hit five grand slam home runs in a season, setting a new major-league record. The previous record of four had been held by nine different players, including a Cub.

Who was the first Cub to hit four grand slams in a season?

The first Cub to accomplish the feat of four grand slams in a season was also the first player to do it at all, and in an era when home runs weren't the grand accomplishment they became later.

Frank "Wildfire" Schulte, who had been the Cubs' primary right-fielder for several seasons, including for four National League champions in 1906, 1907, 1908, and 1910, had the season of his life in 1911.

That year, Schulte hit .300/.384/.534 and led the National League in home runs, RBI, slugging percentage, OPS+, and total bases. For that performance he won the Chalmers Award, sort of a proto-MVP honor given out by Hugh Chalmers' automobile company, largely done to promote the company (it was discontinued after 1914).

The 21 home runs were more than any Chicago NL player had hit since Ed Williamson set his somewhat-tainted NL record of 27 in 1884 (many of them were hit in a ballpark where the home run distance in left field was only 180 feet, and just 196 in right field). Three other White Stockings players also hit more than 20 that year: Abner Dalrymple (22), Cap Anson (21), and Fred Pfeffer (25). Schulte's 21 were also the most by any major-league player since Buck Freeman of Washington hit 25 in 1899.

Here are the details of Schulte's record-setting four grand slams in 1911:

Sunday, June 3, vs. New York Giants at West Side Grounds: *Schulte stepped to the plate in the bottom of the eighth with the game tied 4–4, the bases loaded and two out, and, per the* Chicago Tribune, *"hit the steel score board" in right field for a grand slam. The Cubs won the game 8–4, and the* Tribune *said, "The great crowd roared and rooted so long that not one in twenty saw [Solly] Hofman close the rally with a fly." The win moved the Cubs to within half a game of the first-place Giants.*

Tuesday, July 4, vs. Cincinnati Reds at West Side Grounds: *Schulte's grand slam (also off the right-field scoreboard, per the* Tribune) *was part of an eight-run inning that also featured a two-run homer by Joe Tinker. That accounted for all the scoring in an 8–3 Cubs win in the first game of a doubleheader.*

Tuesday, July 18, vs. Boston Rustlers at Boston: *The Cubs led 7–3 in the top of the sixth when Schulte smacked a home run with the bases loaded (or, as the* Tribune *put it, "with the bases choked with Cubs"). The Cubs went on to win 14–6; Schulte went 3-for-4 with four runs scored.*

Wednesday, August 16, vs. Boston Rustlers at Boston: *This time, the* Tribune *described the bases as "clogged" when Schulte homered in the top of the fourth with the Cubs trailing 3–0. That highlighted an eight-run inning, and the Cubs breezed to a 13–6 win over a Boston club that, truth be told, wasn't very good; they finished 44–107, 54 games out of first place. The Cubs were in first place after this victory, a game ahead of the Pirates and 2 1/2 ahead of the Giants, but the Giants roared to a 37–13 finish and took the pennant by seven games, while the Cubs went 27–25 in the same span.*

In addition to all the grand slams, Schulte also took time to get married that summer. Several of the newspaper recaps referred to him as "Bridegroom F. Schulte."

Schulte continued with the Cubs until the middle of the 1916 season, when he was traded to the Pirates for a backup catcher named Art Wilson, and he later also played for the Philadelphia Phillies and Washington Senators. He played several years in the minors after his major-league career ended, then left baseball after 1923 and settled in Oakland, California, where he died in 1949, aged 67. Schulte, along with 55 other Cubs greats, was named to the new Cubs Hall of Fame in 2021.

Here are the eight other players who hit four grand slams in a season, tying Schulte's record, before Banks broke it in 1955:

Babe Ruth, 1919
Lou Gehrig, 1934
Rudy York, 1938
Vince DiMaggio, 1945
Tommy Henrich, 1948
Ralph Kiner, 1949
Sid Gordon, 1950
Ray Boone, 1953

Jim Gentile tied Banks' record of five in 1961, and it was broken by Don Mattingly, who hit six in 1987. Travis Hafner also hit six, in 2006. Banks' five grand slams in a season remains the National League record, tied by Albert Pujols in 2009.

Walk-off wins are always fun and exciting, and especially so when a hitter smacks a ball out of the ballpark for a walk-off home run.

Who was the first player to hit a walk-off home run at Wrigley Field?

The Cubs moved into their North Side home in 1916, though it was not called "Wrigley Field" at the time. Instead the ballyard was named "Weeghman Park," after team owner Charlie Weeghman, who had bought the Cubs that year as part of a settlement between the existing National and American Leagues and the upstart Federal League, in which Weeghman had owned a team and built the park at Clark and Addison Streets in Chicago to be its home in 1914.

Even though home runs were not yet happening on a regular basis in that era—the entire Cubs team hit just 46 of them in 1916—the first walk-off homer by a Cub at the North Side ballpark was hit by Heinie Zimmerman on Thursday, July 13, 1916, winning the game over the Philadelphia Phillies 6–5.

The Cubs had taken a 4–2 lead into the ninth inning of that game, but the Phillies loaded the bases on two walks and a hit with nobody out and scored a pair on a single by Wilbur Good. Good eventually scored another run in that inning on a Cubs error, and the Phillies took a 5–4 lead.

In the bottom of the ninth, Max Flack walked with one out, and after Cy Williams popped out, Zimmerman smashed his walk-off blast, though, of course, no one called these sorts of hits "walk-offs" in 1916. The *Chicago Tribune* called it a "vicious wallop" and said Zimmerman's homer was "a long, tall fly whaled" over the right-field wall, clearly a reference to Weeghman's Chicago Federal League team known as the Whales, who had inhabited that ballpark the previous year and, in fact, had won that league's championship.

Heinie Zimmerman had been a Cubs infielder, primarily a third baseman, since 1907, and had played for the Cubs in the World Series in 1907 and 1910. He had his best year in 1912, when he batted .372/.418/.571 and led the National League in batting average, slugging percentage, hits, doubles, home runs, RBI, and total bases, becoming the first National League player in the modern era to win baseball's Triple Crown. Despite that, he finished just sixth in the voting for the Chalmers Award, a sort of proto-MVP Award, the award going to Larry Doyle of the Giants.

By 1916, Zimmerman's performance had declined somewhat, though he still led the league with 83 RBI. About six weeks after his walk-off homer, Zimmerman was traded to the Giants—and Doyle was one of the players coming to the Cubs in the deal, along with Herb Hunter and Merwin Jacobson. None of these players had much impact on the Cubs.

Heinie Zimmerman in 1912, when he had another first—the National League's first unofficial Triple Crown.

Zimmerman, though, drove in 100 runs for the pennant-winning Giants in 1917, leading the league again. He became better known for his role in a botched rundown during the World Series against the White Sox. When the Giants' first baseman failed to back up their catcher with the Sox' Eddie Collins in a rundown, Zimmerman wound up chasing Collins to the plate, where he scored a key run in the sixth and deciding game. Though the play wasn't really Zimmerman's fault, the press made him the goat and the tag stuck.

In later days, Zimmerman was accused of throwing games and partly as a result, left baseball and returned to New York City, where he worked a succession of blue-collar jobs before he passed away in 1969 from a heart attack.

Zimmerman's walk-off was technically not in "Wrigley Field," as the ballyard did not officially get that name until December 1926. Thus, the first walk-off home run in Wrigley as we know it by that name today was hit by Kiki Cuyler, a two-run shot in the 10th inning against Brooklyn on Friday, June 27, 1930.

Cuyler was a legitimately great player who is largely forgotten today, even though he's a member of baseball's Hall of Fame. Acquired by the Cubs in a steal of a trade from the Pirates in November 1927 for Sparky Adams and Pete Scott, Cuyler strung together three great seasons for the team from 1928 to 1930, leading the National League in stolen bases all three years. His league-leading total in 1930 was 37 steals. No Cubs player would swipe that many again until Ivan de Jesus had 41 in 1978.

Though his performance had begun to decline by 1932, Cuyler came back from injuries late in the year to put on a streak that perhaps has not been matched by any Cub since then. In his final 28 games in 1932 he hit .373/.408/.568 with five home runs and 27 RBI.

The Cubs capped their pennant drive with 14 wins in a row beginning August 20. Starting August 27, Cuyler put together this weeklong hot streak:

August 27, doubleheader vs. Giants: Three-run homer as the Cubs won, 6–1, their eighth win in a row. In the second game, Cuyler had a single and run scored and the winning streak reached nine.

August 28, vs. Giants: Three hits including an eighth-inning homer. Cuyler's sacrifice fly was the game winner, 5–4 for their 10th straight victory.

August 30, vs. Giants: Two hits, two RBI, yet another eighth-inning homer in another 5–4 win, the 11th straight.

August 31, vs. Giants: Four hits. Cuyler singled in the tying run in the ninth that evened the game at 5–5. The Giants scored four in the top of the tenth, taking a 9–5 lead. In the last of the 10th, after the first two men were routine outs, the Cubs scored two and have two on for Cuyler, who hits a walk-off home run, his second of the season. The Cubs won 10–9, for the 12th consecutive win. This comeback and home run was celebrated in the day as one of the greatest moments in Cubs history, but after Gabby Hartnett hit his famed "Homer in the Gloamin'" six years later, it has been almost forgotten. In addition, there had been a partial eclipse of the sun visible from Chicago that occurred about an hour before the game that afternoon, and newspaper reports noted that Cubs players had (safely) spent some time viewing the eclipse.

September 2, vs. Cardinals: Cuyler homers again, his fifth in six games. The Cubs win 8–5, the winning streak reaching 13. The streak extended one more game to 14, then it ended on a day Cuyler was hitless. Perhaps that wasn't a coincidence.

Further injuries took their toll on Cuyler's career, and the Cubs released him midway through the 1935 season. He played a couple more years with the Reds and Dodgers and retired with a .321 lifetime BA (.325 as a Cub) and 2,299 hits. He passed away in 1950 from a heart attack and was posthumously elected to the Hall of Fame by a veterans committee in 1968.

Grand slam home runs are always exciting, scoring four runs on a single hit.

Who was the first Cub to hit a grand slam as a pinch-hitter?

Often, by their very nature, pinch-hitters are obscure players. Perhaps they're not quite good enough to be everyday regulars, and so serve as bench players and substitutes, called on "in a pinch" (that's the literal origin of the term "pinch-hitter") to try to help the team.

Few Cubs would match this description better than Charles Tolson, who played in parts of four seasons for the Cubs in 1926–1927 and 1929–1930, never having more than 123 plate appearances in any of those years. Sometimes called "Chick" during his playing days, Tolson was a first baseman when he played the field but served as a pinch-hitter in 86 of the 141 games he played for the Cubs.

It was in that role that he stepped to the plate at Wrigley Field Sunday, May 1, 1927, in a game against the Pirates in the bottom of the seventh inning, batting for pitcher Percy Jones with the Cubs trailing 5–2 and the bases loaded.

Irving Vaughan of the *Chicago Tribune* described what happened next:

Like the movie hero who usually arrives at the proper moment, Charles Julius Tolson strolled into Wrigley Field yesterday and delivered one punch. The punch sent the ball spinning into the seats with the bases loaded, a flock of runners scooted home amid the wildest scene that 33,000 customers could possibly create, and it looked like the Cubs were "in."

Tolson's pinch-hit grand slam gave the team a 6–5 lead and indeed, with that lead after seven innings and the team's best pitcher, Charlie Root, on the mound, it looked like a Cubs victory would follow.

Unfortunately, Root walked the bases full of Pirates with two out in the top of the ninth and a single by future Hall of Famer Paul Waner scored two runs. Pittsburgh held on for a 7–6 victory.

That spoiled Tolson's feat, and in becoming the first Cubs hitter to pinch-bat a grand slam, he also set another team first: He became the first Cub whose first two home runs came as a pinch-hitter, the other coming nearly a year earlier, on Wednesday, June 3, 1926, in Cincinnati. On that afternoon, Tolson batted for Cliff Heathcote with a runner on base and the game tied 3–3 in the 10th inning. Not only did he hit a home run, but it was inside the park and gave the Cubs a 5–3 win.

Tolson hit just two other home runs in his brief major-league career, one later in 1927, the other in the Cubs' pennant year of 1929. Tolson played a bit more that year, starting 29 games at first base, and did play in the World Series, though it was just a single pinch-hit at-bat. Tolson was sent up to bat for pitcher Guy Bush with two out in the ninth in Game 1 with the Cubs trailing 3–0 and runners on second and third. With a chance to be a World Series hero, Tolson struck out to end the game.

After playing just 13 games for the Cubs in 1930, Tolson was swapped to the then-independent minor-league Minneapolis Millers for George Kelly. Tolson never played in the major leagues again, and he returned to his hometown of Washington, DC. He passed away there in 1965, aged 66. Despite the same last name and residence in the nation's capital, Charles Tolson was apparently unrelated to Clyde Tolson, who was J. Edgar Hoover's longtime second in command at the FBI.

Twenty-nine Cubs have pinch-hit grand slams through the end of the 2023 season. Here are the most recent 10:

Dwight Smith, July 30, 1989 (first game), vs. Philadelphia Phillies at Philadelphia, seventh inning

Andre Dawson, April 19, 1991, vs. Pittsburgh Pirates at Pittsburgh, ninth inning

Glenallen Hill, August 20, 1998, vs. San Francisco Giants at Wrigley Field, fifth inning

Roosevelt Brown, September 19, 2000, vs. Milwaukee Brewers at Milwaukee, sixth inning

Julio Zuleta, June 5, 2001, vs. St. Louis Cardinals at Wrigley Field, seventh inning

Michael Barrett, May 28, 2004 (first game), vs. Pittsburgh Pirates at Pittsburgh, seventh inning

Derrek Lee, May 19, 2007, vs. Chicago White Sox at Wrigley Field, eighth inning

Mike Fontenot, May 7, 2010, vs. Cincinnati Reds at Cincinnati, eighth inning

David DeJesus, May 11, 2012, vs. Milwaukee Brewers at Milwaukee, seventh inning

David Bote, August 11, 2018, vs. Washington Nationals at Wrigley Field, ninth inning (ultimate grand slam walk-off)

Nineteen different Cubs have hit 40 or more home runs in a season. Who was the first Cubs hitter to accomplish this feat?

Earlier, we learned that Ed Williamson was the first Cub to hit more than 20 home runs in a season (27), and Williamson only accomplished that feat because of the freakish dimensions of Lake Front Park in 1884. When the team was forced to move out of the park the following year, the home runs vanished.

Williamson's 27 home runs remained the National League record until the home-run explosion of the 1920s. Rogers Hornsby, then with the Cardinals, was the man to break that mark, blowing right by 30 homers and smashing 42 in 1922.

But Williamson's 27 remained the Cubs franchise record for a few years after that. Hack Wilson broke it when he hit a league-leading 30 home runs in 1927, and Wilson kept up the barrage and led the NL again in 1928 with 31 round-trippers. He broke his own team mark again in 1929 with 39 dingers but finished third in the league, tied with Hornsby and behind Mel Ott of the Giants (42) and Chuck Klein of the Phillies (43).

In 1930, though, Wilson blew right past 40 and 50 and set both a franchise and league record by hitting 56 home runs.

That number and that year come with quite the story.

The baseball itself had been made "lively" in the early 1920s, and that led to a home-run and run-scoring explosion across the sport, led by Babe Ruth, whose home-run feats helped pack American League ballparks. National League teams were a bit slow to follow, but as noted earlier, the 30- and 40-home-run man was not unusual in the NL by the end of the 1920s.

In 1929 and 1930, though, the "lively ball" led to the two highest-scoring seasons in the history of the game. Teams averaged 5.19 runs per game in 1929 and 5.55 in 1930, and in 1930 the Cubs scored 998 runs, a modern-era franchise record that will likely stand forever (the most any Cubs team has scored since then is 855, in 2008). The entire National League batted .303 that year, and the woeful Phillies, who finished last with 102 losses, were fourth in the league with 944 runs—the losses coming from the 1,199 runs they allowed, a major-league record that should also stand for all time (one recent team has come close, the 1996 Tigers, who allowed 1,103 runs, one of just two clubs to allow more than 1,000 runs since 1939). It was said by some players that the 1930 ball, in particular, had "sunken" seams, meaning the seams on the ball were harder to grip for pitchers and thus breaking balls were far less effective. Presuming that's true, the resulting offensive barrage was totally predictable.

Wilson's 56 home runs lapped the field. He hit "only" four home runs in 16 games in April but followed that with 10 in May, eight in June, 11 in July, and 13 in August (while hitting .398; had there been a Player of the Month Award back then, he surely would have won it).

Wilson became the first Cub—and first NL player—to hit the 50 home-run level when, against all odds, his 50th came in the air off Phillies right-hander Phil Collins in the second game of a doubleheader on September 15, a game the Cubs won 6–4.

No one else hit more than 40 in the NL in 1930, and just two AL greats, Ruth (49) and Lou Gehrig (41), topped 40 in the American League.

Despite Wilson's fantastic season—in addition to leading the league in home runs, he led in RBI (a franchise- and major-league record 191), walks (105—no Cub would walk that many times again until Richie Ashburn had 116 in 1960), and slugging percentage (.723, which remained the club record until Sammy Sosa broke it at .737 in 2001)—the Cubs fell short of a second straight NL pennant. Leading by four games with 17 to go, they lost nine of their next 13 to fall three games behind the Cardinals, who ended the year on a 17–4 run. A six-game Cubs winning streak to end the year wasn't enough, and they finished two games out of first place.

This result would wind up having an effect on the franchise that would last many years. Owner William Wrigley, upset at the team's September collapse, fired manager Joe McCarthy, replacing him with Hornsby as player-manager. McCarthy went on to win eight pennants and seven World Series in 16 years as Yankees manager from 1931 to 1946. Hornsby was so reviled by his players that he wound up fired by mid-1932. There's no way, of course, to know whether the Cubs would have had that sort of success under McCarthy, but it was absolutely a tremendously short-sighted move by ownership.

Wilson's 191 RBI in 1930 has stood the test of time most of all. It remains one of the game's legendary feats and is primarily responsible for his induction into the Hall of Fame in 1977 (the same year as Ernie Banks). While big RBI totals were fairly common in the 1930s, there have been just nine player seasons with 150 or more RBI in the expansion era, the most 165 by Manny Ramirez in 1999. Cubs slugger Sammy Sosa had 160 in 2001, the most by any Cub since Wilson.

A story goes that when Dave Kingman was negotiating his first Cubs contract with then–general manager Bob Kennedy, he experienced a flash of inspiration and asked Kennedy whether a clause could be written into the contract awarding him a large bonus if he broke the team record for RBI in a season. Kennedy readily agreed and wrote the desired language and amounts into the text by hand. After signing and shaking hands, Kingman thought to ask, "By the way, what *is* the team record for RBI in a season?" Kennedy replied, deadpan: "One hundred and ninety." (The official number was updated to 191 in 1999.) Needless to say, Kingman didn't break that record; his best RBI season for the Cubs was 1979, when he had 115.

In 1931, the National League, a bit alarmed at the balance between hitting and pitching being too skewed, introduced a "deader" ball. Offense quickly dropped and the league batting average slipped to a more reasonable .277. Wilson, unable to adjust to Hornsby's strict managerial style, hit just 13 home runs and in August wound up suspended without pay for the rest of the year for his role in an off-field fight involving teammate Pat Malone. He was traded to the Dodgers after the 1931 season and fell on hard times after his playing career ended, passing away in Baltimore in 1948, aged just 48.

After Wilson, no Cub would hit 40 home runs in a season until Hank Sauer hit 41 in 1954. Sosa would break Wilson's team record of 56 with his 66-homer season in 1998, and overall Sosa has the most 40+ home-run seasons in Cubs history, with seven. In three of Sosa's 40+ home-run seasons, he had 60 or more, but he did not lead the league in any of them. His only league-leading totals were 50, in 2000, and 49, in 2003.

Besides Sosa, the only Cub to hit 40 or more home runs in a season more than once is Ernie Banks, who did it five times. No Cub has hit 40 or more home runs in a season since Derrek Lee's 46 in 2005. Besides Wilson, Sosa, Banks, Sauer, and Lee, the other Cubs to hit 40 or more home runs in a season are Billy Williams (42 in 1970), Kingman (48 in 1979), Andre Dawson (49 in 1987), and Ryne Sandberg (40 in 1990).

Pitchers no longer come to the plate and bat in Major League Baseball, but before that era ended after the 2021 season, 96 pitchers had hit grand slams in the sport's modern era (since 1900).
Who was the first Cubs pitcher to hit a grand slam, and what other distinction among all grand slam–hitting pitchers does this pitcher hold?

Pitchers often weren't very good hitters, which made their occasional home runs that much more fun to watch.

Three pitchers hit grand slams off Cubs hurlers before the first Cubs moundsman accomplished that feat: Freddie Fitzsimmons of the New York Giants smashed one off Pat Malone in 1931, Roy Parmelee of the Giants went deep with the bases loaded off Lon Warneke in 1934, and Al Hollingsworth of the Cincinnati Reds hit a slam, also off Warneke, in 1936.

The following year, Cubs right-hander Clay Bryant became the first North Siders hurler to hit a grand slam.

It happened in the second game of a doubleheader on Saturday, August 28, 1937, at Braves Field in Boston, against the team then known as the "Bees."

The Cubs had lost the first game 3–1 but led Game 2 by a 6–3 margin heading to the bottom of the ninth. Charlie Root was on the mound with that lead, but five hits off him, Clyde Shoun, and Bryant tied the game at 6 each. Bryant allowed the hit that scored the tying run before recording the final out of the inning, sending the game to extras.

In the top of the 10th inning, Lonny Frey and Phil Cavarretta singled after the first two hitters were retired. The Bees pitched around

Tuck Stainback, thinking they could dispose of Bryant, the pitcher, batting next.

It wasn't a smart call. Bryant was actually a pretty good hitter, particularly for a pitcher. Entering that game he was batting .303/.343/.364 (10-for-33) with 11 runs scored and had been frequently used as a pinch-hitter and pinch-runner.

Chicago Tribune writer Irving Vaughan described what happened when Bryant stepped to the plate: "Bryant boomed his homer beyond the 368 foot sign close to the left field foul line and there was an impressive parade across the plate."

Even with that, Bryant's day wasn't all good. He walked the first two Boston hitters in the bottom of the 10th, and then he was replaced by Curt Davis. An error scored a run, but Davis finished off the rest of Boston's lineup and the Cubs won 10–7.

At the time, the win allowed the Cubs to maintain a one-game lead in the National League pennant race, but despite going down the stretch with a 20–14 record from September 1 on, they were surpassed by the Giants, who went 24–10 and won the pennant by three games, even though the Cubs posted a 93-win year.

As for Bryant, he would go on to have a fine 19–11 season in 1938 with a 3.10 ERA, helping the Cubs win that year's NL pennant. He also hit .226 with three home runs and finished 15th in NL MVP balloting.

Injuries—specifically, bone chips in Bryant's right elbow—ended his playing career only a couple of years later, and his departure from the Cubs came with some acrimony after they had cut his pay in 1940. Bryant would go on to have a long career coaching and managing in the Dodgers organization, though he was passed over in favor of Walter Alston when it seemed he was line to manage their major-league team in 1954. He continued coaching in both the Dodgers and Cleveland organizations through the 1970s and then retired to Florida, where he passed away in 1999, aged 87.

Bryant's singular distinction among pitchers who hit grand slams: He's the only one in major-league history to ever do so in an extra inning.

Just six other Cubs pitchers hit grand slam home runs—and just three did it at Wrigley Field:

Claude Passeau, May 19, 1941, vs. the Brooklyn Dodgers at Wrigley Field

Ox Miller, September 7, 1947, vs. the Pirates at Pittsburgh

Burt Hooton, September 16, 1972, vs. the Mets at Wrigley Field (off Tom Seaver!)

Kevin Tapani, July 20, 1998, vs. the Braves at Atlanta

Jason Marquis, September 22, 2008, vs. the Mets at New York

Travis Wood, May 30, 2013, vs. the White Sox at Wrigley Field

Pinch-hit home runs are always unexpected and fun. The Cubs have had 355 pinch homers in their history.

When was the first time the Cubs had two pinch-hit home runs in the same game?

Pinch-hitting is an art, and not suited for everyone. It requires focus and preparation, as the player must be ready to enter the game at a moment's notice and bat, having not previously been part of that game. The success level is relatively low, and for home runs, even lower.

Two men who played for one of the worst teams in Cubs franchise history up to that time, the 90-loss 1954 Cubs, were the first men to both hit pinch home runs in the same game. Joe Garagiola and Bill Serena did it for the North Siders against the Philadelphia Phillies at Wrigley Field in the second game of a doubleheader on Wednesday, June 9, 1954.

Garagiola was the first to go deep as a bat off the bench that afternoon when he batted for Bob Rush with one out in the seventh inning. Serena followed two innings later, leading off the ninth as a pinch-hitter for Turk Lown and hitting a ball into the left-field bleachers.

Given that this was a very bad Cubs team, you will not be surprised to learn that the Cubs lost this game anyway, and it wasn't close. The Phillies hammered four home runs and defeated the Cubs soundly, 14–6. The win, in front of 11,238 at Wrigley, completed a doubleheader sweep for the visitors, as they had shut out the Cubs 4–0 in the opener.

Joe Garagiola grew up on what was termed "The Hill" in St. Louis as Yogi Berra's best friend and signed with his hometown Cardinals. It was said by some at the time the two men both signed baseball contracts that Garagiola was the better player as a youth.

Garagiola played five-plus years for St. Louis, eventually being traded to the Pirates in 1951. Two years later he came to the Cubs in a massive trade whose centerpiece was slugger Ralph Kiner. Kiner and Garagiola were sent by Pittsburgh, along with George "Catfish" Metkovich and pitcher Howie Pollet, to the Cubs for Bob Addis, Toby Atwell, George Freese, Gene Hermanski, Bob Schultz, and Preston Ward. The Cubs threw in $150,000, a huge sum in those days and roughly equivalent to $1.7 million today. Massive trades like this were popular in the mid-1950s; in fact, one 17-player deal was completed that same year between the Orioles and Yankees, and in 1956 Baltimore's general manager Paul Richards proposed swapping entire 25-man rosters with the Athletics. That deal failed only because the A's insisted on keeping Roger Maris and Clete Boyer (if only they hadn't later traded them to New York!). These deals rarely helped both teams and eventually fell out of favor.

Garagiola played the rest of 1953 and part of the following year with the Cubs before the team waived him in September 1954 and the Giants claimed him. In 137 games with the Cubs, Garagiola batted .276/.365/.381 with six home runs. After his playing career ended, he joined the Cardinals' radio broadcast team and eventually went on to a decades-long broadcasting career that included stints as host of NBC's *Today* show and calling World Series games for the network.

Bill Serena did not have quite as storied a life; his major-league baseball career lasted six seasons, mostly as a spare-part infielder for the Cubs, though he did hit 17 home runs in 127 games in 1950 and 15 in 122 games in 1952. The White Sox acquired him from the Cubs after the 1954 season, though he never played for them, instead finishing his playing career with three minor-league seasons, following which he became a scout for the Braves and Marlins, serving in that capacity for nearly 40 years before retiring in 1994. Serena passed away in 1996, aged 70.

In recent years, Cubs fans have been thrilled by walk-off grand slams by Jason Heyward and David Bote, the latter an "ultimate grand slam," defined as a player hitting a bases-loaded walk-off homer with his team down by three runs.

Who was the first Cub to hit an ultimate grand slam?

The ultimate grand slam got its name because, indeed, it's the ultimate way to win a game. Make an out in that situation and your team likely loses by three runs. But hit a home run at that point, as Bote did, and you suddenly become a one-run winner and send your home crowd into a frenzy.

Through the end of the 2023 season this has been done just 32 times in major-league history. Hall of Famers Babe Ruth and Alan Trammell accomplished this feat, but ultimate slams have also been hit by guys you otherwise likely have never heard of, including Roger Freed and Brooks Conrad.

Another one of the men who never had a big name in baseball who hit an ultimate grand slam is the answer to this question: Cubs outfielder Ellis Burton, who did it in a win over Houston on Saturday, August 31, 1963.

After a 1962 season in which they set a franchise record for losses with 103, the Cubs got off to a fine start in 1963, actually sitting atop the National League (tied with the Giants) in early June, largely due to solid starting pitching from Dick Ellsworth and Larry Jackson.

While they had fallen into the NL's "second division" (a term given back in the days of divisionless leagues to the teams in the bottom half of the standings) by August, they still had a winning record at 68–64 when the then–Houston Colt .45s visited Wrigley Field for a three-game series beginning August 30.

The Cubs lost the first game of the series 5–1, and Jackson got hit hard early in the second game of the set and didn't make it out of the second inning, departing with a 4–0 deficit.

Meanwhile, the Cubs had all kinds of opportunities through the first eight innings of the game, recording seven hits off Houston starter Hal Brown but could score only once.

Thus, many of the crowd of 9,027 had likely departed by the time the Cubs batted in the bottom of the ninth trailing 5–1.

With one out, Merritt Ranew singled, but that was followed by a fly to right by Dick Bertell. Don Landrum laid down a bunt and beat it out for a hit, putting runners on first and second. A single by Andre Rodgers scored Ranew to make it 5–2. Brown was replaced by another Hal, Woodeshick, who walked Leo Burke to load the bases.

Burton stepped to the plate. Richard Dozer of the *Chicago Tribune* describes what happened:

> *Ellis Burton, the outfielder Houston didn't want last spring, yesterday climaxed a month he will never forget with his happiest moment in baseball.*
>
> *Hal Woodeshick, Houston's ace relief man, threw only one pitch to Burton. It was below the waist—and fast. Burton swung with the vengeance of an angry man, and lined the ball into the left field bleachers, a grand slam home run that gave the Cubs a stunning 6 to 5 victory.*

The *Tribune* quoted Burton as saying, "There's no team in the big leagues I want to beat as bad as this one."

That was Burton's seventh home run of August, during which he also became the eighth player in major-league history (and second Cub, after Augie Galan in 1937) to switch-hit home runs in the same game.

As Dozer wrote, Burton had been discarded by Houston near the end of spring training in 1963, and Cleveland picked him up. He played in just 26 games for them, mostly as a pinch-hitter, before the Cubs acquired him for cash considerations on May 27. Without a true center fielder on the roster, Cubs head coach (still the title for the team's leader despite the official end of the team's College of Coaches) Bob Kennedy installed Burton in that position, and he began to hit, eventually batting .230/.311/.398 in 93 games for the Cubs, with 12 home runs, fourth-most on the team behind future Hall of Famers Ron Santo, Billy Williams, and Ernie Banks.

But a Cubs prospect named Billy Cowan, who had been named Topps Minor League Player of the Year in 1963 when he hit .315/.332/.519 with 25 home runs for Triple-A Salt Lake City, was given the center field job during spring training in 1964, and Burton was relegated to the bench. He played in just 14 games, mostly as a pinch-hitter, and went just 1-for-20 before he was sent to Double-A Fort Worth at the end of May. Returning to the big leagues at the end of August, Burton hit about as well as he had for the Cubs in 1963, but it wasn't enough to allow him to stick in the majors.

Burton then spent time in the Cubs system in Triple-A in 1965, playing just 17 games in the big leagues that year, and the Cubs released him in September. He returned to his native California after his baseball career ended and spent many years as a bank manager before he passed away at age 77 in 2013.

Two players have hit ultimate grand slams against the Cubs, one of those men famous, one not. Future Hall of Famer Roberto Clemente did it July 25, 1956, in just his second year as a major leaguer, and an inside-the-park slam at that. And Houston's Brian Bogusevic got a bit of revenge for Burton's slam 48 years later when he hit an ultimate slam off Cubs closer Carlos Marmol.

The Cubs were supposed to play the inaugural night game under artificial light at Wrigley Field on Monday, August 8, 1988, against the Philadelphia Phillies. Ryne Sandberg homered off Kevin Gross in the bottom of the first inning that night, but that home run was taken out of the record books when the game didn't reach official status due to a torrential rainstorm.

Who hit the first official Cubs home run in a night game at Wrigley Field?

After that Sandberg long ball—it left the yard and went to Waveland!—was wiped out by the downpour that erased the August 8 game from the books, the Cubs played the first official game under the lights the following day against the New York Mets. The Cubs defeated the visitors 6–4, but no Cub homered that evening. Lenny Dykstra went deep for the Mets, becoming the first player to homer in a Wrigley Field night game, and Howard Johnson also homered for New York, so two visiting players homered in a Wrigley night game before a Cub did.

The honor of being the first Cub to homer in a night game at Wrigley went to Damon Berryhill, who smacked a two-run home run off Houston's Mike Scott in the second inning on Monday, August 22, 1988.

Not content with just doing it once for the record books, Berryhill hit a second long ball that night, a three-run job in the bottom of the eighth that gave the Cubs a 6–4 lead. Unfortunately, Goose Gossage, who had a rough year in his only campaign as the Cubs closer, served up a game-tying two-run single in the ninth. The game went to extra innings and the Cubs lost 9–7 in 10.

Damon Berryhill was the Cubs' first-round pick in the old January phase of the MLB Draft in 1984 out of Orange Coast College in Costa Mesa, California. He rose through the system to make his MLB debut in 1987 and by 1988 was sharing time behind the plate for the Cubs with Jody Davis.

With Davis traded away to Atlanta at the end of the 1988 season, Berryhill and Joe Girardi became the Cubs' catching tandem for the 1989 NL East champion Cubs, but Berryhill's season ended early with a shoulder injury that required rotator cuff surgery. We are thus left to wonder whether the Cubs might have had a better NLCS with a healthy Berryhill in the lineup. He spent much of 1990 in the minor leagues rehabbing the injury, playing only 17 games for the Cubs, and then was swapped to the Atlanta Braves in a weird deal that happened only three days before the end of the 1991 season. The Cubs acquired Turk Wendell and Yorkis Perez for Berryhill. Berryhill drifted through the Braves, Red Sox, Reds, and Giants organizations and retired after 1997. He later became a minor-league coach and manager in the Rangers, Dodgers, and Braves organizations.

Berryhill hit 47 home runs in his major-league career. The two-homer game against the Astros in 1988 was the only multihomer game of his career and the five RBI was also a career high.

Including those two home runs by Berryhill against Houston in 1988, the Cubs have hit 973 home runs in 892 games under the lights at Wrigley, through the end of the 2023 season. Sammy Sosa is the individual leader with 60 night-game homers at Wrigley, and Anthony Rizzo is second with 54.

Sixty-two different major-league players have hit two home runs in an inning.
Who was the first Cub to accomplish this feat?

It took more than a century of baseball history before a Chicago Cubs player would hit two home runs in an inning. It happened 32 times—and Willie McCovey, Andre Dawson, and Jeff King would do it twice—before Sammy Sosa became the first Cub to homer twice in an inning. He did it on Thursday, May 16, 1996, against the Houston Astros at Wrigley Field.

The Cubs had taken a 3–0 lead over Houston when Leo Gomez smacked a three-run homer in the second inning off Doug Drabek and extended that to 5–0 in the third on an RBI groundout by Gomez, followed by an error that allowed a second run to score.

The score remained 5–0 Cubs as they came to bat in the bottom of the seventh. Sosa led off the inning against Houston reliever Jeff Tabaka and homered. After Luis Gonzalez walked, Scott Servais also homered to make the score 8–0.

Tabaka recorded the first out of the inning, then issued another walk, this one to Rey Sanchez. That brought Houston manager Terry Collins out of the dugout to lift Tabaka, replacing him with Jim Dougherty. Dougherty allowed a single, then recorded the second out of the inning. That was followed by another walk, loading the bases, and Mark Grace then doubled. That cleared the bases and made the score 11–0. Sosa was the next batter, coming up for the second time in the inning. He blasted Dougherty's first offering out of the ballpark, his second home run of the inning, giving the Cubs a 13–0 lead. Houston scored a consolation run in the ninth, making the final score 13–1.

Oddly, the *Chicago Tribune* recap of this game barely mentioned Sosa's feat, focusing instead on pitcher Amaury Telemaco, who allowed just one hit in seven innings of work.

Since Sosa's accomplishment made him the first Cub to homer twice in an inning, two other Cubs have done it.

Mark Bellhorn hit two home runs in a 10-run fourth inning against the Brewers at Milwaukee on Thursday, August 29, 2002. The first was a three-run shot and the second a solo blast, and the Cubs needed every one of those runs in a 13–10 victory. Bellhorn's feat was unusual in that he switch-hit his two homers. The first was hit right-handed off lefty Andrew Lorraine. When Bellhorn came up again in the inning, his homer was hit left-handed off righty Jose Cabrera. Just two other players have switch-hit two homers in an inning: Carlos Baerga in 1993 and Kendrys Morales in 2012.

Jim Edmonds slammed a pair of homers in a nine-run fourth inning against the White Sox on Saturday, June 21, 2008, at Wrigley Field. The Cubs entered that inning trailing 4–1. Edmonds led off the inning with a homer, which was followed by another long ball from Mike Fontenot. With two runners on and one out, three straight Cubs hit RBI singles, and Aramis Ramirez followed with a three-run homer to make the score 9–4. The White Sox brought in left-hander Boone Logan to face the lefty-hitting Edmonds, but that gambit failed when Edmonds homered for the second time in the inning. The Cubs won the game 11–7.

Here are the four players who have hit two home runs in an inning against the Cubs:

Hank Leiber, New York Giants, August 24, 1935, second inning, off Tex Carleton and Clyde Shoun, at New York. The Giants won 9–4.

Lee May, Houston Astros, April 29, 1974, sixth inning, off Burt Hooton and Jim Kremmel, at Houston. The Astros won 18–2.

Andre Dawson, Montreal Expos, September 24, 1985, fifth inning, off Ray Fontenot and Jon Perlman, at Wrigley Field. The Expos won 17–15. Dawson had previously hit another home run in this game, in the first inning.

Juan Uribe, San Francisco Giants, September 23, 2010, second inning, off Ryan Dempster and Thomas Diamond, at Wrigley Field. The Giants won 13–0.

On April 19, 1969, the Cubs played their first-ever game in Montreal, and Ron Santo homered to become the first Cub to hit a home run outside the United States.

Since then, the Cubs have played numerous games in Canada but also have had seven contests take place outside North America.

Who was the first Cub to hit a home run outside North America?

The Cubs and Mets were chosen to play MLB's first series in Asia, a pair of games that took place on March 29 and 30, 2000, at the Tokyo Dome.

The Mets reached the NLCS the previous season, but the Cubs had come off a rough 1999 season in which they lost 95 games. Why, then, were these teams chosen to face each other in Japan?

At that time, Sammy Sosa had acquired worldwide notoriety due to his 1998 home-run race with Mark McGwire. The Mets had traded for All-Star catcher Mike Piazza during the 1998 season. Both of these players had gained much popularity in Japan, so it was thought these two big-market teams would attract fans to the first-ever major-league games played in Tokyo.

A solid pitching matchup was slated for the opener between Jon Lieber of the Cubs and Mike Hampton of the Mets, and the game went as advertised for the first six innings. An RBI single by Damon Buford gave the Cubs a 1–0 lead in the top of the first, and Lieber held the Mets scoreless until the bottom of the third, when a sacrifice fly by Darryl Hamilton scored Rey Ordonez to tie the game 1–1. A bases-loaded walk in the top of the fifth gave the Cubs a 2–1 lead.

That's where things stood in the top of the seventh. Sosa led off the inning with a walk, and one out later Shane Andrews homered off Mets left-hander Dennis Cook to give the Cubs a 4–1 lead. Andrews thus became the first Cub to homer outside North America. Another homer by Mark Grace in the eighth made it 5–1, and the Cubs hung on for a 5–3 win.

Andrews was the first-round pick (11th overall) of the Montreal Expos in the 1990 draft. Rising through the Expos system, he made his MLB debut in 1995, and by 1998 he seemed ready to become a solid regular if not a star, batting .238/.314/.455 with 25 home runs.

But his numbers declined the following year, and in September 1999, the Expos gave him his unconditional release. The Cubs signed him and in 19 games he hit .254/.329/.537 with five home runs, hinting for a possible big year in 2000 at age 28.

He started the year well, with that home run in Tokyo, and after 39 games was hitting just .212, but with 10 home runs.

It was at that point that Andrews suffered a lower back injury, a herniated disc, which required surgery the following month. He was assigned to Triple-A Iowa for a 15-game rehab stint in which he hit just .184 with two home runs. Upon his return to the Cubs, he batted .257/.341/.446 with four home runs in 27 games the rest of the season, then left the Cubs as a free agent at the end of the season. He played in the Cardinals and Twins organizations and briefly with the Red Sox in the major leagues in 2002 but retired from baseball after 2003.

After his retirement, Andrews returned to his hometown of Carlsbad, New Mexico, where he was inducted into the Carlsbad High School Hall of Fame in 2019.

The Cubs played two games against the Cardinals in London in 2023, and the first Cubs player to homer in the United Kingdom was Ian Happ, who led off the second inning Saturday, June 24 with a home run off Adam Wainwright. Happ added a second long ball in the third inning off Wainwright, and the Cubs went on to win the game 9–1.

Leadoff home runs are always fun and exciting, especially on the road, as they immediately give your team the lead.

Who was the first Cubs player to hit the very first pitch of the entire MLB season for a home run?

This exciting leadoff homer was hit by Ian Happ against the Miami Marlins in Miami on Thursday, March 29, 2018, off Miami right-hander Jose Urena.

There's really no setup for this hit because, as noted, it was the very first pitch of the MLB season. The Cubs and Marlins had been assigned the first spot on a nationally televised schedule by ESPN, so their game was to begin at 12:35 Eastern time. At the time, it was the earliest Opening Day date in major-league history (apart from some special games played outside North America) and the first time since 1968 that all MLB teams had opened on the same day.

Some fans in the crowd of 32,151 at Marlins Park had trouble getting to their seats, as the Miami ballpark was not used to having sellouts, and this was to be Miami's biggest crowd of 2018, including thousands of Cubs fans in attendance for Opening Day in nice weather. Many were not in their seats when Urena delivered a 95-mile-per-hour first-pitch fastball to Happ. On the Cubs TV broadcast, analyst Jim Deshaies said of Happ, "He hit seven home runs in spring training, five of them leading off the game. I expect him to take a pretty healthy cut here if he gets a juicy looking first-pitch fastball from Urena."

The words had barely escaped Deshaies' lips when Happ did exactly that, smashing a home run into the lower deck seats in right field.

The Cubs took a 3–0 lead by the end of that first inning but gave a run back in the bottom of the inning. Anthony Rizzo homered in the second to make it 4–1, but the Marlins scored three off Jon Lester in the third to tie the game. The Cubs went ahead 5–4 in the top of the fourth, and Cubs relievers shut Miami down for the rest of the game. A home run by Kyle Schwarber highlighted a three-run seventh, and the Cubs won that Opening Day game 8–4.

Just one other player in MLB history had previously hit the first pitch of an entire season for a home run: Dwight Evans of the Boston Red Sox off the Detroit Tigers' Jack Morris on Monday, April 7, 1986, at Tiger Stadium. So Happ's blast was the first by a Cub and first by a National League player, and those remain the only two such hits in major-league history.

It was the second consecutive year that Happ had homered in his first game for the Cubs. He made his major-league debut on Saturday, May 13, 2017, in St. Louis and hit a two-run homer off Cardinals right-hander Carlos Martinez in the seventh inning. That cut a Cubs deficit in that game to 5–3, but that's where that game ended.

Happ, who had been the Cubs' No. 1 draft pick out of the University of Cincinnati in 2015, went on to bat .253/.328/.514 (92-for-364) with 24 home runs in 117 games in 2017. That got him eighth place in National League Rookie of the Year voting. But his numbers declined a bit in 2018, to a .761 OPS and 15 home runs in 142 games, and by spring 2019 team management felt he needed to work on some things, so he was sent to Triple-A Iowa, not to return until late July.

In the shortened 2020 pandemic season, Happ was off to a fantastic start, batting .312/.421/.648 with 10 home runs in 37 games when, on September 3, he fouled off a 2–2 pitch in Pittsburgh that hit him in the face. He missed just one game, but when he returned, his batting did not. Happ hit just .171/.259/.276 (13-for-76) with 27 strikeouts the rest of the way. This continued over the first few months of 2021, as Happ hit just .178/.288/.322 (53-for-298) through August 10, 2021, to the point where many fans thought the Cubs should simply nontender him at the end of the season.

But that's just when Happ started to hit again. From August 11, 2021, through season's end, Happ batted .311/.386/.635 (52-for-167) with 14 home runs in 46 games, seemingly picking up where he'd left off before that foul ball in Pittsburgh.

The Cubs retained his services instead of nontendering him for 2022, and they're certainly glad they did so. That year he batted .271/.342/.440 with 42 doubles and 17 home runs, made his first National League All-Star team, and after the season won the National League Gold Glove Award for his good left field play.

About a week after the 2023 season began, the Cubs signed Happ to a three-year, $61 million extension that would begin in 2024, so he'll be in the Cubs outfield through 2026. He's become popular with left field bleacher fans, who signed a baseball for him near the trading deadline in 2022 when there was a chance the team might deal him. They, and Happ, are certainly happy that didn't happen.

CUBS MANAGING/COACHING FIRSTS

One hundred wins is a great benchmark for any baseball team's season, representing great success. It's also a fairly rare feat, and in fact, the century mark in victories has been reached just six times in Cubs franchise history.

Who was the first manager to lead the Cubs to 100 or more wins in a season?

The Cubs had struggled after their longtime leader, Adrian "Cap" Anson, retired from playing and managing after the 1897 season.

After Anson's departure, the team became informally known as "Orphans" and "Remnants." These monikers were hung on the club by newspaper writers in the days before official nicknames were adopted. These names generally reflected the current team reality, often satirically.

After a then-franchise-record 86 defeats in 1901, the team played far better in 1902. Future Hall of Fame manager Frank Selee began his first season at the helm, key players Joe Tinker and Johnny Evers joined the club, and Frank Chance, who had first become a Cub at age 21 in 1898, began to mature into a major star. Selee guided the Cubs to a 68–69 finish that year.

But Selee would not be able to fully enjoy the fruits of his labors. Over the next few years he would be plagued by debilitating illnesses. He had developed pleurisy late in the 1902 season but recovered to manage the 1903 Cubs to an 82–56 mark, good for third place, and the team's best record since 1891. They improved to 93–60 in 1904, a then-franchise record for wins but still finished a distant second, 13 games out, to the Giants, who established a new major-league record for wins (106) that year.

Selee fell ill again in spring training in 1905 and offered to give up his position, but general manager and part-owner Jim Hart convinced him to stay. The illness grew into lung issues and appendicitis, and on July 28, 1905, Selee went on a leave of absence, replaced as manager by first baseman Chance, reprising the role of player-manager that Anson had held.

Selee never returned and passed away in 1909, aged just 49. So it would be Frank Chance who would guide the Cubs to their first 100+ win season in 1906. That year, the Cubs would win a then-major-league record 116 games, which remains the MLB standard, matched only by the 2001 Seattle Mariners, and in a season eight games longer.

The 1906 Cubs, despite being a juggernaut of a team, were stymied in the World Series by the "Hitless Wonders" White Sox. They would cross the century mark again the next year, winning 107 games. In the World Series of 1907, they would win their first title, defeating the Detroit Tigers four games to none (with one tie). A second consecutive World Series title would follow in 1908, the Tigers were again the victims, this time four games to one. But in the regular season that year, the Cubs had fallen one win short of the 100-win milestone, posting 99 victories.

The Cubs would win 104 games again under Chance in 1909, though they failed to win a fourth straight pennant because the Pirates blew past them with 110 victories. The Cubs' 104 wins in 1909 stood as the most victories for a second-place team until the Dodgers broke it with 106 in 2021. Yet another 100-win season happened in 1910, as Chance's Cubs won the National League pennant by again taking 104 games, though they would lose the World Series to the Philadelphia Athletics.

The team fell short of first place in 1911 and 1912, though they won more than 90 games both seasons. Chance and team owner Charles W. Murphy got into a dispute after the 1912 season, and Chance was released as a player and dismissed as manager—at a time when he had been hospitalized for brain surgery, the likely cause of which was all the beanings Chance had suffered as a player in an era long before players

The "Peerless Leader," Cubs first baseman-manager Frank Chance, in 1908.
BAIN NEWS SERVICE, PUBLISHER, PUBLIC DOMAIN, VIA WIKIMEDIA COMMONS.

wore batting helmets. He held the Cubs' season (17) and career (137) records for being hit by a pitch for over a century until Anthony Rizzo broke them in 2015 and 2019, respectively.

Chance later managed the Yankees and White Sox, but health issues caught up with him and he passed away in 1924, aged just 48. His 768 wins as Cubs manager rank third in franchise history, behind Anson (1,282) and Charlie Grimm (946), and his .665 winning percentage is by far the best in franchise history. He was inducted into the Hall of Fame in Cooperstown along with his teammates Tinker and Evers in 1946.

Just two managers have led the Cubs to a 100-win season since 1910: Grimm, 100 in 1935, and Joe Maddon, 103 in 2016.

After the 1960 season, when the Cubs lost 90 games for the seventh time in the previous 13 years, team owner P. K. Wrigley decided to eliminate the position of manager and replace it with a system of leaders dubbed the "College of Coaches," with one of the "college" being

designated "head coach" for a period of time, then rotated out somewhere else in the organization and replaced by someone else.

Who was the first man to serve as Cubs head coach?

The Cubs' College of Coaches is almost certainly the most widely mocked leadership system in baseball history, if not in all of professional sports. The mocking was justifiable—it was a bad idea, and beyond that, it was poorly executed.

The first man to hold the title of head coach was Vedie Himsl.

And no doubt you're saying, "Who?"

A Minnesota native, Himsl had pitched in eight minor-league seasons stretching from 1939 to 1951, with interruptions for World War II service and some years managing in the Cardinals minor-league system.

The Cubs hired Himsl as a scout in 1952, and two years later he became Midwestern scouting director for the team. Eventually he spent a year managing in the Cubs farm system in 1957 at their Class D affiliate, Pulaski (Virginia), and the following year he was named pitching instructor for all Cubs farm clubs. Just 41 at the time, a coaching future in the Cubs organization for Himsl seemed bright.

That's when Himsl got himself caught up in the College of Coaches. Here's how that came about.

After the Cubs had lost 94 games in 1960—their seventh 90+ loss year in the previous 13 seasons (and that was harder to do with only 154 games rather than the current 162)—team owner P. K. Wrigley decided that it must have been the manager's fault, even though he had already changed managers six times in that time span. Saying the manager's role was no longer useful, Wrigley was quoted by reporters: "The dictionary tells you a manager is the one who bosses and a coach is the one who works. We want workers." Another odd Wrigley statement made around the same time: "Managers are expendable. I believe there should be relief managers just like relief pitchers."

Notwithstanding the fact that those statements don't really make any sense, the idea that any business wouldn't have an ultimate "boss" led this idea down the road to failure. The concept of having a system-wide group of coaches who would move up and down from the majors to the minors and thus would develop and teach a "Cubs Way" that would be uniform at every level wasn't bad. In 1963, the Cubs hired a retired Air Force colonel, Robert Whitlow, gave him the title of "Athletic Director," and directed him to develop a plan that might have instituted ideas like these—but he never was permitted to institute some of his ideas. Many years later, under president of baseball operations Theo Epstein, the Cubs again tried this concept, with varying degrees of success.

In fact, if the Cubs had just listened to coach El Tappe, they might have made this all work. Many years after the failure of the College of Coaches, Tappe told *Chicago Tribune* writer Jerome Holtzman that the Cubs needed "stability" in the organization after they had swapped out pitching coaches several years in a row. He said it would be good for the kids coming up through the system, but that "head coach" at the major-league level was all P. K. Wrigley's idea. Tappe added, "I wrote an organizational playbook. He [Wrigley] gave me extra money for that. We had the same signs, except for the keys, the same cutoff and rundown plays for all the clubs in our organization. When a player moved up, he didn't have to learn anything new. We taught from kindergarten all the way through graduation. But I never mentioned anything about rotating managers. It was his idea."

And that's the primary reason the execution of the College of Coaches never worked. Players would complain that they'd just get settled in one place in the lineup and then get swapped out by the next "head coach" when he came in from Wenatchee, Washington—yes, a real place where a real Cubs Class B–level farm team was located in the early 1960s.

Himsl was the first of eight coaches assigned throughout the system to be given the title of head coach. He "head coached" the first 11 games, with the team going 5–6, before he was shipped off for a stint at Double-A San Antonio and Wenatchee, replaced by Harry Craft. Craft was the head coach for 12 games (4–8) before Himsl returned, which *The Sporting News* headlined on May 17 as good for the club: "Players Hail Himsl's Return to Cubs." The paper noted in a positive way his "strong silent type demeanor." It didn't help, though, as Himsl's 17-game stint resulted in a 5–12 mark. He was replaced again by Tappe (0–2) and Craft (3–1) before Himsl returned again for three games at the top spot (0–3).

At that point someone—who knows whether it was Wrigley, general manager John Holland, or just someone they tapped on the shoulder while he was walking down Addison Street—decided they needed a bit of the stability Tappe was talking about, putting him in charge for 78 games (35–43). Lou Klein followed with a 5–6 mark, and Tappe finished the season going 5–11. The 1961 Cubs again lost 90 games, their eighth 90+ loss season in a 14-year span, and then exceeded that in 1962, losing a franchise-record 103 games. That year three different men (Tappe, Klein, and Charlie Metro) served as head coach.

In 1963, the rotating head coach system was ditched. Bob Kennedy headed the team for all of that year and 1964 and into mid-June 1965 before he was fired in favor of Klein, though the title of "manager" wasn't officially used again by the Cubs until Leo Durocher was hired in October 1965. Durocher led off his introductory press conference by saying, quoted by *The Sporting News*: "If no announcement has been made about what my title is, I'm making it here and now. I'm the manager. I'm not a head coach. I'm the manager."

Vedie Himsl, meanwhile, never managed (or "head coached") in the major leagues after 1961, but he did serve as Cubs pitching coach in 1962 and 1963. After that he split time managing in the Cubs minor leagues and serving in the Cubs front office until 1968. He was then named director of MLB's Central Scouting Bureau before returning to the Cubs as director of scouting in 1972, a position he kept through 1985.

Himsl passed away in 2004 at age 87, having devoted the great portion of his life to baseball and the Cubs, and hopefully he is remembered for more than being a footnote as the first head coach of the team's wacky College of Coaches.

The Cubs didn't have a Black manager until the 20th century was almost over. But before that, the team had quite a few Black coaches. Who was the Cubs' first Black coach?

The Cubs created the ill-fated College of Coaches in 1961. The idea wasn't bad—to have a group of coaches who could teach a consistent "Cubs Way" throughout the organization—but in practice it was a miserable failure.

In 1962, the Cubs added the first Black coach to their "College," and in fact, not only was Buck O'Neil the first Black coach for the Cubs, he was the first one for any major-league baseball team.

O'Neil played a dozen years in the Negro Leagues and managed the Kansas City Monarchs, one of the top Negro League teams, for eight seasons. In 1956, after the Monarchs had been sold, O'Neil resigned as manager and became a scout for the Cubs. In that capacity he was renowned for bringing many talented Black players to the Cubs, including Lou Brock, George Altman, and Billy Williams. O'Neil is also credited by some for guiding Ernie Banks, who played for him with the Monarchs, to sign with the Cubs in 1953.

Billy Williams' career might have been saved by O'Neil, who was dispatched to Billy's hometown of Whistler, Alabama, after Williams left the Cubs' minor-league club in San Antonio, Texas, in 1959, reportedly homesick. O'Neil didn't say anything specific to Williams about returning to the club. Instead, after a few days visiting, Buck took Billy to the local park where he played youth baseball, where Williams was surrounded by kids like a celebrity. Williams realized that if he didn't return, there were many ready to take his place. He told O'Neil he was ready to go back to San Antonio and told GM John Holland the good news. Holland offered to send Williams a bus ticket, but O'Neil said he'd drive Billy back to San Antonio himself, just to make sure he arrived. Of course, Billy did, and eventually he was called up to the Cubs later that year, beginning what would become a Hall of Fame career.

O'Neil had served in an unofficial coaching role for the Cubs for a time during his tenure as a scout, but in 1962 the team made him an official coach on the field, though not part of the College of Coaches, who would rotate as acting in the role of field manager. Sadly, O'Neil wasn't even permitted to act as manager when the current head coach, Charlie Metro, and third-base coach El Tappe were both ejected from the second game of a doubleheader on Saturday, July 15, 1962, at Houston in the first inning. O'Neil, serving as a coach in the dugout at the time, would have been the logical choice to take over for the rest of the game, but instead pitching coach Fred Martin was summoned from the bullpen to lead the team for the rest of the game, which the Cubs wound up winning 4–1.

O'Neil returned to scouting duties with the Cubs after 1962, which would be his only year in a big-league uniform. He remained there for many years before leaving for a scouting position with the Kansas City Royals in 1988, where he was named Midwest Scout of the Year in 1998.

In 2006, the Hall of Fame recognized 17 Negro League players, coaches, and executives by inducting them. O'Neil, who had been on the Hall's ballot, didn't get selected by the committee doing the voting, but he was asked to speak in Cooperstown on their behalf. His memorable speech resulted in a standing ovation. He passed away later that year, aged 93, and was at last inducted as a member of the baseball Hall of Fame in 2022.

Jackie Robinson broke Major League Baseball's color barrier in 1947, but it took 28 more years until a major-league team would hire a Black manager, Cleveland's Frank Robinson in 1975.

Who was the Cubs' first Black manager?

A year after a surprise wild-card berth for the Cubs in 1998, the team got off to a good 32–23 start in 1999. After that they collapsed to the worst record in baseball the rest of that season, 35–72, and that poor performance got manager Jim Riggleman fired.

General manager Andy MacPhail scouted around and thought he found a good match for the team in another manager who'd been let go shortly after an unexpected postseason berth for his club. That was Don Baylor, who led the Rockies to the postseason in just their third year of existence in 1995. But Baylor was dumped in Colorado after a losing season in 1998 and took a position as the hitting coach for the Atlanta Braves in 1999.

MacPhail hired Baylor November 1, 1999, and gave him a four-year deal to manage the Cubs from 2000 to 2003, and Baylor thus became the first Black manager in Cubs history.

Baylor had been a fine player during a 19-year playing career, including an MVP Award for the Angels in 1979. He had 2,135 career hits and 338 home runs, and it was hoped that some of his work as batting coach would rub off on the Cubs, who had lost 94+ games two of the previous three seasons.

Make that three seasons in a four-year span in Baylor's first season at the helm in Chicago, as the Cubs would go 65–97 in 2000. The Cubs finished 11th in runs scored but did hit 183 home runs, led by Sammy Sosa's 50. The real issue was with the pitchers. A staff that had Daniel Garibay, Jamie Arnold, Andrew Lorraine, Jerry Spradlin, Phil Norton, and Joey Nation combine for 22 starts allowed a total of 904 runs, not much better than the 920 allowed the previous year and second-worst for any Cubs team in the modern era.

Somehow, Baylor and the team turned things around in 2001. Led by a rejuvenated Kerry Wood and Jon Lieber and closer Tom "Flash" Gordon, the team inhabited first place in the NL Central for most of June, July, and August before fading and finishing third with an 88–74 record.

Hopes were high for the team in 2002, but they got off to a poor start and a nine-game losing streak in mid-May dumped them into fifth place with a 13–27 record, 12 games behind first-place Cincinnati.

As is often the case when teams don't perform up to par, the manager gets put on the hot seat. Such was the case for the old-school Baylor, who often didn't connect with his players. A memorable game from late June seemed to seal Baylor's fate. On Thursday, June 27 at Wrigley Field, the Cubs faced the Reds in the last of a four-game series, having lost two of the first three. The Reds went down 1-2-3 in the top of the first, and Corey Patterson led off the bottom of the inning with a double. Baylor ordered the next hitter, Chris Stynes, to lay down a sacrifice bunt—with a runner in scoring position in a scoreless game, in the first inning! Stynes did so, but the Cubs failed to score, eventually blowing a two-run ninth-inning lead and losing the game in 10 innings. The sac bunt in that situation almost seemed as if Baylor was daring management to fire him, which they did just a week later with a year and a half left on his contract, replacing him with interim manager Bruce Kimm for the rest of the season. It became yet another 95-loss year for the North Siders.

That fall, Dusty Baker was hired as the second Black manager in Cubs history. Baker's tenure in Chicago didn't end well, with a 96-loss season in 2006, but he did get the Cubs to the postseason in his first year at the helm with a division title in 2003.

TEAM ACHIEVEMENTS

The team we now know as the Cubs wasn't always called by the name "Cubs." In fact, when the franchise began National League play in 1876, they were known as "White Stockings." (Imagine that! Had that moniker stuck, you, the Cubs fan, would likely today be a "White Sox" fan.)

When was the very first time the Chicago NL team was called "Cubs"?

To answer this question, it's important to understand that team nicknames as we know them in modern times are far different than the way they were understood in the 19th century. We call that era's Chicago NL team "Chicago White Stockings," but it wasn't as if the team was selling branded caps, shirseys, and other merchandise with that name on them back in the day. That sort of thing didn't become common until the 1950s or 1960s at the earliest.

Team nicknames in the 19th and early 20th centuries were more in use by sportswriters, newspaper headline writers, and editors to find different ways to refer to the teams they were covering. The newspaper was the only way to find out about the team you were rooting for back then, as there was no radio, television, or internet to get information about sports to fans.

Recent Cubs media guides, in fact, note that quite a number of names (in addition to White Stockings) were used to refer to the Chicago NL baseball club at various times before they were known as Cubs. In no particular order: Black Stockings, Colts, Ex-Colts, Rainmakers, Cowboys,

Rough Riders, Remnants, Recruits, Panamas, Zephyrs, Nationals, and Spuds.

A few of those nicknames had meaningful reasons for their use. "Colts" was in common use in the 1890s and early 1900s because of the number of young players on the team. "Remnants" became popular after longtime player-manager Cap Anson left the team after 1897, and what was left behind, well, were considered "remnants." "Orphans" was used around that time for the same reason.

The American League began play in 1901, and many established NL players "jumped" to the new league. With more ballclubs playing and thus more players needed, the Chicago NL team, as well as others in the older league, began to sign younger players.

This gave one Chicago sportswriter an idea. Fred A. Hayner was a writer and editor for the *Chicago Daily News*, and according to a 2016 *Chicago Sun-Times* article by his grandson Don Hayner, also a sportswriter, Fred first wrote the name "Cubs" to refer to the young players on the Chicago NL team in a *Daily News* article on March 27, 1902, a few weeks before the season began.

The article, headlined "SELEE PLACES HIS MEN," had a subhead that read "Manager of the Cubs Is in Doubt Only on Two Positions" and began: "Frank Selee will devote his strongest efforts on the team work of the new Cubs this year."

Among those "new Cubs" were shortstop Joe Tinker and pitcher Carl Lundgren, both of whom would become key players on the Cubs' pennant and World Series winners later in the decade.

Beyond the connection of the word "cubs" to youngsters, newspaper writers were always looking for shorter words to use in headlines, which "Cubs" certainly fit. Some of the previous names, including Colts, were still used by some newspapers for a few years after that, but by 1907 manager Frank Chance had taken to the name Cubs to refer to his ballclub and pushed team owner Charles W. Murphy to make it the official nickname of the team. The team's players were presented with new jackets with a bear cub on the front during the 1907 World Series.

Today, the name Chicago Cubs is a worldwide brand, adorning the famous marquee at Wrigley Field and all sorts of team merchandise.

The name was created to refer to the team more than 120 years ago by a newspaper writer.

The Cubs have scored 20 or more runs in a game 16 times since 1900. When was the first time the Cubs and their opponents *both* scored 20 runs in a game?

The first major-league double 20-run barrage happened over 100 years ago on what was otherwise an ordinary Friday afternoon, August 25, 1922, with the Cubs entering that day's action against the Phillies in third place in the National League, six games out of first place.

What the approximately 7,000 fans (specific attendance figures were not often announced in those days) saw on that Friday afternoon was something not matched before or since in any major-league game. Here's how it all happened.

The Cubs scored a run in the first inning, but starter Tony Kaufmann allowed three Phillies runs in the second.

Then the Cubs offense got to work against Philadelphia's Jimmy Ring. Ten Cubs runs crossed the plate in the second inning. In part due to a pair of Phillies errors in that inning, all 10 of the runs were unearned.

The Phillies added two in the third and one in the fourth to come to within 11–6, which was as close as they would get . . . for a while.

Fourteen Cubs crossed the plate in the bottom of the fourth. Hack Miller, who had homered in the 10-run second, went deep again. Miller went 4-for-5 with six RBI on the afternoon. In addition, there were two walks, a hit batter, and two more Phillies errors in the inning. The Cubs led by 19 at 25–6.

The Phillies did not quit in this one, though. They scored three in the fifth to make it 25–9, and the Cubs added one of their own in the bottom of the inning. That turned out to be the last run the Cubs would score on the day, and they thus entered the top of the eighth with a 17-run lead, 26–9.

You would think such a lead would be safe. Dear reader, I am here to tell you that it wasn't. A 19-year-old pitcher named Uel Eubanks (and per baseball-reference.com, yes, that is his real given first name) was put into the game to begin the eighth inning, just his second MLB appearance.

It turned out to be his last. Eubanks faced 10 batters, and in sequence, this is what happened: walk, batter reached on error, single, walk, fly out, single, bunt groundout, walk, batter reached on error, single.

At that point manager Bill Killefer had mercy and replaced Eubanks with Ed Morris, who was making just his fourth MLB appearance. Entering with the bases loaded and two out, Morris promptly allowed a bases-clearing double. Just two of the eight runs that scored in the inning were earned, but now it was 26–17.

Still, a nine-run lead should be enough, right? Well . . . not exactly.

Morris faced four batters in the ninth, and all of them reached base, via, in order: single, walk, single, double, the last two of those hits scoring runs that made it 26–19.

Killefer, likely quite frustrated with his pitchers, replaced Morris with Tiny Osborne. (Morris pitched in just one more game for the Cubs in 1922, returned to the minor leagues, and didn't pitch in the majors again until 1928 with the Red Sox.)

Osborne didn't have much better luck. He struck out the first batter he faced but then allowed a two-run single that made it 26–21. Yikes, now it's getting too close for comfort. A single and strikeout followed. One out away from victory. But Osborne walked the next hitter, loading the bases, and a single made it 26–22, the bases remaining loaded.

Then, for some inexplicable reason, the Cubs catcher decided it would be a good idea to try to pick the runner off third. A throwing error scored the Phillies' 23rd run. That catcher was future Hall of Famer Gabby Hartnett, who was in his rookie year with the Cubs. In 27 games played and 110 total chances that year, Hartnett made just two errors, actually pretty good for that era. In all, nine errors were made in this game, two on foul popups, and of the 49 runs scored, just 28 were earned. The weather report for that day, per the *Chicago Tribune*, was sunny and quite windy, perhaps helping lead to all the miscues.

Anyway, Osborne, perhaps rattled, walked the hitter who was batting when the error was made. That reloaded the bases, and now the tying run is on base and the Phillies had the lead run at the plate, the charmingly named Bevo LeBourveau, who had entered the game in the fifth inning and gone 3-for-3. Osborne struck LeBourveau out to end the game, and the Cubs had a bizarre 26–23 win.

Of this game, the *Tribune*'s Frank Schreiber wrote in the next day's paper:

> *Nobody will ever know without many hours with the box score and a record book just how many records of ancient and modern baseball were smashed at the north side park yesterday. Cubs and Phillies hooked up in what was advertised as a baseball game, but early on proved to be a comic opera sung to the tune of base hits.*

Actually, we do know how many records were "smashed" during that game, and it didn't take many hours to find them. Here they are, and all but one of them still stand:

- 49 runs combined is still the record for any game of any length, modern era or before.
- 51 hits, still the modern (post-1900) record for a nine-inning game. On April 30, 1887, St. Louis and Cleveland of the American Association combined for 53 hits.
- 14 runs in an inning, the all-time record is still 18 by the Cubs in 1883, a game played at the hitters' paradise of Lake Front Park. 14 is no longer the record for the modern era, it's now 17, set by the Red Sox in 1953. The NL mark is 15 by the Dodgers, set in 1952.
- Three appearances in one inning by one batter (Marty Callaghan, fourth inning) is still the record. No one has appeared four times. The MLB record for batters faced in an inning by a team is 23. In the Cubs' 14-run inning in this game, 19 batters came to the plate. The last player to appear three times in an inning was Johnny Damon for the Red Sox against the Marlins, on June 27, 2003.

Had the Cubs lost that game after leading by 19 runs, it would by far be the biggest blown lead in major-league history. No team has ever blown a lead larger than 12 runs; that happened on August 5, 2001, when Cleveland defeated Seattle 15–14 after trailing 14–2. The Cubs hold the NL record for biggest blown lead; on April 17, 1976, they led the Phillies 13–2, only to lose 18–16 in 10 innings.

This game is one of only two in MLB history where *both* teams scored at least 18 runs. The other one is a game you are probably quite familiar with—it happened at the same ballpark, between the same two teams, 57 years later, when the Phillies got "revenge" for this long-ago loss, defeating the Cubs 23–22 on May 17, 1979.

On Saturday, April 23, 2022, the Cubs shut out the Pirates at Wrigley Field 21–0, recording a franchise record number of runs in a shutout win. That, too, could be considered a bit of "revenge," as the Pirates had set a modern-era MLB record for a shutout win against the Cubs at Wrigley Field, blanking them 22–0 on Tuesday, September 16, 1975.

Today, Cubs baseball can be consumed online, on television, and on radio, with every game available to fans through multiple outlets.

Radio, of course, was the first way for fans to follow games as they were happening without being at the ballpark.

When was the first radio broadcast of a Cubs game?

Commercial radio began in late 1920 with broadcasts of presidential election results, and the following summer, Pittsburgh radio station KDKA would be the first to broadcast a baseball game, carrying the Pirates' 8–5 win over the Phillies at Forbes Field on Friday, August 5, 1921.

It would be a couple of years before commercial radio would take hold in Chicago, but as soon as that happened, Cubs owner William Wrigley encouraged broadcast stations in the city to carry Cubs games, figuring, as did his son P. K. decades later, that it would help promote his baseball team.

A. W. "Sen" Kaney was among the first stars of radio in Chicago, and after the 1924 season radio station WGN, owned then by the *Chicago Tribune*, broadcast the entire Cubs–White Sox City Series.

The first game of that series took place at Wrigley Field on Tuesday, October 1, 1924, so that's the date of the very first time Cubs baseball was heard on the radio. The Cubs won the game 10–7, though they nearly blew a 9–0 lead they held after six innings. Elmer Douglass of the *Chicago Tribune*—clearly not a baseball fan—reported on Kaney's broadcast:

> *Yesterday afternoon, W-G-N introduced us to baseball, with the Cubs and Sox alternately at the bat and "Sen" Kaney continuously at the microphone. Evidently "Sen" knows about as much about baseball as this listener, and that equals the sum of the Sox runs at the close of the sixth inning. Our enthusiasm, however, was equal to the Cubs' lead of nine runs. However, the running comment on the game was good, and reminded the writer of his observations of baseball games from that same high vantage point—the press stand. The yelling by the crowds, the flying pigeons (apparently no airplanes this time), and strikingly through the microphone, the whistles, the chug-chug of railroad trains and engines a block or so west—also the "high winds."*

Despite this so-so review, the station continued broadcasting the remainder of the 1924 City Series, which the Cubs lost to the Sox four games to two.

The next year, the first regular-season Cubs radio broadcast was heard on WGN on Opening Day, on Tuesday, April 14, 1925, with Quin Ryan replacing Kaney at the microphone to call an 8–2 Cubs win over the Pirates.

Over the next few years, games were added to the broadcast schedule, with 1927 the first year the entire Cubs home schedule was broadcast by radio. Succeeding years brought road contests—but generally through "re-creations" done in a Chicago radio studio using play-by-play brought by wire services, with background crowd noise sometimes added. The first such re-creation happened on Tuesday, September 18, 1928, a Cubs game at Braves Field in Boston.

Occasionally, there would be a delay in transmission of these details by wire. When that happened, announcers would have players "foul" balls off until they could receive updated results. Among the men who broadcast Cubs games using this method was future President Ronald

Reagan, who did some recreations of those games for station WHO in Des Moines, Iowa.

In the days before broadcast rights became a thing, there were at times as many as five Chicago radio stations broadcasting Cubs games. In addition to WGN, stations WIND, WBBM, WJJD, and WCFL carried Cubs games from time to time in the 1930s and 1940s before WJJD signed an exclusive rights contract in 1944. Bert Wilson, whose catch phrase was "I don't care who wins as long as it's the Cubs," became the primary play-by-play announcer at that time.

Jack Quinlan had joined the broadcast team in 1953 and in 1955 became the Cubs' primary radio play-by-play voice and moved with the team to WGN when that station signed a rights deal in 1958. Quinlan and Lou Boudreau became a popular broadcast team, except for 1960 when the Cubs made an unusual trade: They swapped Boudreau to the manager's office and put manager Charlie Grimm in the radio booth. Neither move worked out, and Boudreau returned to radio in 1961, pairing with Quinlan until Quinlan's untimely death in a car accident during spring training in 1965. At that time Vince Lloyd moved from WGN-TV to radio, and he and "Good Kid" Boudreau were the radio voices of the Cubs through 1986.

Milo Hamilton joined both the radio and TV crew in the early 1980s but departed not long after being passed over for the main WGN-TV play-by-play job in favor of Harry Caray. In 1985, DeWayne Staats joined WGN, doing both TV and radio, before leaving after 1989, succeeded by Thom Brennaman. Brennaman left for Fox-TV and a gig in Arizona after 1995, and Pat Hughes took over the radio chair in 1996. Former Cubs great Ron Santo joined the radio team in 1990, and he and Hughes were a beloved partnership until Santo's passing in 2010.

For the first time in almost 60 years, Cubs games began to be heard on a station other than WGN in 2015. The rights were bought by CBS radio, and games were broadcast on WBBM in 2015, but after the White Sox moved their radio broadcasts from CBS-owned WSCR ("The Score") to WGN after that year, Cubs radio moved to The Score, where the broadcasts still originate. Hughes, who won the Hall of Fame's

Ford C. Frick Award for broadcast excellence in 2023, still carries on play-by-play duties, assisted by Zach Zaidman and analyst Ron Coomer.

The numbers 10, 14, 23, 26, and 31 are famous in Chicago Cubs history. To be precise, they are the only numbers specifically retired by the team for Hall of Fame Cubs: Ron Santo, Ernie Banks, Ryne Sandberg, Billy Williams, and both Fergie Jenkins and Greg Maddux for No. 31.
    When was the first time the Cubs sported numbers on the backs of their jerseys?

In the early days of Major League Baseball, players simply wore jerseys with the name of their team or the city where they played on the front, but no personally identifying information on the back.

Slowly, the idea of having numbers on the back to identify players caught on, first with American League teams. Cleveland did it briefly in 1916, then the Yankees were next in 1929, famously giving Babe Ruth No. 3 and Lou Gehrig No. 4 to correspond with their spots in the batting order. Two years later all AL teams had numbers, but the National League dragged its feet, back in a time when the leagues had separate rule and more power than they do today.

The Sporting News urged the National League to catch up with the times in its edition of November 26, 1931:

> *The big leagues have always been slow about adopting innovations. The magnates hemmed and hawed for a long time before they put into effect the foul-strike rule, and one circuit delayed a year or two after the other had adopted this boon to modern baseball.*
>
> *It is proper that the powers that be in baseball should jealously guard the game's traditions, but there is such a thing as bending over backward in refusing to adopt improvements, the value of which can hardly be denied.*

The following year, the Boston Braves became the first NL team to break the logjam, and at a meeting of NL owners in June 1932, the league voted to require teams to add uniform numbers. Most teams did it right away, but the Cubs, who were on a 19-game road trip that took up nearly the entire month of June, chose to wait until they returned to Wrigley Field.

Thus, it was that for their game of Thursday, June 30, 1932, the team first took the field with numbers on their backs. The *Tribune* reported: "None of them felt like defying fate by wearing 13, so the number was eliminated." No Cub wore No. 13 until Claude Passeau took it in 1939, and to this day, just 11 others have worn No. 13 for the Cubs, the fewest for any number other than No. 0, first taken by Marcus Stroman in 2022. Those 11 are: Hal Manders (1946), Bill Faul (1965–1966), Turk Wendell (1993–1997), Jeff Fassero (2001–2002), Rey Ordonez (2004), Neifi Perez (2004–2006), Will Ohman (2006–2007), Andres Blanco (2009), Starlin Castro (2010–2015), Alex Avila (2017), and David Bote (2018–2022).

As was the case with the Yankees, most of the Cubs' 1932 numbers were assigned by their typical batting-order spot, but with one regular sitting out, the first day's batting order went by number: 1, 2, 3, 4, 49, 6, 7, and 11, with pitcher Guy Bush finishing up the order wearing No. 14. The odd-number-out player was outfielder Vince Barton, substituting that afternoon for Johnny Moore, who was the Cubs' first player to wear No. 5 and who typically hit fifth. The Cubs won that first uniform-numbered game over the Reds 7–0 and eventually wound up taking the NL pennant that year with a 90–64 record.

Numbers are generally sacrosanct today, with players mostly keeping their digits when moving from team to team via trade or free agency. But back then, ballclubs realized that they could boost scorecard sales by players switching numbers around. In fact, perhaps-apocryphal stories were told of teams actually *asking* players to swap numbers to boost scorecard sales. No matter the reason, the old vendor cry, "You can't tell the players without a scorecard!" was *literally* true in some instances. Well-known Cubs of the day often swapped numbers. Charlie Grimm wore 6, 7, and 8 at different times; future Hall of Famer Billy Herman wore 2 and 4; fellow future Hall of Famer Gabby Hartnett wore 2, 7, and 9; and all-time Cubs wins leader Charlie Root had four different numbers in various years: 12, 14, 17, and 19, quite the selection considering the fact that he had played his first six Cubs seasons wearing no number at all.

Regarding retiring numbers, that honor had begun with the Yankees retiring No. 4 for Lou Gehrig in 1939 and later Babe Ruth's No. 3 in 1948.

The Cubs were going to begin this tradition for the franchise in April 1954 by retiring No. 44 for Phil Cavarretta in honor of his stellar playing career. Cavarretta, who had managed the Cubs from 1951 to 1953, made the mistake of being honest with a reporter when asked how the team would do in 1954, answering "not very well." Cavarretta was fired and the number retirement ceremony was canceled—and so was the idea of the Cubs retiring numbers while the Wrigleys still owned the team, as no Cubs number retirement ceremonies happened until after the Wrigleys sold the team to the Tribune Company. Even so, clubhouse manager Yosh Kawano, who was in charge of assigning numbers, kept No. 44 out of circulation until 1971, when Burt Hooton, who had worn the number at the University of Texas, requested it. Yosh had Hooton call Cavarretta and ask permission to wear the number.

The first Cubs number retirement ceremony happened at Wrigley Field on Sunday, August 22, 1982, when Ernie Banks' No. 14 was retired, five years after Mr. Cub was elected to the Hall of Fame.

The number 14 remained popular, though. When Ryne Sandberg was traded to the Cubs, he requested No. 14, which he had worn as a high school quarterback in Spokane, Washington. Kawano gently explained to Sandberg who Banks was and assigned Sandberg No. 23, telling Ryno that was a "fine infielder's number." Now, of course, Sandberg's number has joined Banks' flying atop a Wrigley flagpole.

Here are the other Cubs number retirement ceremony dates:

August 13, 1987: Billy Williams, No. 26

September 28, 2003: Ron Santo, No. 10

August 28, 2005: Ryne Sandberg, No. 23

May 3, 2009: Fergie Jenkins and Greg Maddux, No. 31

No. 42 is retired for the Cubs as well as all MLB teams in honor of Jackie Robinson.

The Cubs were a television mainstay with WGN-TV carrying their games for more than 70 years. Now most of the team's games are seen

on their own TV channel, Marquee Sports Network. But the first tele-vised Cubs game wasn't broadcast on WGN-TV.

What channel aired that game, and when did it happen?

The defending National League champion Cubs came home on Saturday, April 20, 1946, after sweeping an opening three-game series in Cincinnati, to take on their archrivals, the St. Louis Cardinals, in the home opener at Wrigley Field.

There were plans for another special event that afternoon, beyond Opening Day—a live TV broadcast of the game on WBKB, to begin with a pregame show at 1 p.m. and then the entire nine-inning game at 1:25 p.m., with Jack Gibney as the solo announcer.

Unfortunately, only the people who worked at the station saw the game (and not very well), as the *Tribune* reported that "electrical interfer-ence in the State-Lake building where the transmitter is located resulted in such poor images that William C. Eddy, director, declined to put them on the air." Apparently, there were too many people using the elevators in WBKB's building, and in those early days of TV the pictures being relayed downtown from Wrigley Field were unsuitable for broadcast due to that interference. The *Chicago Tribune* headlined an article about this attempt the next day: "Fail in Effort on Television of Cubs Game."

The Cubs failed that day too, losing 2–0 to the Cardinals.

They did tests again the following week, but technical issues con-tinued to plague WBKB, then broadcasting on Channel 4. (Chicago no longer has a Channel 4, but that's a topic for a different book.)

It took nearly three more months before a successful Cubs television broadcast actually happened. The station did several more tests before the game on Saturday, July 13, 1946, against the Brooklyn Dodgers was actually aired on WBKB, so that's the actual date of the first televised Cubs game from Wrigley Field. There was just one camera, situated in "an upper tier position looking across home plate down the first base line, with the pitcher in view on the mound," per Larry Wolters of the *Tribune*.

Wolters also noted in the newspaper that the "lookers" (not "viewers," as we would call them today) got "good views of players leading off from first, of Leo Durocher rushing out to argue with an umpire [they looked like black bears], of the dust raised when a runner slid home."

If you could see this broadcast now, and of course there was no way to preserve that in the early days of television, it wouldn't look anything like the baseball broadcasts you know today. There was just the one camera at Wrigley, situated as described previously, and it didn't have a zoom lens; that wouldn't be developed for another decade or so.

Also, consider the mention of Leo Durocher, then the Dodgers manager. No Cubs fan in 1946 would likely ever have dreamed that Durocher would take over the Cubs 20 years later. And wouldn't it be nice if baseball announcers calling games on TV today did this at times, as Wolters wrote:

Jack Gibney, the commentator, judiciously let the pictures speak for themselves. His comment was limited largely to describing action out of range of the camera, to statistics, recapitulations, and crowd color and reaction.

The Cubs wound up losing the game 4–3 to the Dodgers, and Wolters concluded:

Because of the considerable area of action in baseball, this sport is much less satisfactory for telecasting at present than wrestling or boxing. Eddy was satisfied, however, with the result.

Millions of Cubs fans would be more than just satisfied with televised baseball over the years, being treated to thousands of game broadcasts, many more than other teams. Most major-league ballclubs shied away from television in those early days because they feared it would eat into game attendance.

Cubs owner P. K. Wrigley, though he didn't invest much into the team in his later years, was prescient in his view of televised baseball, looking at it as a marketing tool for his ballclub. In a *Tribune* article reporting on WGN-TV's first Cubs broadcast on April 23, 1948, Wrigley was quoted as saying:

We are confident that television, handled with imagination and under-standing, will bring baseball closer to vast numbers of Americans. It will result eventually in bringing many more persons to ball parks to get a close-up, personal view of the dramatic scenes and colorful characters they become acquainted with on the television screens.

That is, of course, exactly what happened. Cubs broadcasts filled Chicago-area living rooms and dens in the 1940s, 1950s, and 1960s, and, because the team played all its games in the afternoon, kids could watch the endings when they got home from school. It's those kids, asking their parents to take them to Wrigley Field, who helped create generations of Cubs fans, lasting to this day.

For a time, in an era before the broadcast rights fee became a profit center for baseball clubs, Chicagoans could see Cubs games on three different Chicago TV stations—WGN, WBKB, and WENR. All three channels carried many Cubs games, largely simply because they'd fill a couple of hours of air time, until network television commitments left WGN-TV to itself for Cubs TV by 1953. WGN-TV would televise 7,115 Cubs games before the relationship between the team and station ended after the 2019 season.

To the modern fan, the Cubs' reputation before their World Series win in 2016 was one of almost unrelenting losing and futility, but that was not the case through much of the team's history.

When was the team's first 90-loss season?

For the first several decades of their existence, the Cubs were generally among the top franchises in the National League, and in the World Series era beginning in 1903, they won 10 pennants in a 40-season span from 1906 to 1945. Among NL teams, only the Giants had more league pennants in that time frame.

Despite winning just two World Series in those 10 pennant-winning years, in 1945 the Cubs were generally seen to be one of the most successful Major League Baseball franchises. In addition to those 10 league titles, the Cubs had won at least 90 games and finished second or third in the National League six other times in that 40-season span, and in one of those years (1909) they established a record for most wins by a second-place team (104) that stood for more than a century until the Dodgers (106) broke it in 2021.

And with all that success, the Cubs finished in last place in the National League just once over the first seven decades of their existence, in 1925 with a 68–86 record. Even in that poor season, one more win would have vaulted them out of the cellar, as they finished just half a game behind Brooklyn and Philadelphia, who both ended up 68–85.

They wouldn't finish last in the league again until 1948, which was the first season in Cubs franchise history in which they would lose 90 games. The Cubs thus became the last of the "Original 16" major-league teams to lose 90 in a season; the previous "last" of this type belonged to the Giants, who had their first 90-loss season (98) in 1943.

Truth be told, the 1945 NL pennant won by the Cubs was something of a fluke. At that time, they hadn't had a winning season since 1939 and won in 1945 largely due to league MVP Phil Cavarretta's great season, a fine year from Andy Pafko and the excellent midseason acquisition of Hank Borowy from the Yankees. Basically, the Cubs lost fewer good players to World War II than other teams, but when those other players returned to their ballclubs, the Cubs began heading south.

They managed a winning record (82–71) and a third-place finish in 1946 but slipped back under .500 at 69–85 and fell to sixth place in 1947 as Borowy got old and injured and other star Cubs either got old, or injured, or both.

The Cubs were still a popular draw among Chicago fans, though; 1947 attendance totaled 1,364,039, third-best in franchise history and the most since 1930.

Charlie Grimm, who managed the 1945 team to the pennant and in a previous managerial stint had managed Cubs pennant winners in 1932 and 1935, was still at the helm as the 1948 season began.

The 1948 Cubs won four of their first seven games but eventually dropped into the NL basement with a doubleheader loss to the Reds on May 30. They'd exit eighth place just twice more the rest of the year, and for only a single day each time.

Still, they won five of seven in early September to bring them to a 57–75 mark after a win over the Cardinals on September 8. Had they maintained that winning percentage (.432) for the rest of the year, they'd have finished 66–88, bad enough but not crossing that 90-loss mark.

Unfortunately, the day after that victory over St. Louis, the Cubs embarked on a 10-game losing streak in which they were outscored 66–32 by the Cardinals (one game), Pirates (twice), Dodgers (once), Braves (twice), Dodgers again (twice), and Giants (once) before defeating the Giants 3–2 in the second game of a doubleheader on September 21—and they had to score those three runs in the ninth on a three-run homer by Pafko and hold off a Giants' rally in the bottom of the inning to win that contest.

That victory left the Cubs at 58–85 with 10 games remaining. A 5–3 run put them at 63–88 heading into a season-ending three-game series at St. Louis, needing to win two of three to avoid a 90-loss season.

It didn't happen. A 6–4 loss on October 1 left them one short of the 90-loss plateau and the Cardinals defeated the Cubs again on October 2, with Al Brazle and Jim Hearn shutting out the North Siders on just five hits. The star hurler of 1945, Hank Borowy, got pounded for six runs in three innings in what would turn out to be his final game as a Cub. That December, Borowy was traded to the Phillies along with Eddie Waitkus for Monk Dubiel and Dutch Leonard.

All of this happened for the reason you'd guess: The Cubs really didn't have many good players. Andy Pafko hit .312/.375/.516 with 26 home runs and 101 RBI, one of the best years of his career, but all that got him was a distant 16th-place finish in MVP voting. Bill Nicholson, who led the league in home runs in 1943 and 1944, had suffered injuries in the interim and managed just 19 long balls and a .261 BA in 1948, his last good year, and no other Cub homered in double digits. The team total of 87 round-trippers was dead last in the National League, just a bit more than half the league-leading total of 164 by the Giants. The Cubs weren't last in the NL in runs scored in 1948, but their 597 runs scored was just nine more than the Reds, who scored a league-worst 588.

The pitching staff? Horrid. Johnny Schmitz had a very good 18–13, 2.64 ERA season with a pair of shutouts that got him an All-Star nod and 12th place in MVP voting (there was no Cy Young Award back then), and Russ Meyer was 10–10 with a 3.66 ERA, decent enough, but the rest of the starters (Dutch McCall, Ralph Hamner, Doyle Lade, Bob Rush, and a fading Borowy) were all terrible. They allowed 701 runs, which, surprisingly, was just third worst in the National League, tied with the Pirates.

This 90-loss season, the first in Cubs franchise history, would unfortunately turn out to become commonplace as the decades went by. Much of this was caused by increasing desperation to try to bring a winner, any winner, back to Wrigley Field. A succession of Cubs general managers would pick up players who had starred in the past, such as Johnny Vander Meer, Jim Hegan, Lew Burdette, and Robin Roberts, hoping they'd recapture their former glory—but that scenario always failed. Or they'd make panic trades, such as the dealing off of the popular and productive Pafko in 1951 for a bunch of nobodies, or the most famous and possibly the worst deal in baseball history, the swapping of Lou Brock for Ernie Broglio in 1964. All of that, combined with poor amateur scouting and unwillingness to finance a robust minor-league system, were the reasons the Cubs produced only one winning year (82–80 in 1963) in the 20 seasons between 1947 and 1966. In those 20 seasons, the Cubs would lose 90 or more games 11 times, including a franchise-worst 103 defeats in 1962 and 1966.

Cubs attendance held up for a while after they drew 1,036,386 in 1945, their first season of a million or more admissions since 1931. Soon after, though, it would begin to decline. In 1948, 1,237,792 entered the turnstiles at Wrigley Field. By the time the team had that awful 103-loss 1962 season, the Cubs sold fewer than half as many tickets as they had in the 90-loss year of 1948, just 609,802. The Cubs wouldn't sell as many as that 1948 number in a season again until 1969, when they set a franchise record with 1,674,993, breaking a mark that had been set in 1929.

Cubs spring training has been a tradition in Mesa, Arizona, for seven decades. But they didn't always hold preseason camp in Mesa.

Andy Pafko's baseball card in 1951, the year the Cubs traded him away.

What was the first date that the Cubs played a home spring training game in Mesa?

The Chicago NL franchise pretty much invented what we now know as spring training. In 1886, team president Albert Spalding and manager Cap Anson brought the then–White Stockings to Hot Springs, Arkansas, for preparation for the upcoming season. SABR member Mike Dugan, a Hot Springs resident, was quoted in 2013: "Anson had learned about our mineral waters and spas and the reason he brought the team to Hot Springs was so they could 'boil out the alcoholic microbes' in his hard-living players."

The team traveled there for preseason workouts from 1886 to 1888 and again in 1890 and 1892. It's unclear if they had similar camps for the rest of the 1890s (though Hot Springs would host other teams for spring camps off and on through around 1940), but in 1901, 1902, and 1906 they gathered for this purpose in Champaign, Illinois, only a few hours by train from Chicago. Other early spring training locations for the team, by then known as the Cubs: Los Angeles, 1903–1904, and Santa Monica, California, in 1905. Then they headed south, to New Orleans (1907); Vicksburg, Mississippi (1908); back to Hot Springs (1909–10); back to New Orleans in 1911 and 1912; and in Tampa, Florida, from 1913 to 1916.

Then followed a long stretch of Cubs spring camps in California. They trained in Pasadena from 1917 to 1921 and moved to the Wrigley-owned Catalina Island in 1922 once William Wrigley completed his purchase of the team. That would be the team's spring home through 1951, except for three years during World War II, 1943 to 1945, when wartime travel restrictions forced them to hold spring practice in French Lick, Indiana.

Teams were beginning to hold spring practice in Arizona in the late 1940s, and the Cubs and New York Yankees had played a spring series there in 1951, prompting Dwight Patterson, owner of a Mesa ranch, to try to lure the Cubs to move to Mesa. That's when Patterson formed the Mesa HoHoKams, a civic organization that raised $22,000 to offer the Cubs if they would move their training location to Rendezvous Park in the Arizona city.

The offer was accepted, and so the Cubs relocated their spring camp to Mesa for the 1952 season. The first Cubs spring training game in their new Arizona home was played on Saturday, March 8, 1952, against the Cleveland Indians. The Rendezvous Park crowd was reported to be about 4,000, quite a large gathering for a park that officially held just 3,000.

The Cubs won the game 5–4, holding off a three-run ninth-inning Cleveland rally. Harvey Gentry, who had been selected as a Rule 5 pick from the Giants during the offseason, became the first Cubs player to hit a spring home run in Arizona in the seventh inning. The *Chicago Tribune* reported that the HoHoKams had offered a "gold mine share" to the first Cub to homer in a Mesa spring game, and so it was given to Gentry, though *Tribune* writer Irving Vaughan also noted that "it is in Superstition country, legendary home of the Lost Dutchman mine, and all prospectors who ever searched for it never returned."

Gentry did return, but to the Giants from the Cubs after spring training, never playing in a regular-season game for the Cubs (though five for the Giants in 1954). He lived for a long time after his baseball career, passing away in Ohio in 2018, aged 92.

As for the Cubs' spring homes, they held camp at Rendezvous Park through 1965, after which new manager Leo Durocher, a California resident, had them relocate to Long Beach in 1966. That proved unsatisfactory largely due to unexpected rains, and the Cubs moved spring training back to Arizona in 1967, though to Scottsdale, where they played spring games through 1978. In 1979 they moved back to Mesa, in the first incarnation of HoHoKam Park, which was demolished after 1996. A new ballpark also christened HoHoKam Park was erected on the same site in 1997, and the Cubs played there through 2013, before moving to their current spring home of Sloan Park for the 2014 season.

Through the end of the 2023 season, 52 games in MLB history have had a total game time of six hours or longer.

When was the first Cubs game that lasted that long?

The Cubs had played many long extra-inning games in the first century or so of their history, but none took longer than six hours to complete until 1982—and it can be argued that the game actually took more than 24 hours to finish, because the first game in Cubs history that took longer than six hours of game time was suspended due to darkness at Wrigley Field and finished the following afternoon.

This game began on Tuesday, August 17, 1982, as the Cubs hosted the Dodgers at Wrigley Field in the opener of a three-game series, six years before lights were installed at the North Side ball yard. A National League rule instituted in 1969 stated that any game that couldn't be completed due to darkness at Wrigley would be suspended and finished before the next scheduled game between the two clubs.

In this afternoon contest, the Cubs began by scoring a first-inning run on an infield groundout by Bill Buckner. In the top of the second, the Dodgers tied the game on an RBI single by Mike Scioscia.

And then the two ballclubs went through a long, *long*, **long** stretch without being able to score at all. A few runners reached scoring position through the regulation nine innings, but none could cross the plate. Cubs manager Lee Elia was ejected in the bottom of the eighth after Larry Bowa had tried to score what could have been the winning run. Bowa was ruled out by plate umpire Eric Gregg, though newspaper reports indicated he had beat the throw and got his foot under Scioscia's tag.

More ejections were to follow. Cubs outfielder Jay Johnstone was tossed by Gregg in the ninth for arguing balls and strikes. Then neither team scored through the first eight extra innings, at which time darkness began to fall on Wrigley Field. At 6:45 p.m., about an hour before sunset, the umpires determined it was getting too dark to play, with sunset on that day coming up at 7:47 p.m. and players likely being exhausted. The teams had completed 17 innings, and the game was suspended with the score still 1–1.

The next day, Wednesday, August 18, play resumed at 12:05 p.m., with the regularly scheduled Cubs vs. Dodgers game still to follow.

No one scored in the 18th, and in the 19th, Cubs coach John Vukovich, serving as manager after Elia's ejection, was also thrown out, for—what else?—arguing balls and strikes.

In the top of the 20th inning, LA third baseman Ron Cey—who would be traded to the Cubs for a couple of minor leaguers after the season—led off with a single. He was picked off, which led to another argument and his ejection after he bumped first base umpire Dave Pallone, as well as the ejection of Dodgers manager Tommy Lasorda.

The ejection of Cey caused a dilemma for the Dodgers, as they had no position players remaining on the bench. They did have an outfielder, Pedro Guerrero, who could also play third base, so he moved there in the bottom of the 20th, replacing Cey. But that left them short in the outfield, so the Dodgers used starting pitchers Fernando Valenzuela (20th inning) and Bob Welch (21st inning) as outfielders, shifting them between left field and right field depending on the side of the plate from which the Cubs hitter was batting. (Irony: The actual Dodgers outfielder who switched back and forth with the pitchers was future Cubs manager Dusty Baker.)

In the top of the 21st inning with one out, Steve Sax doubled and was wild pitched to third base. After Ken Landreaux walked, Baker came to bat and hit a fly ball to right field. Sax tagged up and despite the throw to Jody Davis beating Sax to the plate, he was ruled safe by Eric Gregg.

Chicago Tribune reporter Robert Markus wrote: "Davis slapped the tag on Sax, and Gregg, to his eternal chagrin, had his right arm three quarters up in the air to call Sax out when he suddenly flattened his palms and called him safe."

Obviously, in modern baseball this play would be reviewed, but no such thing existed in 1982 and the call stood, even though it was strongly disputed by everyone connected with the Cubs. Television replays appeared to show Davis tagging Sax out before he touched the plate.

The Cubs went out 1-2-3 in the bottom of the 21st and the game ended in a 2–1 Cubs loss, with a total game time of six hours, 10 minutes. That game time was surpassed in Cubs history on Tuesday, July 29, 2014, when the Cubs and Rockies played a 16-inning affair in six hours,

27 minutes. That game became known as the "John Baker Game" when the backup catcher both pitched and scored the winning run.

The 21-inning affair played by the Cubs and Dodgers in 1982 remains the longest game by innings in the history of Wrigley Field.

With the "placed runner" in extra innings, which began in 2020, being made a permanent MLB rule before the 2023 season, it's unlikely any games will be added to that list. No MLB game has taken more than six hours to complete since Tuesday, September 24, 2019, when the Diamondbacks and Cardinals played a 19-inning game in six hours, 53 minutes, won by Arizona 3–2.

The Cubs have had many years over the long history of their franchise when they have finished in first place. And they have also had many years when they've had the worst record in the league.

When was the first time they went worst-to-first?

When the Cubs were winning pennants in the early part of the 20th century, they were a solid, good team for many years, coming close in years they didn't win. This happened again from the late 1920s through the late 1930s, an era when the Cubs won four National League pennants and finished second or third seven other times.

But there was also a time when Cubs playoff appearances came as somewhat of a surprise. Even the 98-win 1945 NL pennant winners were coming off a losing season the previous year (75–79), though that 1944 team was not the NL's worst.

Then followed a long postseason drought of 39 years. But when it ended in 1984 with another 96-win season that also came off a losing season of 71–91. Again, though, the 1983 Cubs didn't have the worst record in the league.

It happened again the next time the Cubs made the postseason:
1988: 77–85
1989: 93–69
Though again, the 1988 Cubs weren't the worst team in the league.

The next time the Cubs made the postseason after that, in 1998, they did have the worst record in the league the previous year, 68–94, tied with the Phillies. But the 1998 Cubs didn't finish first—they were a second-place wild-card team.

In 2002, the Cubs again had a terrible season, going 67–95, then finishing first in the NL Central in 2003 with an 88–74 mark. But that 95-loss season wasn't worst in the league—the Brewers' 106-loss season topped it.

So that first Cubs "worst-to-first" season would have to wait until 2007. The 2006 Cubs were one of the worst teams in franchise history, losing 96 games. At the time, that tied the 1974 team for fifth most in the history of the Cubs.

The 2006 Cubs were a strange mélange of a team. Derrek Lee had come off a third-place finish in MVP voting in 2005 when he hit .335/.418/.662 with 50 doubles and 46 home runs, but he suffered a serious wrist injury in Los Angeles in April and played in only 50 games. The rest of the offense couldn't make up for Lee's absence and finished 28th in runs scored—and the pitching played along by allowing 834 runs, fifth most in the major leagues. After starting out 12–7, the team went 16–40 in May and June and at one point in May they lost eight in a row and scored nine runs—total—in the eight losses.

That skid dumped the 2006 Cubs into fifth place in the NL Central, where they remained until September, when an 11–17 finish dropped them into the cellar with the league's worst record, one game behind the Pirates. Dusty Baker, who had been a hero in 2003—for a while, anyway—had his contract expire at the end of the season and it was not renewed. Instead, general manager Jim Hendry went outside the organization again for a "big-name" manager, this time Lou Piniella, who had managed the Yankees, Reds, and Mariners to multiple postseason appearances and won a World Series in Cincinnati.

Then Hendry got to work on free agent contracts, signing Alfonso Soriano to an eight-year deal that was at the time the biggest in Cubs franchise history. Left-hander Ted Lilly was inked to a four-year contract by Hendry literally while he was on a gurney in a hospital, where he'd been taken from the Winter Meetings after complaining about not feeling well.

Hendry also added versatile infielder/outfielder Mark DeRosa and signed Jason Marquis to bolster the rotation.

And then the year started with a clunk. The 2007 Cubs went 10–14 in April and 12–15 in May, somehow ending the latter month in third place in a division so bad only one team was over .500, making it dubbed by some the "Comedy Central." The Cubs began June by dropping the first two games of a weekend series to the Braves at Wrigley Field. In the second of those defeats, the Cubs were trailing 4–3 in the bottom of the eighth when Angel Pagan was called out on a close play at third base. In those pre-replay review days, situations like that often called for a managerial tirade, and Piniella gave one of the better ones in recent years. He stormed out of the dugout, threw his cap to the ground, and went face to face screaming with umpire Mark Wegner, who claimed Piniella kicked him. Fans threw trash onto the field to the point that the game was delayed several minutes for cleanup. The Cubs lost 5–3, and afterward, Piniella admitted that the call was correct and he was simply trying to "fire up" his team.

Whether that was responsible for what the Cubs did next or not might never be known, but the team, nine games under .500 after that loss to Atlanta, went on a remarkable streak that peaked on August 1 when they defeated the Phillies to get to 57–49—a 35–18 run that put them in first place in the division. Among the wins in that stretch was a June 29 comeback against the Brewers at Wrigley Field where they trailed 5–0 after the first inning and 5–3 going to the bottom of the ninth. Two singles with one out put runners on first and third, and Lee plated one run with a sacrifice fly. Aramis Ramirez then smashed Francisco Cordero's first pitch into the left-field bleachers for a walk-off home run, and those who attended that game will tell you that was among the loudest roars in Wrigley history.

The Cubs remained in a tight race with the Brewers for the top spot in the NL Central for most of August and September but finally pulled away with a 15–8 run from September 1 to 23, which put them at 83–73, 3 1/2 games ahead with six remaining. They got swept by the Marlins in Miami after that but clinched the division title on Friday, September 28 in Cincinnati on the strength of seven shutout innings by Carlos

Zambrano and homers from Soriano and Lee. Their first-place record was a modest 85–77, but it was the first time in franchise history they'd gone from worst-to-first.

Unfortunately, the postseason did not go well. Matched in a Division Series with the NL West champion Diamondbacks, the first two games were played in Arizona. Zambrano threw six shutout innings, and the Cubs nursed a 1–0 lead into the seventh, but Piniella pulled Big Z after just 85 pitches, claiming later he was "saving" Zambrano to start Game 4 at Wrigley Field—a game that never happened when the Cubs got swept. The D-Backs scored a pair off Carlos Marmol to win Game 1, and then after the Cubs took a 2–0 lead early in Game 2 on a Geovany Soto home run, Lilly served up a three-run homer to Chris Young and famously slammed his glove to the ground, upset with himself. The Diamondbacks won 8–4, and the Cubs would have to take three straight to move on.

Young began Game 3 at Wrigley Field by homering off Rich Hill, and the Cubs were never in the ballgame, losing 5–1, and Zambrano had to wait until the following season for his next start.

Nevertheless, the Cubs had gone worst-to-first and would finish first in the NL Central again in 2008, winning 97 games, their most since 1945, and that made for the team's first back-to-back postseason appearances since three straight in 1906–1907–1908. Sadly, that year, the 100th anniversary of the Cubs' most recent World Series win, also ended badly, with a three-game division series sweep at the hands of the Dodgers.

AWARD FIRSTS

When the Cubs won the World Series in 2016, Kris Bryant was named National League Most Valuable Player.

Who was the first Cub to win the National League MVP Award?

The answer to this question is, "It depends."

Depends on what? You're no doubt asking this question.

It depends on your definition of the MVP Award, because there have been several iterations of it in MLB history, and so you shall have a bit of a history lesson before I tell you who's generally considered the first Cubs player to win the MVP Award.

In 1910, there had been a car given to the major-league player with the highest batting average, sponsored by Hugh Chalmers, owner of a well-known automobile company of the time. There was some controversy over this award, primarily because there was some dispute over whether Ty Cobb or Napoleon Lajoie had the highest batting average, and in the end both players were given a car. The next year, Chalmers created an award that was supposed to be voted on by writers for "the most important and useful player to the club and the league," one award per league—so something a bit similar to a modern Most Valuable Player. The Chalmers Award was given out for four years before Chalmers apparently decided it wasn't giving his car company as much publicity as he wanted, and he discontinued it.

Frank Schulte of the Cubs won the Chalmers Award in 1911, but this isn't really a "Most Valuable Player" as we know it today.

The American League created an award in 1922 that was supposed to honor "the baseball player who is of the greatest all-around service to his club." The winner was to get a medal and cash prize and previous winners were ineligible, resulting in Babe Ruth winning it only once in the seven years it was awarded. The National League joined the AL in presenting such an award in 1923, and Rogers Hornsby of the Cubs won it in 1929, the last year this "League Award" was handed out. (The NL had no restrictions on previous winners; Hornsby had also won it in 1925.)

Finally, after this award had fallen into some disarray, Commissioner Kenesaw Mountain Landis recommended that the Baseball Writers Association of America vote for a Most Valuable Player Award, one for each league, in 1931. The voting format has changed a bit over time, but this award, now handed out by the BBWAA for more than 90 years, is the one most fans consider the true MVP Award, and in fact, on Major League Baseball's website, they acknowledge MVPs going back only to 1931.

These award criteria were given to BBWAA voters in 1931 and remain in effect today:

(1) actual value of a player to his team, that is, strength of offense and defense; (2) number of games played; (3) general character, disposition, loyalty and effort; (4) former winners are eligible; and (5) members of the committee may vote for more than one member of a team.

These criteria have been interpreted in myriad ways over the past nine decades by various writers and often cause controversy in the voting. It can be argued that such controversy is good for baseball, using the old saw "there's no such thing as bad publicity."

In any case, the first Cub to win the BBWAA's version of the MVP was catcher Gabby Hartnett, who won the NL Award in 1935, and so Hartnett is generally considered the first Cub to be named Most Valuable Player.

By 1935, Hartnett was an established star in baseball and widely considered the best catcher in NL history. It was his 14th season as a Cub and he'd been the Cubs' primary catcher for the previous 12 years, except for 1929, when he played in just 25 games due to a mysterious injury that was never truly diagnosed. (One wonders whether the Cubs might have won the 1929 World Series with a healthy Hartnett.)

The 1935 season was a great one for the Cubs. A 21-game winning streak—to this day the NL record for the longest without tie games being included—brought them to the pennant and a 100-win season, their first since 1910 and the last time they'd hit the century mark in wins until 2016. Hartnett batted .344/.404/.545 with 34 doubles, six triples, and 13 home runs. The MVP vote was quite close, though: Hartnett received 75 points from the writers to Dizzy Dean's 66.

Three years later, with the Cubs floundering in third place, manager Charlie Grimm was replaced by Hartnett, who served as player-manager. He guided the Cubs to a 44–27 mark the rest of the year and on September 28, 1938, hit the famous "Homer in the Gloamin'" that defeated the Pirates and put the Cubs in first place for the first time since June 7. (Contrary to popular belief, this home run didn't win the pennant for the Cubs; they'd have to wait three more days, defeating the Cardinals in St. Louis, to clinch the NL title.)

The team fell on hard times over the next couple of seasons, and Hartnett was fired as manager at the end of the 1940 season and also released as a player. He signed and played one final season with the Giants. At the time of his retirement as a player he was considered the greatest catcher in National League history, and even today he ranks probably no lower than fourth best (Johnny Bench, Mike Piazza, and Gary Carter are generally recognized to be ahead of Hartnett).

After his playing days were over, Hartnett managed in the minor leagues through much of the 1940s, then returned to the Chicago area where he opened Gabby Hartnett's Recreation Center in suburban Lincolnwood, a bowling alley that also included a sporting-goods store and remained open long after Hartnett's death in 1972.

Hartnett was elected to baseball's Hall of Fame in 1955, in a class that included Joe DiMaggio, Ted Lyons, and Dazzy Vance.

Other Cubs who have been named NL Most Valuable Player:

Hank Sauer, 1952

Ernie Banks, 1958 and 1959 (the first NL player to win consecutive MVP Awards)

Ryne Sandberg, 1984
Andre Dawson, 1987
Sammy Sosa, 1998
Kris Bryant, 2016

Major League Baseball, in conjunction with Rawlings, created the Gold Glove Award for fielding excellence in 1957.
Who was the first Cubs player to win a Gold Glove?
In 1957, the first year Gold Gloves were awarded, Rawlings made one award to the top fielder at each position in the major leagues. The following year, the awards were expanded to honor the best fielder at each position in both major leagues.

Two years after that, in 1960, future Hall of Famer Ernie Banks became the first Cubs player to win a Gold Glove for his play at shortstop.

Banks was signed to a Cubs contract by Buck O'Neil, the legendary scout who also brought Billy Williams, George Altman, and Lou Brock to the North Side.

Making his MLB debut in September 1953, Ernie became the Cubs' regular shortstop the following year and finished second in Rookie of the Year voting. He hit .275/.326/.427 with 19 home runs and, truth be told, probably had a better overall year than the player who won that award, Cardinals outfielder Wally Moon. But the Cubs were a floundering franchise in the mid-1950s, and so a player from such a team wouldn't necessarily get the recognition due.

Banks got even better in 1955, hitting .295/.345/.596 with 44 home runs and finishing third in MVP voting behind Roy Campanella and Duke Snider of the Dodgers, again, players from the pennant-winning team beating out the guy from a sixth-place club. (To be fair, Snider and Campanella probably did have better years than Banks in 1955.) Banks set a major-league record by hitting five grand slams that year. That still stands as the National League record, though American Leaguers Don Mattingly (1987) and Travis Hafner (2006) both hit six slams in a season.

Ernie continued his solid, everyday play—over the next several seasons he'd play in 717 consecutive games—and in 1958 and 1959 his excellent play got him named National League MVP, the first time any NL player had won back-to-back MVP Awards.

The following year, Banks' overall numbers were just a tick lower than his MVP seasons, and he finished fourth in the balloting, though he led the NL in home runs with 41, his last 40-homer season. The Gold Glove he won that season was the only one in his career, and he would play shortstop for just one more season, 1961, before injuries forced his move to first base, where he'd finish his 19-year career with the Cubs in 1971.

After his playing career ended, Banks served as a Cubs coach for a few years and later became a popular team ambassador. He passed away on Friday, January 23, 2015, a bit more than year or so short of seeing his beloved Cubs win the World Series.

Since Banks in 1960, 20 other Cubs have won Gold Gloves, most recently Ian Happ, Dansby Swanson, and Nico Hoerner in 2023. This created yet another Cubs first—it was the first time three Cubs had won Gold Gloves in a single season.

The National League created its Player of the Month Award in 1958. Who was the first Cub to win this award?

Interestingly, Ernie Banks, who won the NL's MVP Award in both 1958 and 1959, didn't win the National League Player of the Month Award in any calendar month in either of those years.

Instead, George Altman became the first Cub to receive this honor when he was named National League Player of the Month in June 1961. He hit .355/.393/.718 (44-for-124) that month with nine doubles, three triples, and 10 home runs. That performance helped get him All-Star honors for both games that year (from 1959 to 1962, two All-Star Games were played annually), and overall in 1961 Altman batted .303/.353/.560 with 27 home runs. He led the National League in triples with 12 and finished 14th in MVP balloting.

Like Banks, Altman was signed for the Cubs by Buck O'Neil. He played one year in the Cubs system in 1956 before being drafted into the US Army. After one year there, he returned to baseball in 1958 to play for Pueblo (Colorado) in the Cubs system, batting .325 with 11 triples and 14 home runs in just 89 games.

He made his major-league debut in 1959 at age 26 and became the Cubs' primary center fielder. Altman hit .245 with 12 home runs in his rookie season and upped those numbers to .266 with 13 home runs in 119 games in 1960.

His 1961 season, described earlier, was his finest in the major leagues. He continued that good performance in 1962, now mostly playing right field, by batting a career-high .318, good for sixth in the National League, and his .904 OPS ranked seventh. He hit 22 home runs and stole a career-high 19 bases, even though the 1962 Cubs established a franchise record with 103 losses.

Altman was to turn 30 in March 1963, so the Cubs thought perhaps they'd be better off trading him at his peak value. Not long after the 1962 season ended, on October 17, the Cubs traded Altman and Moe Thacker to the Cardinals for Larry Jackson, Lindy McDaniel, and Jimmie Schaffer.

That turned out to be one of the better trades for the Cubs in the 1960s. Jackson won 24 games for the Cubs in 1964 and was eventually traded to the Phillies in the deal that brought Fergie Jenkins to the Cubs. McDaniel had a couple of good years in relief in Chicago and then was sent to the Giants in the trade that brought Bill Hands and Randy Hundley to the North Side.

Altman, though, did not do well playing in St. Louis. Management there thought he should uppercut the ball more to take advantage of a short right-field porch in the old Busch Stadium, and this messed with Altman's swing to the point that his numbers declined to .274/.339/.401 with just nine home runs in 135 games. The disappointed Cardinals traded Altman to the Mets for Roger Craig in November 1963, but Altman's one year in New York produced a poor .594 OPS and the Cubs were able to reacquire Altman in January 1965 for outfielder Billy Cowan.

Unfortunately, injuries had taken a toll on Altman, and he hit just five home runs in 1965 and four in 1966 as a part-time player. After just 15 games with the Cubs in 1967, he spent most of that year with Triple-A Tacoma and was let go by the team after the season.

But that was not the end of George Altman's playing career. In 1968 he signed with the Tokyo Orions of Japan's Nippon Pro Baseball and in nine seasons in NPB hit .309 with 213 home runs, becoming one of the first true American stars to succeed over a several-year period in Japan.

After his playing career ended, Altman returned to Chicago and became a commodities trader at the Chicago Board of Trade, later retiring and settling in the St. Louis area.

Other Cubs to win the National League Player of the Month:
Dick Ellsworth: May 1963
Ron Santo: June 1963, July 1964, June 1969
Billy Williams: May 1964, July 1972
Ken Holtzman: May 1969
Fergie Jenkins: July 1971
Andre Thornton: September 1975
Dave Kingman: April 1980
Bill Buckner: August 1982
Mel Hall: August 1983
Leon Durham: May 1984
Ryne Sandberg: June 1984, June 1990
Keith Moreland: August 1984
Andre Dawson: August 1987, May 1990
Mark Grace: July 1989
Sammy Sosa: July 1996, June 1998, May 1999, July 2000, August 2001
Derrek Lee: April 2005, September 2009
Alfonso Soriano: June 2007
Kris Bryant: August 2016
Cody Bellinger: July 2023

The first MLB Rookie of the Year Award was given in 1947. It's now named after its first recipient, Brooklyn Dodgers star Jackie Robinson.

Who was the first Cub to be named National League Rookie of the Year?

Billy Williams, now enshrined in the Hall of Fame in Cooperstown, was the first Cubs Rookie of the Year, winning the award in 1961.

Williams had been signed by famed scout Buck O'Neil out of the Mobile, Alabama, area in 1956. After a few years of minor-league ball in the Cubs system, he got homesick playing in San Antonio in 1959 and went home. O'Neil was dispatched to Mobile to talk Williams into returning. In O'Neil's book *I Was Right on Time*, he wrote that he had to do just one simple thing to show Billy he should go back to Texas:

> *I said to Billy, "C'mon. Let's go out to the ballyard. There's a player I want you to see." This was just a pretense, of course, although you never knew what you might find in Mobile, the garden of such delights as Henry Aaron and Willie McCovey. When we got to the ballpark—it was just a little sandlot league—Billy was mobbed by the younger ballplayers. "Billy, we hear you're doin' great." "Billy, have you met Ernie Banks?" "Billy, what brings you home?"*
>
> *They treated him like a superstar, and I could see that Billy enjoyed the attention. I spent five days in Mobile with the Williams family, and I never said one word about him going back to San Antonio. I never had to. What sold him was those other hungry young ballplayers. He saw what a great thing he had going, and he knew that if he blew it, there were a hundred guys waiting in line to take his place.*

Earlier that same year, Hall of Famer Rogers Hornsby, then a Cubs spring training instructor, called together a group of prospects at the end of camp to critique them. Hornsby treated most of the prospects roughly, but when he got to Williams, he said, "You can play in the big leagues right now." He said the same thing to another prospect in that group—Ron Santo.

Williams returned to San Antonio, began hitting the ball well, and was called up to the Cubs late in 1959 for an 18-game trial in which he hit just .177, though in so doing he established a milestone in Cubs history—he became the 1,000th player in Cubs history when he made his major-league debut on Thursday, August 6, 1959, playing left field against the Philadelphia Phillies, batting third and going 0-for-4 with one RBI. Another September callup in 1960 produced better results—a

.277 batting average and a pair of home runs hit in the season's final two games in Los Angeles.

In 1961, the Cubs switched from having a manager to the infamous College of Coaches system, which was a giant flop, but one thing the "college" did right was install Williams in the Cubs' starting lineup full time. The team, as it had been for nearly a decade and a half, was terrible, losing 90 games, but Williams flourished as a starting player in the major leagues at age 23, playing mostly left field along with a few games in right. He hit .278/.338/.484 with 25 home runs and received 10 of the 16 first-place votes for Rookie of the Year, winning the award over another fellow future Hall of Famer, Joe Torre.

Williams' 25 home runs established a record for Cubs rookies, breaking the previous club record of 19 that had been set by his teammate Ernie Banks in 1954. The record stood until 2008 when it was broken by Geovany Soto, who hit 26. That mark was matched by Kris Bryant in 2015 and broken by Patrick Wisdom, who hit 28 in 2021.

Two years after Williams' Rookie of the Year season, he began a streak of consecutive games on Sunday, September 22, 1963, that would not end for nearly seven years, when he asked to sit out a game on Wednesday, September 2, 1970. The 1,117 games established a National League record that was later broken by Steve Garvey in 1983.

From 1962 to 1973, Billy was named to the NL All-Star team six times and finished second in MVP voting twice, both to Johnny Bench of the Reds, though it's arguable he had better seasons both times. In 1970 Williams hit 42 home runs, the only time a left-handed Cubs hitter has hit 40 or more, and in 1972 he led the NL in BA (.333), SLG (.606), OPS (1.005), and total bases (348). He became revered by Cubs fans for the swing that got him nicknamed "Sweet Swingin' Billy" and for his classy demeanor on and off the field.

Williams was traded to the Oakland Athletics after the 1974 season, where he would become the only position player from the star-crossed late 1960s Cubs team to play in the postseason, three games for the 1975 A's in the ALCS.

Billy settled in northern California after he retired from the A's, but when he was hired as a Cubs coach in 1980, he and his family returned

Future Hall of Famer Billy Williams at Wrigley Field.
JAY PUBLISHING VIA TRADINGCARDDB.COM, PUBLIC DOMAIN, VIA WIKIMEDIA COMMONS.

to Chicago. Eventually, Williams spent 15 seasons as a Cubs coach. It's estimated he wore the Cubs uniform as a player or coach for around 5,000 games, more than any other single individual.

In 1983, Williams was asked to compete in an Old-Timers' Game as part of All-Star celebrations in Chicago marking the 50th anniversary of the All-Star Game. Still just 44 years old and trim as he had been in his playing days, Billy smashed a home run into the upper deck at old Comiskey Park, off former White Sox hurler Hoyt Wilhelm, then aged 60.

Now, consider what sort of game this was and who the pitcher was. Nevertheless, this home run got national attention, as well as the attention of some writers who were Hall of Fame voters. Some say that this Old-Timers' Game home run was a factor in Williams' election to the Hall of Fame in 1987, and his subsequent number retirement by the Cubs.

Williams serves to this day as a special advisor to Cubs management and ownership and continues to make his home in the Chicago suburbs, and he often makes appearances at Wrigley Field as an esteemed elder statesman. He and his teammate Fergie Jenkins were given World Series rings in 2016 and participated in the festivities at the invitation of the winning players, given a special shout-out by Anthony Rizzo at the championship rally as one of the most beloved Cubs in franchise history.

Other Cubs who have won the Rookie of the Year Award:

Ken Hubbs, 1962
Jerome Walton, 1989
Kerry Wood, 1998
Geovany Soto, 2008
Kris Bryant, 2015

An award honoring the best reliever in baseball was created by *The Sporting News* in 1960, titled "Fireman of the Year," after the idea that a relief pitcher put out "fires" created by previous pitchers.

Who was the first Cub honored as Fireman of the Year?

It didn't take too long for a Cubs reliever to win this award.

The Cubs had been a bad team for a decade and a half beginning in 1947, bottoming out with a franchise record 103 losses in 1962.

The 1963 Cubs, though, started out at least on an even keel, playing .500 ball for most of the first two months and sneaking into a first-place tie on June 6 and 7—the latest in the season they'd been even in a tie for the top spot since 1947.

One of the reasons for that good play was a reliever who had been acquired the previous offseason from the Cardinals, Lindy McDaniel, in one of the Cubs' better deals in that era. They also acquired starter Larry Jackson and infielder Jimmie Schaffer in exchange for George Altman, Don Cardwell, and Moe Thacker.

McDaniel went on to have one of his best seasons in 1963 and was named NL Fireman of the Year, the first Cub to win that award.

A starter for some of his early career in St. Louis, McDaniel pitched exclusively in relief for the Cubs in 1963, appearing in 57 games with an ERA of 2.86 and a WHIP of 1.239, walking just 2.8 per nine innings. Though the save was not yet an official stat in 1963, McDaniel led the league with 22.

McDaniel played a big role in the Cubs' win over the Giants on June 6, the day they went into a first-place tie with San Francisco and St. Louis.

The Cubs were facing the Giants at Wrigley Field that afternoon. Billy Williams had hit a two-run homer off Juan Marichal in the bottom of the eighth to tie the game 2–2, and from there the game went into extra innings.

McDaniel entered the game with the bases loaded and one out in the top of the 10th. With Ed Bailey at bat, McDaniel picked Willie Mays off second base. He then struck out Bailey to end the inning.

The Giants sent Billy Pierce, normally a starter, to throw the bottom of the 10th. He ran a 2–2 count on McDaniel, and then Lindy hit a walk-off homer. If ever a baseball player can be said to have singlehandedly won a game for his team, McDaniel surely did so on that day. It's the only walk-off home run ever hit by a Cubs relief pitcher.

The Cubs maintained the first-place tie for another day and remained within three games of first place for another month before fading and finishing seventh in the 10-team National League with an 82–80 record. It was the Cubs' first winning season in 17 years.

McDaniel had good years for the Cubs in 1964 and 1965, though not quite as good as his 1963 season, and the team faded back under .500. After the 1965 season, McDaniel and Don Landrum were traded to the Giants for Bill Hands and Randy Hundley, another outstanding deal from that era. Though McDaniel would pitch in the major leagues for another decade after leaving the Cubs, Hands and Hundley were productive Cubs for many years.

The Fireman of the Year Award was renamed Reliever of the Year in 2001, and the award was discontinued after 2010. A new award titled Relief Pitcher of the Year was created in 2013 and has been issued continuously since then. No Cubs pitcher has won the new award to date, so when that happens, it'll create another Cubs first!

The Cy Young Award, created to honor great pitching, was first given to MLB's best pitcher in 1956. For its first 11 seasons there was just one Cy Young Award for both major leagues, but beginning in 1967, one pitcher in each league was named a Cy Young winner.

Who was the first Cub to win the Cy Young Award?

Fergie Jenkins had six straight seasons of winning 20 or more games for the Cubs, beginning in his first full year with the team in 1967. Those six years were all outstanding, but his best season was probably 1971, and that's the year he won the Cy Young Award, becoming the first Cubs pitcher to get that honor.

That season, Fergie set career highs in wins (24), games started (39), innings pitched (325, an unimaginable number in modern baseball), and complete games (30). That last number is also inconceivable as baseball is played in the 21st century—in 2023, all 30 major-league teams combined for just 35 complete games.

But back then, completing what you started was considered a badge of honor for starting pitchers. Jenkins completed 10 of his first 11 starts in 1971, the clunker coming in an April 16 outing in San Francisco when he allowed the Giants six hits and five runs and didn't make it out of the third inning.

On June 13, Fergie threw an 11-inning complete game against the Reds at Wrigley Field; unfortunately, an RBI single by Lee May plated a Cincinnati run in the top of the 11th and the Cubs lost the game 4–3. Since that afternoon, just two other Cubs games have featured a starting pitcher throwing at least 11 innings: Fergie threw 12 innings in a 4–1 loss to the Giants on July 22, 1973, and Rick Sutcliffe threw an 11-inning complete-game win in the first game of a doubleheader against the Expos at Wrigley Field on September 20, 1988.

The best game of Jenkins' Cy Young season was a two-hit, seven-strikeout shutout thrown against the Braves on August 16 at Wrigley Field. A bit more than a month earlier, he set a career high with 14 strikeouts in a 2–1 win over the Phillies at Veterans Stadium, and he matched that total in the same venue on September 19.

No Cubs pitcher in the past half-century has come close to the 325 innings Fergie threw in 1971; the most since then is 289, also by

Jenkins, in 1973. No Cubs pitcher has thrown more than 250 innings since 2000, when Jon Lieber piled up 251.

Jenkins added to the luster of his Cy Young pitching in 1971 by having the best batting season of his career. Always a good hitter, Jenkins batted .243/.282/.478 in 1971 with seven doubles, a triple, and six home runs. Baseball-reference.com says that batting performance was good for 1.7 bWAR, which was better than at least three position-player regulars on that team: Joe Pepitone, Jim Hickman, and Don Kessinger. The six homers are a franchise record for a pitcher, matched by Carlos Zambrano in 2006. Had the Silver Slugger Award existed at the time (it wasn't created until 1980), Fergie no doubt would have won that award in 1971 too.

Fergie's performance declined in 1973 and he was traded to the Texas Rangers after that season, where he bested his 1971 career high by winning 25 games in 1974, which remains Texas' franchise record. After two years toiling in Texas he was traded to the Red Sox, where he pitched for two seasons before being swapped back to the Rangers. Before the 1982 season, Jenkins considered retirement but was coaxed to return to the Cubs as a free agent by Cubs general manager Dallas Green, who had been a minor-league teammate of Fergie's in the Phillies organization in 1964 and 1965. Jenkins responded with a fine season, posting a 3.15 ERA and registering his 3,000th career strikeout against Garry Templeton of the Padres in San Diego on May 25, 1982. His 1983 season, though, wasn't as good, and Fergie was let go early in spring training in 1984, just a few months before he might have become the first 1969 Cub to go to the postseason with the team.

After his retirement, Jenkins coached in the minor leagues and also served as Cubs pitching coach in 1996. He was elected to the Hall of Fame in 1991 and the Cubs retired his No. 31 in 2009. He shares that number retirement honor with Greg Maddux, who wore the number with distinction for the Cubs from 1986 to 1992 and again from 2004 to 2006.

Future Hall of Famer Fergie Jenkins at Wrigley Field in 1973.

Other Cubs pitchers who have won the National League Cy Young Award:

Bruce Sutter, 1979
Rick Sutcliffe, 1984
Greg Maddux, 1992
Jake Arrieta, 2015

It should be noted that one other Cubs pitcher might have won a Cy Young Award during the time there was only one such award for both major leagues. In 1964, Cubs right-hander Larry Jackson posted a great season, with 24 wins (which led both leagues) and a 3.15 ERA. Jackson finished 12th in NL MVP voting and second in Cy Young voting. Dean Chance of the Angels won the award and received 17 of the 20 first-place votes. Jackson received two first-place votes, and Sandy Koufax got the other one. By modern standards Koufax probably had a better season than Jackson, but in those days, pitcher wins got most voters' attention, and had there been separate votes for both leagues, Jackson likely would have won the National League Cy Young Award.

The National League began honoring a player's performance with a Player of the Week Award in 1973, and the American League followed suit a year later.

Who was the first Cubs player to be named NL Player of the Week?

The star-crossed group of Cubs who played well but never won anything in the late 1960s and early 1970s had been held together for one last run at a division title in 1973.

They got off to a fantastic start, holding first place from late April through mid-July, at one point in late June leading the NL East by 8 1/2 games and hitting the midway point of the season July 1 with a 48–33 record.

It was just before then, for the week ending on Friday, June 29, 1973, that Ron Santo became the first Cub to be named National League Player of the Week. For that week, Santo hit .355/.412/.677 (11-for-31) with four doubles and two home runs. Both of Santo's home runs that week came in what wound up as an 18-inning, 5–4 loss to the Montreal

Expos in the second game of a doubleheader June 27—but both had been game-tying homers, one in the ninth inning, the other in the 13th.

Santo's performance had peaked from 1963 to 1969, during which time he won five Gold Gloves, made six All-Star teams, and finished in the top 10 of NL MVP voting four times, but by 1973 he had begun to decline. Santo was batting .304/.385/.487 in 1973 at the time he was named NL Player of the Week, but for the rest of that season batted just .231/.312/.396, perhaps one of the biggest reasons the Cubs fell apart during the second half that year. At one point they lost 31 of 39 and wound up going 29–52 in the second half, finishing 77–85, their first losing record since 1966.

After the 1973 season, the Cubs "backed up the truck" (the following spring, WGN-TV aired a season preview that at one point showed a truck literally backing up toward Wrigley Field) and traded away quite a few of the popular players from the late 1960s/early 1970s era. General manager John Holland had a deal in place to trade Santo to the California Angels for two young pitchers, Andy Hassler and Bruce Heinbechner. But the previous year's collective bargaining agreement between the players' union and owners had given players with 10 years in the major leagues and at least the past five with the same team the right to veto trades. Santo, who had business interests in the Chicago area, didn't want to relocate to California and exercised his "10-and-5 rights," as they became called—and the CBA trade veto right was for a time dubbed "The Santo Clause."

Santo eventually consented to a trade to the White Sox for Steve Stone, Ken Frailing, and Steve Swisher. Santo, though, played poorly in his only year on the South Side in 1974 and retired after that season. Ironically, both Stone and Santo later became Cubs broadcasters, Santo becoming beloved as Pat Hughes' WGN radio partner until his death in December 2010 from complications from juvenile diabetes, something he'd battled throughout his baseball career. Santo was elected posthumously to the Hall of Fame by a veterans committee in 2012.

The NL Player of the Week Award has been given to a Cubs player 96 times in the half-century it has existed. Three Cubs have won the award five or more times: Sammy Sosa (11), Ryne Sandberg (seven), and

Andre Dawson (five). Five Cubs pitchers have been named NL Player of the Week more than once: Jake Arrieta (four times), Greg Maddux (three times), Bruce Sutter (three times), Kyle Hendricks (twice), and Matt Clement (twice).

The National League began the Pitcher of the Month Award in 1975 (the American League followed in 1979).
Who was the first Cub to be named NL Pitcher of the Month?
Before we learn the identity of this Cubs pitcher, a former Cubs pitcher won it twice in the year it was created.

Burt Hooton, who had been the Cubs' No. 1 draft pick in 1971 and who threw a no-hitter for them in his fourth major-league start in 1972, had some up-and-down years for the team through 1974. When he posted a mediocre 4.80 ERA in 1974 and got off to a bad start in 1975, the Cubs traded him to the Dodgers for Geoff Zahn and Eddie Solomon. That deal would have been okay if the Cubs had just kept Zahn, who went on to have some decent years in Minnesota and Anaheim, but they outright released him in January 1977.

Meanwhile, Hooton had a fine year for the Dodgers in 1975, winning NL Pitcher of the Month honors in both August and September; he would go on to pitch in three World Series for LA and win a ring in 1981.

For the Cubs, it would have to wait until the following year for one of their pitchers to be named NL Pitcher of the Month. The award was won by Ray Burris in August 1976, when he went 6–1 with a 1.88 ERA in seven starts, with four complete games and a shutout. That was following a July when he had a 1.91 ERA in five starts with three CG. Overall, in Burris' final 20 outings (19 starts) in 1976, he posted a 2.03 ERA and a 12–3 record, back when pitcher wins really meant something.

The Cubs weren't a very good team in 1976, going 75–87, but Burris' good pitching helped lead them to a 32–28 mark after July 31.

It was hoped that Burris would lead a Cubs pitching staff that could produce winning teams again. He had been the team's 17th-round draft pick in 1972 out of Southwestern Oklahoma State and had been an off-and-on starter with the team from 1973 through 1975 until his 1976 breakthrough.

Unfortunately, it didn't last. Burris got off to a rough start in 1977 and by midseason was being pounded with regularity. He did remain in the Cubs' rotation through 1978, with similar poor results (combining for a 4.74 ERA over 79 appearances—71 starts—in 1977 and 1978). Moved to the bullpen in 1979, Burris pitched even worse—a 6.23 ERA in 14 appearances—and in May general manager Bob Kennedy traded him to the Yankees for Dick Tidrow.

That actually turned out to be a decent deal for the Cubs. Tidrow had very good years for the Cubs in 1979 and 1980 and in the latter year tied the franchise record with 84 appearances.

It took a while, but Burris eventually got back to pitching well. In 1984 he posted a 3.10 ERA and had 13 wins for the A's, retiring after a 15-year career that also had him appearing for the Mets, Expos, Brewers, and Cardinals.

Other Cubs pitchers who have been named NL Pitcher of the Month:

Bruce Sutter: May 1977

Rick Reuschel: June 1977, July 1977, August 1979, August 1980

Dick Tidrow: July 1979

Rick Sutcliffe: August 1984

Greg Maddux: August 1988, April 2006

Mike Morgan: May 1992

Mark Prior: August 2003, September 2003

Carlos Zambrano: September 2004, July 2006, July 2007

Jake Arrieta: August 2015, September 2015, April 2016, August 2017

Jon Lester: June 2016, September 2016

Kyle Hendricks: August 2016

Cole Hamels: August 2018

Yu Darvish: July/August 2020

Gold Glove Awards for fielding excellence have been given to MLB players since 1957, and the Silver Slugger Award for the best batter at each position began in 1980.

Who was the first Cub to win both awards in the same year?

Ryne Sandberg, who burst on the national scene with the famous "Sandberg Game" in 1984, was the first Cubs player to win a Gold Glove and Silver Slugger in the same season. His .314/.367/.520 season with 36 doubles, 19 triples, 19 home runs, and 32 stolen bases got him named National League MVP with 22 of the 24 first-place votes, and Sandberg also won the second of nine Gold Gloves and the first of seven Silver Slugger Awards that year.

Sandberg, along with Larry Bowa, came to the Cubs on January 27, 1982, in exchange for Ivan de Jesus in one of several deals new Cubs general manager Dallas Green made in bringing over players he was familiar with from his former team in Philadelphia.

At the time of the trade, Bowa was seen as the main target, a longtime All-Star who was seen as having something left in him at age 36. Sandberg, a 20th-round draft pick of the Phillies in 1978, had just middling numbers in the minor leagues and was considered a throw-in by Phillies management. Green, though, thought Sandberg, then just 22 years old, might be a solid Cubs infielder of the future. (Ironically, Sandberg had his first MLB hit as a member of the Phillies off Cubs right-hander Mike Krukow in a 14–0 loss to the Cubs on September 27, 1981, at Wrigley Field. It turned out to be the only hit he had as a Phillie.)

Sandberg had two decent if unspectacular years for the Cubs in 1982 and 1983, finishing sixth in Rookie of the Year voting in 1982 as a third baseman, then shifting to second in 1983, when he won his first Gold Glove.

The Cubs hired Jim Frey to manage the ballclub in 1984, and Frey, a longtime hitting coach, saw something in Sandberg that made him think Sandberg could hit with more power. He encouraged Sandberg to be more aggressive and hit more line drives, and that helped result in Sandberg's MVP season, which included the famous "Sandberg Game" on Saturday, June 23, 1984, in which he hit two home runs off Cardinals

Future Hall of Famer Ryne Sandberg at Wrigley Field in 1983.
AL YELLON.

closer (and former Cub) Bruce Sutter, going 5-for-6 with seven RBI to help win that game 12–11. (Many think the second of Sandberg's homers won that game, but the winning run was actually driven in on a 12th-inning walk-off single by backup infielder Dave Owen.)

Sandberg continued having good-to-great seasons after 1984, with more All-Star appearances, Gold Gloves, and Silver Sluggers. He led the National League in home runs in 1990 with 40, and then his career got derailed a bit when he was hit on the hand by a pitch from San Francisco's Mike Jackson during spring training in 1993. His power dipped that year as a result—he hit only nine home runs—and that was one of the factors that prompted him to retire midseason in 1994.

Two years later, Sandberg had the itch to play again and returned for two final seasons with the Cubs, retiring after the 1997 season and being elected to the Hall of Fame in 2005. Sandberg later expressed an interest in managing, and so Cubs general manager Jim Hendry hired him to manage in the team's farm system in 2007. Eventually he was named Pacific Coast League Manager of the Year in 2010 and was widely praised by Cubs prospects who played for him. Passed over for the Cubs' managing job when the team hired Mike Quade, Sandberg took a position managing in the Phillies' system, eventually becoming the Philadelphia manager in 2013. That gig lasted one full season and parts of two others before he resigned.

Today, Sandberg is a beloved Cubs ambassador who makes frequent appearances at Wrigley Field.

Sandberg also won a Gold Glove and Silver Slugger in the same season in 1988, 1989, 1990, and 1991.

Other Cubs to win both awards in the same year:

Andre Dawson, 1987
Derrek Lee, 2005
Anthony Rizzo, 2016

Previously, we learned that after the creation of the Gold Glove Award by Rawlings in 1957, the first Gold Glove earned by a Cub was won by

Ernie Banks in 1960. In all, the first 12 Gold Gloves collected by Cubs were awarded to infielders or catchers.

Who was the first Cubs outfielder to win a Gold Glove?

From the inception of the Gold Glove through 1983, Ryne Sandberg (one), Ernie Banks (one), Ron Santo (five), Glenn Beckert (one), Don Kessinger (two), Randy Hundley (one), and Ken Hubbs (one) won those 12 fielding awards, all but one of those by infielders (the other by catcher Hundley).

The Cubs ended a 39-year postseason drought in 1984 and along with that division championship season came the first outfielder from the team to win a Gold Glove, Bob Dernier.

Dernier was the Reds' 12th-round selection in the January 1977 draft but didn't sign, instead inking a deal as an amateur free agent with the Phillies later that year. First coming to the major leagues in 1980, he became a decent fourth outfielder in Philadelphia, mostly known for his speed—stealing 42 bases in 1982 and 35 in 1983.

Just before Opening Day 1984, Cubs general manager Dallas Green, panicked because the team had lost 11 straight spring training games (at a time when spring results meant more than they do today), engineered a trade with his former team, the Phillies, bringing Dernier, outfielder Gary Matthews, and reliever Porfi Altamirano to Chicago in exchange for reliever Bill Campbell and utilityman Mike Diaz.

This trade worked out spectacularly well for the Cubs during their 1984 National League East title season. Matthews became a fan favorite nicknamed "Sarge" and led the National League with 103 walks and a .410 on-base percentage, becoming the first Cub to walk 100 or more times in a season since Richie Ashburn in 1960.

And the Cubs, who hadn't really had a competent center fielder since they had traded Rick Monday to the Dodgers in January 1977, installed Dernier as the regular center fielder and leadoff man.

At age 27, Dernier blossomed in his first full-time role. He batted .278/.356/.362, drew 63 walks, and stole a career-high 45 bases, in so doing becoming just the sixth Cub to swipe that many since 1900 (and only four others have had as many or more since then).

With Sandberg batting behind him, they began to be called the "Daily Double" by WGN-TV's Harry Caray for the numerous occasions on which they'd begin games by getting on base together and being followed by Matthews, Leon Durham, and Jody Davis driving them in. Sandberg led the NL in runs scored with 114, and Dernier finished seventh with 94.

Dernier's speed helped him create great defensive range in center field, and that got him the Gold Glove nod at the position. He also finished 17th in MVP voting. Then he got the Cubs' postseason going with a splash, homering in Game 1 of the NLCS and scoring three runs as the Cubs defeated the Padres 13–0. Dernier went 4-for-17 with two doubles, a homer, and five walks in that NLCS, but it wasn't enough to help the Cubs win the series.

Unfortunately, 1984 was Dernier's only truly great season. His offensive numbers declined, in part due to foot and hamstring injuries, to the point where he became a part-time player and he departed the Cubs via free agency after the 1987 season, re-signing with the Phillies, who he played for as a spare-part outfielder for two more years, hanging it up after 1989.

After his playing career, Dernier had a couple of coaching stints, first with the Texas Rangers in 1997 and 1998 and then with the Cubs from 2004 to 2011. The coaching stint with the team where he had his best year included time as a minor-league coordinator as well as a couple of years as a major-league coach under manager Mike Quade in 2010 and 2011. Now, as a Cubs alumni ambassador, Dernier makes frequent appearances at Wrigley Field, signing autographs and mingling with fans.

Since Dernier's Gold Glove in 1984, three other Cubs outfielders have won that fielding award: Andre Dawson (1987–1988), Jason Heyward (2016–2017), and Ian Happ (2022–2023).

The Manager of the Year Award was first bestowed on an MLB field boss by the Baseball Writers Association of America in 1983.

Who was the first Cubs manager to receive Manager of the Year honors?

.

It didn't take too long for a Cubs skipper to receive a Manager of the Year Award after its creation in 1983.

Jim Frey led the Cubs to the National League East title in 1984, their first postseason appearance in 39 years, and for this accomplishment he was named NL Manager of the Year. Frey received 16 of the 24 first-place votes, with four each going to Davey Johnson of the New York Mets and Dick Williams of the San Diego Padres. The latter would wind up defeating the Cubs in the NLCS.

Frey, who had a 14-year career in the minor leagues (including seven at Triple-A) as an outfielder, never played in the majors. After his playing career ended in 1963, the Baltimore Orioles hired him as a scout and manager in their minor-league system. He joined Earl Weaver's major-league coaching staff in Baltimore in 1970 and served there as the Orioles won three pennants and the 1970 World Series, including several years as hitting coach.

After the 1979 season, Frey was named manager of the Kansas City Royals, his first major-league managing position, at age 48. Kansas City had won three division titles from 1976 to 1978 but fell short in 1979, and manager Whitey Herzog was fired.

It did not take long for Frey to turn things around in Kansas City. The 1980 Royals won 97 games and ran away with the AL West, 14 games ahead of the second-place Athletics. They then swept the Yankees in the ALCS, only to fall short to the Phillies in the World Series.

Still, the Royals' future seemed bright under Frey. Unfortunately, they got off to a poor start in 1981, falling into last place early and sitting at 20–30 when the players' strike interrupted the season. When the Royals didn't play much better when the season resumed, Frey was fired August 31. In a *Washington Post* article, Royals general manager Joe Burke said this about Frey after dismissing him:

> *"I think it was a case of an excellent manager at the wrong club,"* *Burke said in a telephone interview, calling the hiring of Frey a* *'mistake.' He was the type of manager the players here just didn't* *respond to.*

"I don't think they were responding to him last season, either, but it wasn't evident because all the players were having such remarkable seasons."

After Frey served as hitting coach for the Mets in 1982 and 1983, he was hired by Cubs general manager Dallas Green on October 7, 1983, to manage the team in 1984. "Jim was raised in the Baltimore organization," Green said at the time, "and had their caliber of training, which is obviously very successful."

Green had drawn on his Philadelphia experience and coaches to staff the Cubs when he first took the GM job in late 1981 but seemed to realize he needed an outside voice after two losing seasons.

One of the things Frey did when he first took over as manager was to use his Baltimore and New York experience as hitting coach and take Ryne Sandberg under his wing. Sandberg had a couple of solid but unspectacular seasons for the Cubs in 1982 and 1983, but Frey thought he saw that Sandberg could do more. NBC Sports Chicago quoted Sandberg after Frey passed away in 2020:

"After watching a couple weeks of spring training games, he took me aside and asked me to change my mindset as far as driving the baseball, being aggressive on certain pitches and hitting baseballs in the gaps and hitting home runs," Sandberg said.

That's exactly what happened with Sandberg, who started hitting doubles, triples, and home runs on his way to the 1984 National League MVP Award and an eventual election to the Hall of Fame in 2005. It's not too much of a stretch to say that Sandberg might not have made it to Cooperstown without Frey's tutelage.

Frey's leadership and careful use of the stars Green had given him in 1984 helped the Cubs to the NL East title, Frey's second division championship as a manager. The Cubs flopped in that year's NLCS, and we won't belabor that here; the failure of the players in that series wasn't Frey's fault, although many felt Frey should have used Rick Sutcliffe to start Game 4 instead of saving him for Game 5.

Hopes were high for a repeat in 1985, but injuries did that team in—every single member of the starting rotation wound up injured, and Frey was forced to use men like Johnny Abrego, Derek Botelho, Jay Baller, Steve Engel, and Reggie Patterson as starters. The team finished 77–85, far out of first place.

More woes followed in 1986 as the team began to show its age and the injury bug continued to bite, and Frey was fired on June 12 with the team mired in fifth place with a 23–33 record.

Frey was still popular with Cubs fans, and so the following year he was hired as an analyst on WGN radio broadcasts of Cubs games. He was ill equipped for a job he had never done before. In fact, his radio colleagues had to teach him how to keep a scorecard, as he had never previously done that.

The radio gig lasted only a few months before Frey was hired to replace his predecessor, Green, as Cubs general manager. That turned out to be another job Frey wasn't well suited for; he had never before worked for a baseball team in any nonfield position. His tenure as general manager was marked with controversial trades, such as his swap of Lee Smith to the Boston Red Sox for Al Nipper and Calvin Schiraldi and his late 1988 trade of Rafael Palmeiro and Jamie Moyer to the Texas Rangers for Mitch Williams, Paul Kilgus, Curtis Wilkerson, and Steve Wilson. While Williams did help the Cubs win the NL East again in 1989, Palmeiro and Moyer both had long MLB careers, Moyer still active in the major leagues more than 20 years after Frey sent him away.

In 1991, with the Cubs floundering, Frey was forced—reportedly by Tribune Company higher-ups—to fire his lifelong friend Don Zimmer as manager. Jim Essian, promoted from Triple-A Iowa to replace Zimmer, didn't do well, and both Essian and Frey were let go after the 1991 season. He left baseball in 1992, quoted years later in retirement as saying, "I just got worn out" after 43 years in the game.

In his later years, Frey was reported to have been "instrumental" in the creation of the Somerset (Massachusetts) Patriots of the Atlantic League and served as the team's vice chairman for a time.

Frey passed away on April 12, 2020, in his Florida home, aged 88.

Major League Baseball's Rookie of the Year Award was created in 1947 and first won by Jackie Robinson, after whom the award is now named.

Six Cubs have won this award. Who was the first Cubs pitcher to be named National League Rookie of the Year?

Kerry Wood won the NL Rookie of the Year Award in 1998, the first Cubs pitcher to do so, and Wood's story is one of great talent that never quite lived up to its promise because of major injuries.

Wood was the Cubs' No. 1 pick (fourth overall) in 1995 out of Grand Prairie High School in Texas. In the Cubs' minor-league system, Wood struck out a lot of batters—417 in 338 2/3 innings—but also issued quite a number of walks, 234, including an astonishingly high total of 131 in just 151 2/3 innings combined between Double-A Orlando and Triple-A Iowa in 1997.

Nevertheless, Wood was put on the 40-man roster and dazzled opposing hitters in spring training in 1998. Because he was just 20 years old with just 10 Triple-A starts at the time, he was optioned to Iowa before the 1998 season, leading Angels manager Terry Collins to say "The Cubs" when asked who would win that year's World Series. Asked why, Collins replied, "If the Cubs have five starters better than Kerry Wood, they'll certainly win it all."

That seemed a crazy statement given the Cubs' 94-loss season in 1997, but the team, led in part by Wood, did make the postseason.

Wood made just one start at Iowa in 1998, striking out 11 in five innings, before the Cubs called him up to start a game against the Expos at Montreal on April 12. He didn't make it out of the fifth inning, allowing seven runs, but struck out seven. Five days later he made his Wrigley Field debut, throwing five shutout innings against the Dodgers, again with seven strikeouts. A poor outing against the Dodgers at Los Angeles followed, then a strong seven-inning effort (one run, nine strikeouts) against the Cardinals at Wrigley Field.

It was a cloudy, mild, off-and-on rainy Wednesday afternoon when Wood made his fifth major-league start at Wrigley against the Astros on May 6. And in this game, strikeout after strikeout began to happen. Just one hit came off Wood, a third-inning single by Ricky Gutierrez that could have been ruled an error on third baseman Kevin Orie. Wood struck out nine of the last ten batters he faced, and the final out, a K of Derek Bell, was Wood's 20th, tying the major-league record set by Roger Clemens eleven years earlier. Wood's game is arguably the most dominant pitching performance in major-league history.

After the game, Wood spoke to his high school coach and said he was most proud of the fact that he didn't walk any Astros hitters.

Wood had other dominant games during 1998, striking out at least 13 four other times and winding up with 233 strikeouts. Still, his Rookie of the Year win was a close vote, as he got just 16 of the 32 first-place votes. Todd Helton of the Rockies received 15, and Kerry Ligtenberg of Atlanta got the other one.

Even with his dominance in 1998, Wood missed the last month of the regular season with elbow issues. He returned to throw five innings in Game 3 of the NLDS against the Braves, allowing one run, but the Cubs lost the game 6–2 and the series to Atlanta.

Before the 1999 season, Wood's elbow required Tommy John surgery, and he missed the entire year. He would return to the major leagues on May 2, 2000, nearly two years to the day after his 20-K game, facing the same team, Houston, at Wrigley Field. Not only did he throw six strong innings, he hit a two-run homer in his first plate appearance, helping lead the Cubs to an 11–1 win.

Wood continued to pitch well for the Cubs for the next few years, including a league-leading 266 strikeouts and an All-Star appearance in 2003, a year when he also threw a shutdown game (eight innings, one run) in the decisive Game 5 of the NLDS against the Braves.

Injuries began to show up after that, as Wood made only 22 starts in 2004 and missed a lot of time in 2005 and 2006, largely with shoulder issues. He contemplated retirement but instead came back as a relief pitcher in 2007, throwing 22 games out of the bullpen that year as the Cubs returned to the postseason, then posting 34 saves (matching his uniform number!) in 2008 as the Cubs won 97 games and an NL Central title.

He departed as a free agent after that year and spent 2009 and 2010 with Cleveland and the Yankees, then returned to the Cubs in 2011, the signing announced with great fanfare at that year's Cubs Convention.

But the shoulder issues would not go away, and after pitching poorly in nine games in relief in early 2012, Wood and the Cubs announced that he would retire after making one last appearance against the White Sox in a game at Wrigley Field on Friday, May 18, 2012. The rebuilding Cubs had already fallen into last place in the NL Central by then, but the

Kerry Wood pitching during spring training 2012.
MIKE LACHANCE VIA WIKIMEDIA COMMONS.

Wrigley crowd gave Wood a standing ovation when he entered in the top of the eighth inning with the game tied 2–2 to face Sox slugger Dayan Viciedo. Wood struck out Viciedo on three pitches, then left to another ovation and scooped up his then five-year-old son on leaving the field, a wonderful final coda to a career that could have been really special if not for all the injuries.

Other Cubs pitchers who have received Rookie of the Year votes:

Dick Drott had three voting points in 1957 and finished third. Les Lancaster had one point in 1987 and tied with three others for sixth. Mike Harkey had seven points in 1990, good for fifth place. Chuck McElroy had three points in 1991, tied for fifth place. Steve Trachsel had 22 points in 1994, good for fourth place.

Mark Prior had three points in 2002, tied for seventh place.

Kyle Hendricks had two points in 2014 and tied with two others for seventh place.

Major League Baseball's amateur draft began in 1965. The Cubs, at least in its early years, didn't have much luck selecting good players, though in recent years, the team added stars such as Javier Baez, Kris Bryant, Kyle Schwarber, Ian Happ, and Nico Hoerner.

Who was the first player drafted by the Cubs to be elected to baseball's Hall of Fame?

To say the Cubs didn't have much luck in the early years of the draft is understating it. Whether it was poor scouting or poor player development (or both!), of the first eight men who were Cubs No. 1 picks, from 1965 to 1972, four of them never played in the major leagues at all, and only one of the other four (Roger Metzger) had any sort of decent MLB career, and that for another team (Astros).

The Cubs didn't make a No. 1 pick who had a long, successful MLB career until they selected Joe Carter in 1981, and of course he also had most of that career for other teams, though the Cubs did get value when they traded him to Cleveland as part of the Rick Sutcliffe deal.

Lee Smith, a second-round pick in 1975, is in the Hall of Fame, but he wasn't the first Cubs selection to be inducted in Cooperstown. Smith entered the Hall in 2019.

The honor of being the first Cubs draft pick to be elected to the Hall of Fame goes to right-hander Greg Maddux, who was the Cubs' second-round choice out of Valley High School in Las Vegas in 1984. Maddux was inducted into the Hall of Fame in 2014, a first-ballot selection with 97.2 percent of the vote.

A retired scout named Ralph Meder had moved to Las Vegas and began a series of pickup games for the top high school players in the area, which included Mike Maddux, Greg's older brother. Greg was good enough to play in some of these games at age 13. When a scout came calling on the Maddux family, interested in drafting Mike, the boys' father Dave told the scout, "You will be back for the little one." While Mike Maddux had a solid MLB playing career and an even longer one as a pitching coach, it was his younger brother who was the real talent in the family.

After his selection by the Cubs at age 18, Greg Maddux dominated the Appalachian League at Pikeville, then did the same the following year at Peoria in the Midwest League. Doing the same the following year combined between Double-A Pittsfield and Triple-A Iowa, Maddux found himself called up to the Cubs in September, back when teams could add a dozen or so players to their final month roster.

He made his major-league debut not as a pitcher but as a pinch-runner in the 17th inning of the completion of a suspended game at Wrigley Field on September 3, 1986. Remaining in the game to pitch, the second batter Maddux faced, former Cub Billy Hatcher, homered to win the game for Houston.

Maddux was placed in the Cubs rotation in 1987, at age 21, and he looked younger, so he grew a mustache, which just made him look silly. The facial hair didn't last long, and he struggled to the point where he was sent back to Iowa in early August. Four starts there with a 0.98 ERA brought him back to the Cubs, where he struggled again the rest of the year.

But 1988 brought a new approach for Maddux, who went 18–8 with a 3.18 ERA and made the National League All-Star team, the first of five straight good-to-excellent years with the Cubs, which included playing in the NLCS in 1989 and culminating in a 20-win season in 1992, where he won the NL Cy Young Award.

That was also Maddux's final season before free agency, and he made it known he wanted to stay in Chicago. Cubs general manager Larry Himes made Maddux a $27.5 million, five-year offer in July of that year, which Maddux rejected, and after some further back and forth, Himes stated the team wouldn't be making another offer and would use the money elsewhere. Another slightly larger offer was made in November, also rejected by Maddux, and then Maddux received offers from the New York Yankees and Atlanta Braves. Maddux, who prized his hitting abilities, wanted to stay in the National League, so he was going to accept the Braves' offer of $28.5 million. He contacted the Cubs to see if they would match the offer—comparable money to what Himes had offered him in November—but was told the team had already spent the money on other free agents.

It was one of the most colossal mistakes in Cubs franchise history. Maddux went on to spend 11 years in Atlanta, helping them win 10 division titles, three NL pennants, and a World Series in 1995. He would win three more Cy Young Awards in Atlanta and had two of the greatest pitching seasons in modern MLB history in 1994 and 1995, though both were marred by being shortened by a players' strike. Over those two seasons, Maddux posted a 1.60 ERA and 20 complete games over 53 starts, during which he allowed just 12 home runs in 411 2/3 innings.

Among the stellar games Maddux threw during his time in Atlanta was a 78-pitch complete game against the Cubs in the first game of a doubleheader at Wrigley Field on July 22, 1997. The Braves won 5–1; apparently Cubs hitters' game plan was to be aggressive against Maddux, who generally threw first-pitch strikes.

While the Cubs did make the postseason in 1998 and 2003 during Maddux's time in Atlanta—and wound up playing the Braves in a division series both times, losing in 1998 but winning in 2003—it seems likely they might have done better with Maddux in their rotation.

After the Cubs blew a three-games-to-one lead in the NLCS in 2003, general manager Jim Hendry wanted to bolster the rotation, so he brought Maddux back to the Cubs on a three-year deal. Even though

Maddux was then 38, he remained a capable MLB starter and he won 16 games with a 4.02 ERA in 2004 (and only three bad September starts pushed that ERA over 4.00). He essentially repeated that year in 2005, though he and the Cubs both finished with losing records. For Maddux it broke an MLB record of 17 consecutive seasons in which he had won at least 15 games.

During his second stint with the Cubs, Maddux recorded his 300th career win on August 7, 2004, against the Giants in San Francisco and registered his 3,000th career strikeout on July 26, 2005, at Wrigley Field, vs. Omar Vizquel, then playing for the Giants.

In 2006, the Cubs fell out of contention early and it became clear Maddux, then 40, was going to be traded at the deadline. On July 29, he started at Wrigley Field against the Cardinals and threw a vintage game, allowing just one run and no walks in six innings, and received a mighty ovation when removed from the game after allowing a leadoff double in

Future Hall of Famer Greg Maddux in 2004.
JEFFREY HAYES VIA WIKIMEDIA COMMONS.

the top of the seventh. Two days later, Maddux was traded to the Dodgers for infielder Cesar Izturis, who played just 87 games for the Cubs before he was sent to the Pirates for cash considerations in June 2007.

Maddux wound up playing in the postseason for the Dodgers in 2006 and 2008, with an interim stop in San Diego in 2007, and ironically his final appearance at Wrigley Field was as a member of the Dodgers in Game 1 of a 2008 Division Series between the two clubs, mopping up the ninth inning of a 7–2 LA blowout win.

In between his start as a Cubs pinch runner and end as a Dodgers reliever, Maddux won 355 games, struck out 3,371 batters, and is recognized as one of the greatest pitchers of his generation.

In Cubs history, Maddux ranks 13th in wins (133), fifth in games started (298), and sixth in strikeouts (1,305). His No. 31, shared with fellow Hall of Famer Fergie Jenkins, was retired by the Cubs on May 3, 2009.

ALL-STAR GAME FIRSTS

Three Hall of Famers have homered in the All-Star Game for the Cubs: Ernie Banks, Billy Williams, and Andre Dawson.
Who was the first Cub to homer in an All-Star Game?
The MLB All-Star Game was in just its fourth year when a Cubs player went deep for the first time in a Midsummer Classic.

Augie Galan was the Cub who first smacked a baseball out of the yard in an All-Star Game, doing it in the 1936 contest at Braves Field in Boston. The National League had taken a 2–0 lead in the second inning, with two other Cubs involved in scoring that pair of runs. Cubs outfielder Frank Demaree led off with a single and catcher Gabby Hartnett tripled him in to give the National League a 1–0 advantage. Hartnett subsequently scored on a single by Pinky Whitney of the Phillies to increase that NL lead to 2–0.

In the fifth inning with one out, Galan came to the plate and smashed a ball over the right-field wall off Schoolboy Rowe of the Tigers. Of this blast, Irving Vaughan of the *Chicago Tribune* wrote:

Galan, batting left-handed, crashed against Rowe's first pitch and it sailed into right, hitting the flag pole which serves as a foul line mark and caroming into the pavilion for a homer. The American leaguers protested that the drive was foul but made no headway.

The switch-hitting Galan's drive thus could be said to be the difference in that game, won by the NL 4–3. It was the first National League All-Star win after three losses in the annual game that began in 1933.

Augie Galan, a northern California native, began his professional baseball career with the San Francisco Seals, a then-independent team in the Pacific Coast League. After hitting .356 with 51 doubles in 1933, he was traded by the Seals to the Cubs for Win Ballou, Sam Gibson, Leroy Herrmann, Hugh McMullen, Larry Woodall, and minor-leaguer Lonny Backer.

With a haul like that sent to the PCL, the Cubs were hopeful the 22-year-old Galan would make a big splash at Wrigley Field. He played in just 66 games that year, largely as a backup second baseman, but because future Hall of Famer Billy Herman was ensconced at second base, a fortuitous move to center field for Galan turned him into an everyday regular, and a star.

In 1935, when the Cubs won the NL pennant, Galan led the league in runs scored (113) and stolen bases (22) and finished ninth in MVP voting. He led the league in steals again the following year with 23. Just one other Cub (Stan Hack, 1936 through 1940, and with fairly low totals, 18, 19, 15, 18, and 22 in those five seasons) has led the NL in steals since then.

Knee injuries would take their toll on Galan, and in the middle of the 1941 season he was traded to the Brooklyn Dodgers. Once restored to health, he had All-Star seasons for Brooklyn in 1942 and 1943, finally playing for both the Reds and A's before retiring from MLB after 1949, though he played and managed again in the PCL through 1953. After one year coaching for the Philadelphia A's, Galan returned to his native Bay Area and went into private business for many years. He passed away in 1993, aged 81.

Besides Galan, Banks, Williams, and Dawson, the five other Cubs who have homered in an All-Star Game are Hank Sauer (1952), George Altman (1961), Alfonso Soriano (2007), Kris Bryant (2016), and Willson Contreras (2018).

The Major League Baseball All-Star Game has been a midsummer tradition for more than 90 years since its creation in 1933.

When was the first All-Star Game hosted by the Cubs at Wrigley Field?

The answer to this question could have been "the very first game in 1933" because the impetus behind the creation of the All-Star Game came from *Chicago Tribune* sports editor Arch Ward.

The world was in the throes of the Great Depression in 1933, and in that same year the city of Chicago was to host a World's Fair, an event that attracted thousands of people with exhibits from around the globe. The Chicago World's Fair was called "A Century of Progress," referring to the city's beginnings 100 years earlier.

City leaders thought a sporting event in connection with the fair would be a good idea, and Mayor Ed Kelly and *Tribune* publisher Robert McCormick approached Ward, who thought an exhibition baseball game involving the game's biggest stars would be a great attraction.

Officials from the city of Chicago and baseball owners eventually agreed on such a game, and the 1933 affair might have been held at Wrigley Field—the decision between the Cubs' home and the White Sox' Comiskey Park was settled by a coin flip. The White Sox won that flip and thus the honor of hosting.

It was such a success that baseball's moguls decided to make it an annual affair. But Wrigley Field would have to wait quite some time after that first game in 1933 to be the host of the All-Star Game.

That wouldn't happen until Tuesday, July 8, 1947, so instead of becoming the first ballpark to host the Midsummer Classic, it was the 13th (the Polo Grounds in New York had hosted twice by then, in 1934 and 1942). It was the second-to-last of the 14 then-existing stadiums (the ballparks in St. Louis and Philadelphia both were home to two teams back then) to host an All-Star Game. Ebbets Field in Brooklyn wouldn't be the site of an All-Star Game until 1949.

The first two All-Star Games in 1933 and 1934 had featured fan voting via newspapers across the country for the starting players, and managers selected the rest of the roster. But after that, managers selected all the players until the 1947 game at Wrigley Field, when fan voting returned. In 1957, there was a voting scandal when Cincinnati newspaper readers stuffed the ballot box for local players, and selection was returned to managers until 1970, when a computerized punch-card system was instituted. Now All-Star voting is all done online or via the MLB app.

The 1947 Cubs, then just two years past their most recent National League pennant, placed two men on the NL All-Star squad: outfielder Andy Pafko, making his first of four consecutive All-Star appearances, and first baseman Phil Cavarretta. It was the last of three All-Star nods for Cavarretta.

The NL scored first in the 1947 contest on a home run by the Giants' John Mize off Yankees hurler Spec Shea. Mize, largely a forgotten figure today, was a fearsome power hitter in that era. His 51 home runs in 1947 would lead the league.

The American Leaguers tied the game in the sixth inning on a double-play ball that scored a run, and they'd score another in the seventh that proved to be the game winner. With one out, Bobby Doerr singled and stole second. Doerr was picked off second but reached third on a throwing error by NL pitcher Johnny Sain. He then scored on a single by Stan Spence, a four-time All-Star for the Washington Senators in the 1940s.

The game drew 41,123 to Wrigley Field, a crowd that would be a sellout today, but one that was about 5,000 fewer than the ballpark could hold in that era. Wrigley Field would host All-Star Games again in 1962 and 1990 but still awaits its fourth All-Star Game as 2024 begins.

Many great Cubs pitchers have appeared in All-Star Games, from Claude Passeau to Fergie Jenkins to Bruce Sutter to Greg Maddux to Jake Arrieta.

Who was the first Cub to post a pitching win in the All-Star Game?

A lot of those great Cubs pitchers had bad All-Star outings. Fergie, for example, got roughed up in the 1971 Midsummer Classic in Detroit, allowing two runs in his single inning of work—in a year he'd go on to win the National League Cy Young Award. Maddux posted a 6.75 ERA in his only All-Star appearance as a Cub in 1991.

The honor of the first All-Star win by a Cubs pitcher in an All-Star Game went to Bob Rush, who was the pitcher of record for the National League in the 1952 contest at Shibe Park in Philadelphia. It was his second All-Star nod, as he'd been on the NL All-Star roster in 1950, though he did not appear in that year's contest.

It took rain and a home run from a Cubs teammate to make Rush the winner in the game played on Tuesday, July 8, 1952.

Rush entered the game to throw the fourth inning and allowed three hits and two runs, the runs scoring on RBI singles by Eddie Robinson and Bobby Avila, the Cubs' right-hander perhaps distracted a bit by a drizzle that fell throughout the game. That gave the American League a 2–1 lead. In the bottom of the fourth, Stan Musial was hit by a pitch, and Hank Sauer, on his way to an MVP season, smashed a two-run homer to put the NL in front.

Rush threw a scoreless fifth and the NL went out in order in the bottom of the inning and then the drizzle turned into a harder, steadier rainfall. They waited 56 minutes and then called the game off with the Nationals winning, and Rush was credited with the victory.

While the Cubs weren't very good—honestly, pretty bad—through most of the 1950s, their 1952 season was decent enough. They finished at .500–77–77—their only nonlosing season between 1947 and 1962. Rush had his best overall season, going 17–13 with a 2.70 ERA and posting 5.2 bWAR, fifth-best among all National League hurlers that year. He was the Cubs' best pitcher through this sad span, pitching well for a decade's worth of seasons from 1948 to 1957. Though his W/L record wasn't good—110–140—he posted a decent 3.70 ERA and accumulated 33.5 bWAR as a Cub. To this day, the WAR figure is ninth-best among all Cubs pitchers in the modern era, just barely below Greg Maddux in eighth place, 33.7.

After the 1957 season, the Cubs traded Rush, Eddie Haas, and Don Kaiser to the Braves for Taylor Phillips and Sammy Taylor. Neither of the "Taylors" did anything significant for the Cubs, but Rush had a fine year with Milwaukee in 1957, winning a World Series ring, though he didn't appear in the Series that year. He did start one World Series game for the Braves against the Yankees in 1958.

Other Cubs pitchers who recorded wins in the All-Star Game:
Larry Jackson, 1963
Bruce Sutter, 1978 and 1979
Lee Smith, 1987
Cubs pitchers who recorded losses in the All-Star Game:
Bill Lee, 1939
Claude Passeau, 1941 and 1946
Johnny Schmitz, 1948
Wade Davis, 2017

Many great Cubs hitters have played in the All-Star Game, including Hall of Famers Ernie Banks, Ron Santo, and Billy Williams, as well as World Series heroes Anthony Rizzo, Javier Baez, Kris Bryant, and Willson Contreras.

Who was the first Cub to be named All-Star Game MVP?

The All-Star Game is a curious thing, for piling up great performances and statistics at least. As it's a single game played in a stadium many are unfamiliar with, even great players can produce poor numbers in the Midsummer Classic. Santo, for example, never homered in eight All-Star appearances, and Banks just once in 13 All-Star Games.

The first All-Star Game MVP Award given to a Cub went to Bill Madlock in the game played on Tuesday, July 15, 1975, at County Stadium in Milwaukee. It was his only All-Star appearance as a Cub, though he would go on to two others later with the Pirates.

Madlock was not the starting third baseman for the National League that year. Ron Cey of the Dodgers, who would become a Cub eight years later, got the starting nod at third in the first of six consecutive All-Star appearances.

Madlock entered the game in the bottom of the sixth inning at third base with the National League up 3–0. Carl Yastrzemski smacked a three-run homer in that inning to tie the game. Madlock came to bat in the top of the seventh and flied to center.

The game was still tied in the top of the ninth when the Nationals loaded the bases on a single by Reggie Smith, double by Al Oliver, and Larry Bowa being hit by a pitch. Madlock, the next hitter, slapped a

2–2 pitch from White Sox reliever Rich Gossage down the left-field line for two runs. A sacrifice fly made it 6–3 NL, which is where the game ended.

Madlock was named MVP for his game-winning hit—but there was a catch. The voters wound up in a tie, and Madlock had to share his MVP Award with Mets pitcher Jon Matlack—yes, there were plenty of Madlock/Matlack name jokes—for his two innings of scoreless relief, recording the win. Still, Madlock's hit seemed more important.

Madlock won the first of two batting titles with the Cubs in 1975. His .354 batting average that year is the best for any Cub since 1930, when Riggs Stephenson hit .367 and Hack Wilson hit .356. (1930 season batting numbers come with a lot of caveats because of a supposed "juiced" baseball that year.) He followed that up with another batting title and a .336 BA in 1976. No Cub has had that high a BA since. Derrek Lee's .335 in 2005, Mark Grace's .331 in 1996, and Glenn Beckert's .342 in 1971 are the only other Cubs BAs higher than .330 since 1945.

The Cubs seemingly had something going with Madlock's good hitting (he finished sixth in MVP voting in 1976), but they got into a contract dispute with him. Madlock was seeking a multiyear contract extension for $200,000 a year, big money in those days and far more than any Cub had ever earned. Unhappy with that, new Cubs GM Bob Kennedy swapped Madlock and Rob Sperring to the Giants for Bobby Murcer and Steve Ontiveros—and then gave Murcer a five-year, $1.6 million extension. The trade was one of the worst in Cubs history.

Madlock was given a five-year, $1.3 million deal by the Giants but was traded to the Pirates in midseason 1979, where he went on to be one of the key parts of the "We Are Family" World Series champions that year in Pittsburgh. He had other good years with the Pirates and wrapped up a 15-year career with the Dodgers and Tigers, with a career BA of .305 and 2,008 career hits. It's left to Cubs fans to wonder how Madlock would have done playing his entire career in hitter-friendly Wrigley Field. He'd certainly have made the almost-contenders of 1977, 1978, and 1979 better teams.

To this day, Bill Madlock is the only Cubs player to be named All-Star Game Most Valuable Player.

The Home Run Derby is a somewhat silly but fun event that has taken place at the All-Star Game site since 1985.

Who was the first Cub to win the Home Run Derby?

The Home Run Derby had been created in 1985, and back then was a shorter event held in conjunction with "All-Star Workout Day," the day before the All-Star Game. It wasn't televised and took place in the afternoon. Before 1991, the Derby was structured as a two-inning event with each player allowed five outs per "inning," without tiebreakers. In fact, this resulted in cowinners in 1986, Wally Joyner and Darryl Strawberry.

It was under this format that Andre Dawson became the first Cub to win the Home Run Derby. He did it on Monday, July 13, 1987, at Oakland-Alameda County Coliseum.

The format did not encourage home runs to be hit. Just four players were selected to participate in 1987: Dawson, Ozzie Virgil Jr. of the Atlanta Braves, George Bell of the Toronto Blue Jays, and Mark McGwire of the host Oakland A's.

Then, calling "outs" on swings that did not produce home runs made the proceedings move along quickly, and also led to low home run totals. The four players, who combined for 172 home runs during the 1987 regular season, hit a total of eight home runs in this "derby," which must have seemed like a bad team's batting practice. Dawson was the winner— he hit four. Virgil had two, and Bell and McGwire hit one each.

Fans must not have been too disappointed, then, when the following year's Derby in Cincinnati was canceled due to rain.

Two years after that, in 1990, the All-Star Game and Home Run Derby came to Wrigley Field. In order to help increase the number of home runs, the field of participants was increased to eight. Ryne Sandberg of the host Cubs participated, along with Matt Williams, Bobby Bonilla, and Darryl Strawberry representing the National League. Cecil Fielder, Ken Griffey Jr., Mark McGwire, and Jose Canseco were the four American Leaguers chosen. Those eight combined to hit 291 home runs during the 1990 regular season. Fielder hit 51, becoming the first player to hit 50 or more since George Foster in 1977.

This would not be the case at Wrigley Field on Monday, July 9, 1990. That afternoon, those eight players combined for five home runs, three of them by Sandberg, who became the Derby champion, fun for the hometown crowd. The only other dingers were hit by Williams and McGwire, one each.

Why did this happen? Chicago's notoriously capricious weather. The day before the Derby, Sunday, July 8, had been hot and humid, with temperatures in the 90s and strong southwest winds. Too bad the Derby couldn't have been held that day, Waveland and Sheffield would have been annihilated by baseballs. But overnight Sunday into Monday, a cold front came crashing through. Temperatures dropped into the low 70s, well below average for that time of year, with strong winds blowing from the north.

This author was there that afternoon. It felt more like September than July. And the howling winds kept blowing baseballs back into the yard. Sandberg, who was quite familiar with Wrigley's winds, knew how to slash line drives into the bleachers.

That Home Run Derby—ranked one of the worst ever by MLB.com writer Chris Landers in 2017—convinced baseball officials to change the format. The following year the event was expanded to three rounds, and from 1991 to 2006 eight to ten players were selected and instead of five outs, 10 were allowed for each round, after which the count was reset, with the top four advancing to the second round, and the top two advancing to the final.

The difference was immediate—27 home runs were hit in the 1991 Derby in Toronto, with Cal Ripken Jr. the winner with 12, and 40 were hit in 1992 in San Diego. Other format change tweaks over the next few years continued to increase the number of home runs hit.

Since 2015 the Home Run Derby has had time limits instead of outs, and many players routinely hit double digits in home runs.

The only other Cub besides Dawson and Sandberg to win the Home Run Derby was Sammy Sosa, who was the champion at Turner Field in Atlanta in 2000. Sosa finished second in 2001 and 2002 and thrilled fans at Miller Park in Milwaukee by smashing one blast 524 feet. Kyle Schwarber made the final in 2018 but lost by one home run to hometown favorite Bryce Harper at Nationals Park in Washington.

THE DRAFT

Who was the first player selected by the Cubs in the very first MLB Draft?

For its first 90 years or so, Major League Baseball teams signed talent for their teams simply by offering amateur players contracts or by acquiring them from independent minor-league teams. Over time, this system began to favor wealthier teams like the New York Yankees, who could afford to sign many more players than others.

And so, in 1965 a draft system was created, in which teams would select players in reverse order of standings from the previous year, at first, alternating picks between American League and National League clubs.

The Cubs, by virtue of a 76–86 record in 1964, got the sixth selection in the first draft.

They chose Rick James, a right-handed pitcher from Coffee High School in Florence, Alabama. The draft was an inexact science in those days, as scouting was an entirely different animal than it is today, with video and analytics available to teams. The Cubs under the Wrigley ownership didn't have as many scouts as other teams, and it showed in some of the players they selected.

James was signed upon graduation and sent to a Cubs minor-league team in Treasure Valley, Idaho, in the Pioneer League, then a rookie-level league. He was still just 17 years old, and his lack of experience showed. He made nine appearances (eight starts) and posted a 5.66 ERA. He did strike out 39 batters in 36 innings, but walked 26. That wasn't uncommon for teenage pitchers going pro—they could throw hard but often didn't know where the ball was going.

With Leo Durocher taking over as Cubs manager the following year, many players, young and old, cycled through the Cubs system, and many young players got a chance to play in the major leagues perhaps before they were ready. James split his 1966 season between A-ball and Double-A and had better numbers, a 3.91 ERA in 24 games (21 starts), and so the following year was promoted to Triple-A. Again, his ERA dropped, to 3.20 in 22 games (19 starts), though his strikeout rate dropped from 8.0 per nine innings to 4.4—often that was a sign of injury.

Nevertheless, this got James a September promotion to Wrigley Field. He was a few weeks short of his 20th birthday. He made his major-league debut throwing the fifth inning of a 7–1 loss to the Giants at Wrigley Field on September 20, throwing just one pitch to Ollie Brown, who hit into an inning-ending double play. Six days later he threw a scoreless sixth inning in an 8–7 win over the Cardinals at Wrigley, and then he was given a start October 1 against the Reds in Cincinnati, the last game of the season. It did not go well; James gave up nine hits and eight runs to the Reds in just three innings and the Cubs wound up losing 10–3.

James returned to Double-A in 1968 and had a mediocre season, posting a 4.02 ERA in 19 starts. After the season he was exposed to the expansion draft and was selected by the Padres. Eventually he wound up in the Royals organization and pitched there in 1969 and in the Giants organization in 1970 before leaving baseball. He had just turned 23; the three games he threw for the Cubs in 1967 were his only appearances in the major leagues.

The Cubs made many other poor choices in the first round of the draft over the next decade and a half. Here are the rest of the team's first-round picks through the end of the Wrigley ownership in 1981:

1966: Dean Burk
1967: Terry Hughes
1968: Ralph Rickey
1969: Roger Metzger
1970: Gene Hiser
1971: Jeff Wehmeier
1972: Brian Vernoy
1973: Jerry Tabb

1974: Scot Thompson
1975: Brian Rosinski
1976: Herman Segelke
1977: Randy Martz
1978: Bill Hayes
1979: Jon Perlman
1980: Don Schulze
1981: Joe Carter and Vance Lovelace (the latter a compensation pick)

Of those 16 players, only nine (Metzger, Hiser, Tabb, Thompson, Segelke, Martz, Hayes, Perlman, Schulze, and Carter) ever played even one game for the Cubs, and none really had any sort of impactful career on the North Side. Six (Burk, Hughes, Rickey, Wehmeier, Vernoy, and Rosinski) never played in the major leagues at all. The Cubs did draft some impactful players in other rounds in those years, notably Burt Hooton (first round of the old secondary phase of the draft, 1971) and Lee Smith (second round, 1975).

In recent years, of course, the Cubs have had quite a number of successful and impactful first picks, including Javier Baez, Kris Bryant, Kyle Schwarber, and Ian Happ.

And the Cubs did get some value out of that very first draft in 1965 a few years later. The first overall pick in that draft, Rick Monday, went to the A's but eventually was traded to the Cubs and played five productive seasons on the North Side from 1972 to 1976, hitting 106 home runs, a total that to this day ranks 25th in franchise history.

The Cubs, though having had quite a few rough years after the MLB Draft was instituted in 1965, had to wait quite some time before they had the No. 1 overall pick.

Who was the first player the Cubs drafted No. 1 overall?

During the first few decades of the MLB Draft, the leagues alternated having the No. 1 overall pick.

The Cubs' .369 winning percentage in the strike-shortened 1981 season was the worst in the National League, but the Toronto Blue Jays were a tick worse at .364. Nevertheless, because the American League's Seattle Mariners had the No. 1 overall pick in 1980 (and selected pitcher Mike

Moore, while the Cubs, picking second, chose outfielder Joe Carter), the Cubs were granted the No. 1 overall pick in 1982.

That was the first year of Tribune Company ownership of the team and Dallas Green's first year as general manager, which brought new executives overseeing the team's farm system and draft.

Those executives chose Shawon Dunston, a high school player from Brooklyn, New York, as the first overall pick in the 1982 draft, the first Cubs No. 1 overall pick.

It was a risk because high school players from northern cities play in far fewer games than those from warm-weather areas like Florida, Texas, California, and Arizona. Dunston turned heads even while playing in just 26 games his senior season by hitting .790 with 10 home runs and 37 stolen bases without being caught stealing. He became the first player from the New York City area to be chosen with the No. 1 overall pick in the MLB draft.

The Cubs signed him with a then team-record $100,000 bonus and assigned him to their Rookie League team in the Gulf Coast League, where he hit .321/.354/.411 with two home runs and 32 stolen bases.

Continuing to hit with some power and lots of steals, Dunston worked his way through the Cubs system, and there were some who thought he should have been added to the roster in September 1984 as the team headed to an NL East title, perhaps as a help during the postseason.

But Green and the brass didn't want to put Dunston, who was then just 21 years old, through that sort of pressure. They did bring him to the major leagues and gave him a share of the starting shortstop job the following year, to be mentored by veteran Larry Bowa. Dunston played in 74 games in 1985 and hit .260/310/.388 with four home runs and 11 stolen bases, and he spent some time at Triple-A Iowa when he struggled early.

Given the full-time shortstop position in 1986, Dunston hit reasonably well—.250/.278/.411 with 17 home runs—but also made 32 errors. It was said by some that Dunston had such a good arm that he should be tried as a pitcher. His scattershot throws continued to produce a lot of throwing errors until slick-fielding Mark Grace took over as the

Cubs' full-time first baseman; Grace helped prevent quite a few Dunston throws from heading toward the first-base dugout.

Dunston got a NL All-Star nod in 1988, and in 1989 Cubs fan Jim Cywul created the "Shawon-O-Meter," a sign held up in the Wrigley Field bleachers that was updated with Dunston's batting average after every plate appearance. Dunston, who was quoted as saying he "loved those Cubs fans," hit .278 in 1989. A version of the Shawon-O-Meter is on display at the Baseball Hall of Fame in Cooperstown.

Dunston played with the Cubs through 1995. After that season he signed with the Giants as a free agent, but two years later he returned to the Cubs, although that didn't even last one full year, as he was shipped to the Pirates in August 1997.

Overall with the Cubs Dunston played in 1,254 games, all but seven at shortstop (he was put in left field for a few games just before the trade to Pittsburgh), and batted .267/.295/.407 with 107 home runs and 175 stolen bases, though that produced just 9.7 career bWAR,

Popular Cubs shortstop Shawon Dunston.
KASEY IGNARSKI.

likely because of his 183 errors as a Cub that produced negative defensive WAR.

Dunston settled in the Bay Area after retirement and has worked for many years as a special assistant in the Giants organization.

In choosing Dunston with the No. 1 overall pick in 1982, the Cubs passed on choosing Dwight Gooden, chosen fifth overall by the Mets. Despite injury and other troubles, Gooden posted 53.0 bWAR in a 16-year MLB career.

The Cubs have never again had the No. 1 overall pick in the MLB Draft. Since 1982 they have had the No. 2 overall choice twice, selecting Mark Prior in 2002 and Kris Bryant in 2013.

POSTSEASON FIRSTS

The Cubs have participated in 11 World Series since that baseball championship was created in 1903, winning three times.

Who was the first Cub to homer in a World Series game?

This answer might surprise you, as it came in the midst of the Deadball Era, when home runs—and even run-scoring itself—were at a premium.

The first Chicago Cub to hit a home run in a World Series game was shortstop Joe Tinker, part of the famous Tinker-to-Evers-to-Chance double-play combination, who homered in Game 2 of the 1908 World Series on Sunday, October 11, 1908, at West Side Grounds in front of 17,760 delighted Cubs rooters.

The *Chicago Tribune* recap of the game called Tinker's homer "a mighty hit into the bleachers." It broke up a scoreless tie in the bottom of the eighth inning. With one out in that frame, Solly Hofman reached base on an infield single toward Detroit third baseman Germany Schaefer. Tinker followed with his homer, called by the *Tribune* one of his "justly renowned home runs." The Cubs went on to score six runs in that inning and win the game 6–1 on their way to their second straight World Series title, becoming the first team to win Series back-to-back.

About Tinker being "justly renowned" for home runs, you have to remember the context of that comment. Tinker hit six home runs in 1908, a career high, and that led the team and was tied for fourth most in the National League. The Cubs as a team hit just 19 home runs that year; it would be more than a decade before the home-run revolution would come to baseball, led by Babe Ruth.

Tinker was the stalwart shortstop for four Cubs pennant winners, in 1906–1907–1908 and 1910, and in all manned the position for the team for 12 years, from 1902 to 1912 and a cameo in 1916 when he was also the team's manager. He and Evers were the closest of friends for quite some time until a fistfight happened on the field late in the 1905 season because, according to some reports, Evers had taken a taxi to the field and left his teammates waiting at a hotel. Apart from necessary conversation regarding play on the field, Tinker and Evers didn't speak to each other for more than 30 years before reuniting for an Old-Timers' event at Wrigley Field in 1937. At the time the two men had not seen each other in 14 years. They ended the feud with a tearful embrace at a Chicago hotel.

While Tinker, Evers, and Chance's overall numbers might not have rated Hall of Fame induction, their play for Cubs World Series teams and their notoriety from Franklin P. Adams' famous 1910 poem "Baseball's Sad Lexicon" got them installed as Hall of Famers in Cooperstown together in 1947.

No Cub would homer again in a World Series game until Charlie Grimm went deep in a 10–8 loss to the Philadelphia Athletics in Game 4 of the 1929 World Series.

Other Cubs to homer in a World Series game:
Gabby Hartnett, Game 3, 1932; and Game 4, 1935
Kiki Cuyler, Game 3, 1932
Frank Demaree, Game 4, 1932; Game 1, 1935; and Game 3, 1935
Chuck Klein, Game 5, 1935
Billy Herman, Game 6, 1935
Joe Marty, Game 3, 1938
Ken O'Dea, Game 4, 1938
Phil Cavarretta, Game 1, 1945
Dexter Fowler, Game 4, 2016; and Game 7, 2016
Kris Bryant, Game 5, 2016; and Game 6, 2016
Addison Russell, Game 6, 2016
Anthony Rizzo, Game 6, 2016
David Ross, Game 7, 2016
Javier Baez, Game 7, 2016

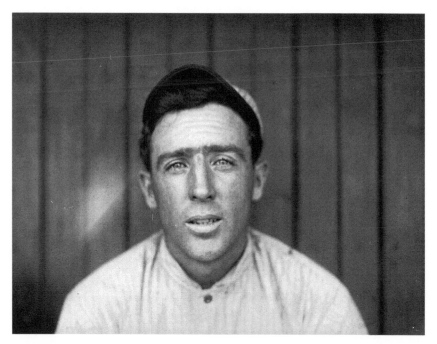

Early 20th-Century Cubs shortstop Joe Tinker had a piercing look about him.
PAUL THOMPSON, PUBLIC DOMAIN, VIA WIKIMEDIA COMMONS.

An unusual feat in baseball is for a pitcher to strike out four batters in an inning. This is usually accomplished by having a hitter strike out but reach base on a wild pitch or passed ball. Through the end of the 2023 season, this has been done 101 times in MLB history.

Who is the first Cubs pitcher to accomplish this feat, and what is unique about that accomplishment?

Orval Overall, an alliteratively named Cubs right-hander, struck out four Detroit Tigers in the first inning on Wednesday, October 14, 1908.

If that date seems unusual for this sort of baseball feat, it is. It happened in Game 5 of the 1908 World Series, and it was the game that clinched that Fall Classic win for the Cubs, their last world title until 2016.

Most games from that long ago don't have play-by-play data available, but because it's a World Series game, we do know how Overall struck out four in that initial inning, a wild frame in which he walked the leadoff hitter and allowed a single before Claude Rossman reached on a strikeout and wild pitch to load the bases. Rossman's K should have been the third out of the inning, but with the bases jammed, Overall had to strike out Germany Schaefer to end the frame and record that fourth K. It was the only real scoring threat the Tigers had in that Series-clinching game. Eventually, Overall settled down and threw a three-hit shutout, striking out 10. More than a century later, just two other Cubs pitchers have struck out 10 in a postseason game: Kerry Wood in National League Division Series Game 1 against the Braves in 2003 and Jake Arrieta in the National League Wild Card Game against the Pirates in 2015.

Orval Overall, born in California in 1881, played college baseball at Cal and signed with Tacoma, then an independent club in the Pacific Coast League, in 1904. He helped lead Tacoma to the PCL pennant and then was subject to a bidding war between the Reds and Cubs for his professional services.

The Reds won the battle but lost the war. Overall posted an 18–23 record with a 2.86 ERA in 1905, but after he got off to a poor start in 1905, Cincinnati traded him to the Cubs in June 1906 for Bob Wicker, another righty, who was done in the major leagues after 1906.

Overall had thrown over 300 innings in 1905, and Cubs manager Frank Chance helped Overall blossom by using him a bit less often. Overall made just 18 appearances (14 starts) in 1906, throwing 144 innings and posting a 1.86 ERA, then going 12 innings in two relief outings in that year's World Series with a 1.50 ERA.

In 1907, when the Cubs had probably the best season in franchise history with 107 wins and a World Series title, so did Overall. He went 23–7 with a 1.68 ERA and eight shutouts and was part of a rotation with Mordecai Brown and Ed Reulbach that steamrolled the Tigers in the World Series. He wasn't quite as good in 1908, but the performance in the decisive Game 5 of the World Series included the unusual feat noted earlier. Orval's four-strikeout inning is unique—to this day it's

Orval Overall was a stalwart of the early 20th-century Cubs. Here he is in 1910.

the only time a pitcher has struck out four hitters in an inning in a World Series game.

Overall's career got derailed with arm trouble after 1910, and as was the case with many players in that era, he left baseball because he thought he could make more money elsewhere—in this case, working in a gold mine he owned with teammate Mordecai Brown. He returned briefly to the Cubs in 1913, didn't pitch well, and retired.

Overall, though, Overall pitched in four World Series for the Cubs, posting a 1.58 ERA in eight games covering 51 1/3 innings.

He went on to become a wealthy man working in the banking industry in his native California and died of a heart attack in 1947, aged 66.

Other Cubs pitchers who have struck out four hitters in an inning:

May 27, 1956, Jim Davis, vs. Cardinals at St. Louis, sixth inning (first game of doubleheader)

July 31, 1974, Bill Bonham, vs. Montreal Expos at Wrigley Field, second inning (first game of doubleheader)

September 2, 2002, Kerry Wood, vs. Milwaukee Brewers at Wrigley Field, fourth inning (second game of doubleheader)

October 4, 2009, Ryan Dempster, vs. Arizona Diamondbacks at Wrigley Field, fifth inning

September 20, 2012, Jason Berken, vs. Cincinnati Reds at Wrigley Field, second inning

August 29, 2014, Justin Grimm, vs. Cardinals at St. Louis, ninth inning

April 30, 2022, Michael Rucker, vs. Brewers at Milwaukee, fifth inning

Walk-off wins are always exciting, bringing a team to victory on a run scored in a game's final at-bat. That's especially true in the postseason, where the stakes for each game are much higher.

The Cubs have had two postseason walk-off wins. When was the first?

In the first decade of the 20th century, the Cubs were a powerhouse team. They won four pennants in five years, missing only in 1909 when they won 104 games (and that established a record for most wins by a second-place team that stood until 2021 when the Giants broke it with 106 wins). They'd won two of three World Series chances in that era, in 1907 and 1908, and in 1910 returned to the Fall Classic with a 104–50 mark to face their American League equals, the Philadelphia Athletics, who went 102–50 in the regular season.

Unfortunately, the 1910 World Series didn't start out well for the Cubs. Games 1 and 2 took place in what was then a brand-new baseball palace, Shibe Park in Philadelphia, which had opened the previous year. In Game 1, the A's knocked Orval Overall out of the game after the third inning and won 4–1. The Cubs kept Game 2 close, trailing just 3–2 heading to the bottom of the seventh, but the host A's put up six against Cubs ace Mordecai Brown in that seventh inning and won 9–3.

The Series shifted to West Side Grounds in Chicago for Game 3, and unfortunately, the results weren't much better for the Chicagoans. The teams matched single runs in the first inning and both put up a two-spot in the second, but the 3–3 tie was broken by a five-run Philadelphia third that included a rare (for that era) three-run homer by Danny Murphy. The A's went on to win 12–5.

So the Cubs had their proverbial backs to the wall when Game 4 took place on Saturday, October 22, 1910, in front of 19,150 at West Side Grounds.

The Cubs struck first, taking a 1–0 first-inning lead on an RBI single by Solly Hofman. The A's tied the game up off Cubs starter King Cole in the third and scored two in the fourth on a double by Murphy to take a 3–1 lead. Frank Chance singled in a run in the last of the fourth to make it 3–2.

And there the game stayed until the bottom of the ninth, the Cubs three outs away from being swept out of the World Series by the visitors.

Frank "Wildfire" Schulte, who would win the Chalmers Award the following year when he hit .300/.384/.534 with 21 home runs, led off that ninth inning with a double.

That was followed by something you'd never see in modern baseball—a sacrifice bunt. With nobody out and a runner in scoring position! But more than a century ago, this sort of thing was common. Schulte was 90 feet away from tying the game with one out, and Chance made that

Jimmy Sheckard, shown in the Cubs' first World Series year, 1906.

base advance irrelevant by smacking a triple over A's center fielder Amos Strunk's head. Schulte scored to tie the game 3–3, but Chance, representing the winning run, was stranded when the next two Cubs popped out.

Brown had relieved King Cole in the ninth and held the A's scoreless in the 10th despite a one-out double.

In the bottom of the 10th, Jimmy Archer hit a ground-rule double with one out and advanced to third on an infield grounder.

Jimmy Sheckard was the next hitter. He lined a single to center, scoring Archer with the game winner, the first walk-off postseason win in Cubs history—not that anyone called them "walk-offs" more than a century ago. Instead, the *Chicago Tribune* described the scene after Sheckard's hit this way: "Out of the stands and field seats like a flood bursting through a dam poured frenzied fans from everywhere, madly intent on getting close enough to Chance and those Cubs to slap them on the back and mayhap carry them off the field."

They certainly don't write 'em like that anymore, that's for sure, in addition to the fact that fans pouring onto the field after wins no longer happens (and that's almost certainly for the best).

The Cubs staved off World Series elimination for one game but dropped Game 5 in 1910 to the A's the next day. Philadelphia broke up a close 2–1 game with a five-spot in the top of the eighth in front of 27,374 at West Side Grounds on their way to a 7–2 win. No Cubs fan, knowing the team was just two years removed from their previous World Series win in 1908 at the time, would have believed you in 1910 had you told him (and yes, they were almost all men back then) that they wouldn't win again until 2016.

There is just one other postseason walk-off win in Cubs history. That, too, happened with the team on the verge of elimination, down three games to two to the Detroit Tigers in the 1945 World Series. Game 6 was at Wrigley Field, and it looked like an easy win for the Cubs, leading 7–3 heading to the top of the eighth. But Detroit tied it with four in that inning and the game again headed to extras.

No one could score in the ninth, 10th, or 11th, and the Cubs also held Detroit scoreless in the 12th. In the bottom of the 12th, Frank Secory (later to become a National League umpire!) singled with one out.

After pitcher Hank Borowy struck out for the second out, Stan Hack hit what looked like a single to left, just past Detroit third baseman Jimmy Outlaw. But the ball took a crazy bounce over the shoulder of Hank Greenberg in left field and Secory scored the game-winning run, Hack credited with a double, and the World Series was tied at three wins each.

Of course, you know the 1945 Game 7 story, the Cubs lost and wouldn't return to the Fall Classic again for 71 years.

The Cubs played in four World Series in five years in the first decade of the 20th century, but all their home games for those Fall Classics were played at West Side Grounds, the team's home from 1893 to 1915. When was the first World Series game played at Wrigley Field?

The Cubs moved to Wrigley Field in 1916 and won the National League pennant two years later, in the shadow of World War I, when the season was cut short in early September and teams played around 130 games.

The 1918 World Series began September 5 with the Cubs as the home team—in Comiskey Park!

The choice to play Cubs World Series home games at the home of the White Sox wasn't made because of any issues at Weeghman Park on the North Side, the park that would eventually be renamed Wrigley Field.

Instead, that choice was strictly money driven. The Cubs' North Side home had a capacity of about 20,000 at that time, with no upper deck (that wasn't completed until 1927). Comiskey Park held about 32,000, so it was thought more tickets could be sold.

They might as well have not bothered, at least for the first two games. Game 1 attracted 19,274 and Game 2, the next day, 20,040 attended on the South Side. Both crowds could have fit into the Cubs' home park. For Game 3, held on a Saturday, the teams did draw 27,054, a larger gathering than the Cubs could have had on the North Side.

Thus, it would have to wait until the next time the Cubs won a National League pennant, in 1929, for Wrigley Field to host a World Series game.

That happened on Tuesday, October 8, 1929, Game 1 of that year's World Series.

At the time, Wrigley Field had only rudimentary outfield seats, not the iconic bleachers that wouldn't be built until 1937, so temporary stands were constructed beyond the outfield walls and over Waveland and Sheffield Avenues, closing off both streets for the duration of the Series. That allowed 50,740 to attend that day's game, the largest-ever crowd for a World Series game at Wrigley Field. The *Chicago Tribune* reported that about 3,000 fans were in line waiting for bleacher ticket sales to begin at 8:30 a.m., a line "stretching for four blocks, from the ticket window at Sheffield and Waveland Avenues completely around the walls of the park."

Unfortunately, the huge throng of Cubs rooters couldn't rally their team to victory. Connie Mack, manager of the Philadelphia Athletics, had come up with the unusual idea of sending one of his older pitchers, Howard Ehmke, to scout the Cubs during the month of September. Then he started Ehmke in Game 1 instead of one of his better starters (Lefty Grove or George Earnshaw).

The gambit worked. Ehmke knew all the proclivities of Cubs hitters from his scouting tour and threw a complete-game 3–1 victory, striking out 13. That established a World Series record that stood for 24 years, until Carl Erskine of the Dodgers struck out 14 Yankees in Game 3 in 1952. Even today, Ehmke's 13 strikeouts rank tied for fourth most by anyone in a World Series game.

A slightly smaller crowd of 49,987 attended the next day's Game 2, also lost by the Cubs to the A's by a 9–3 score.

The Cubs constructed the temporary bleachers over Waveland and Sheffield again in 1932 and 1935 and had the following paid crowds for World Series games:

Game 3, Saturday, October 1, 1932: 49,982
Game 4, Sunday, October 2, 1932: 49,844
Game 3, Friday, October 4, 1935: 45,532
Game 4, Saturday, October 5, 1935: 49,350
Game 5, Sunday, October 6, 1935: 49,237

With the construction of the iconic bleachers in 1937, attendance figures for Wrigley Field home games in the 1938 and 1945 World Series ranged from 41,708 (Game 6, 1945) to 43,463 (Game 5, 1945).

Renovations at Wrigley Field in the late 1960s and early 1970s turned the outfield grandstand seats to face home plate and reduced the capacity of the ballpark so that no game at Wrigley can attract as many fans as attended the World Series games in 1929, 1932, 1938, and 1945. For the three World Series games played at Wrigley Field in 2016, attendance figures were 41,703 (Game 3), 41,706 (Game 4), and 41,711 (Game 5).

The designated hitter has been part of baseball since 1973 but hasn't always been used in World Series games.

Who was the first Cub to serve as a designated hitter in a World Series game?

The DH, created in 1973, wasn't used in the World Series until 1976, and then it was used in even-numbered years through 1985. The practice of playing by the home team's rules (DH in AL parks, pitchers batting in NL parks during the World Series) began in 1986.

And so when the Cubs and Cleveland Indians met in the 2016 World Series, the Cubs' first Fall Classic appearance since 1945, the teams used the DH in the four games played in Cleveland but not in the three games played at Wrigley Field.

The first Cub to serve as a designated hitter in the World Series was Kyle Schwarber, and that's the story of one of the most amazing recoveries from an injury in baseball history.

After a solid debut season in 2015, when he batted .246/.355/.487 with 16 home runs in 69 games and five more home runs in the Cubs' post-season run that year, Schwarber was made the Cubs' starting left fielder to begin 2016.

In just the second game he played that year, Schwarber and center fielder Dexter Fowler collided in the outfield chasing a ball at Chase Field in Arizona, and Schwarber fell to the ground with a serious knee injury. Diagnosed with a torn ACL, Schwarber was ruled out for the season.

He spent much of 2016 rehabbing the injury at the Cubs' brand-new clubhouse facility in Wrigley Field, significant as it allowed him to be with the team for most of the season. If not for those new facilities in Chicago, Schwarber probably would have spent the year rehabbing at the Cubs' training facility in Mesa, Arizona, unable to share in the dramatic events of that season and the comradeship of his teammates.

Schwarber's rehab went better and more quickly than anyone had hoped. Between Games 2 and 3 of the NLCS, Schwarber went to Dallas to visit the doctor who had performed the surgery. Reminiscing about this visit several years later, Schwarber was quoted by NBC Sports Chicago: "He looks at me and goes 'You know, your knee looks really great. I'm really surprised at how well this is going. I know you guys are on a big run here. I wouldn't be against you pinch-hitting or something if you guys make it to the World Series.'"

Kyle Schwarber taking batting practice during the 2016 World Series.
ARTURO PARDAVILA VIA WIKIMEDIA COMMONS.

That got the wheels spinning in the Cubs front office after president of baseball operations Theo Epstein got the news. Schwarber began taking batting practice and was sent to the Arizona Fall League, where he went 1-for-6 with a pair of walks.

Deemed ready to play, Schwarber was added to the Cubs' active roster for the World Series and thus became the first Fall Classic designated hitter for the team in Game 1, played in Cleveland on Tuesday, October 25, 2016. He struck out in his first at-bat in the second inning, then doubled in the fourth, the first hit by a Cubs DH in a World Series game. Schwarber finished that game going 1-for-3 with a walk, his first major-league game action in more than six months.

As a DH in the World Series, Schwarber went 7-for-17 (.412) with three walks and two RBI in the four games played in Cleveland, and also went 0-for-1 as a pinch-hitter at Wrigley Field. None of the seven hits was more important than Schwarber's leadoff single in the 10th inning of Game 7. Albert Almora Jr. ran for Schwarber and tagged up, taking second on a deep fly ball by Kris Bryant, and eventually scoring the lead run on Ben Zobrist's double.

Schwarber hit 121 home runs in six years as a Cub before he was nontendered after the 2020 season in a cost-cutting move widely derided by Cubs fans. Those 121 home runs rank 22nd in Cubs history through the end of the 2023 season. Kyle has gone on to success in Philadelphia, where he led the National League in home runs with 46 in 2022 and played in another World Series that year, but his amazing comeback from injury to playing in the 2016 World Series only six months later will be forever remembered by Cubs fans.

WRIGLEY FIELD FIRSTS

The Cubs franchise dates to 1876 and was created as the White Stockings. They played in several different locations over their first four decades of existence.

When was the first game played by the Cubs in what is now called Wrigley Field?

The Chicago NL franchise, interestingly enough because they're now a North Side institution in the city, began play in 1876 on the South Side, in a ballpark located at what is now 23rd and State Street, called, simply enough, "23rd Street Grounds."

They next moved to Lake Front Park, which was located close to where the "Bean" (or "Cloud Gate") is in Millennium Park now, at the southeast corner of Michigan and Randolph, playing there from 1878 to 1884.

From 1885 to 1890, the first iteration of West Side Grounds was home to the Chicago NL ballclub. That park was located at Congress and Throop Streets. In 1891, the team played just Mondays, Wednesdays, and Fridays there, playing the other days at South Side Park, which was located at 35th St. and Wentworth, only a block or so from where the modern-day White Sox play. The team played on the West Side full time in 1892 and in 1893 moved to a different West Side Grounds, located at Polk and Wolcott. (Wolcott was called Lincoln Street at that time.) That's where the team had some of its greatest glory years, rebranded as "Cubs" and winning four pennants and two World Series titles from 1906 to 1910. In September 2008, a historical marker was placed on the site near Polk and Wolcott. The area is now home to some buildings connected with the University of Illinois at Chicago Medical Center.

Various medical buildings have been on that site for many years, and during the existence of West Side Grounds, its left-field wall was bounded by the campus of the Cook County College of Medicine's mental health facility. That led to a historical curiosity regarding the Cubs' ballpark, that it is the origin of the phrase "out of left field," meaning something strange, eccentric, or unexpected. The curious sounds made by the hospital patients were often heard from that direction during games.

There was no effective treatment for virtually any kind of mental illness then. Due to the lack of available drugs and therapies, such illnesses could develop into forms not seen today. An "asylum," as most such institutions were called, was exactly what the name implied in its original meaning, a refuge of safety for the afflicted and endangered. It is true that some asylums in that time raised funds by selling admissions to those desiring to observe the inmates for entertainment or shock value. The elimination of that abuse was one of the early triumphs of the nascent progressive and social reform movements. That such behavior could be heard and commented upon during the days the Cubs played at West Side Grounds was part of the common currency of its times.

By 1915, the Cubs had fallen on hard times. They finished that season with a 73–80 mark, their first losing season since 1902, and attendance had dropped to only a bit over 200,000 after peaking at 665,325 in the World Series title year of 1908. The 1915 Cubs were in first place with a 40–29 record and a 2 1/2 game lead on July 7, but they then lost 15 of their next 18. They got back to shouting distance of the lead at the end of July, but a 14–15 August and 12–19 September did them in.

The Cubs won their final game of the 1915 season 7–2 over the Cardinals. Baseball fans in Chicago, though, had turned much of their attention to the Chicago Whales, the Federal League team owned by Charles Weeghman that had built a lovely new ballpark on the North Side of the city. Weeghman had the new facility named after him, Weeghman Park. The Whales, or Chi-Feds as they were sometimes known, had finished in a first-place tie with St. Louis in 1915, managed by former Cubs star Joe Tinker.

Federal League owners had brought an antitrust suit against the American and National Leagues, which would eventually end up in a Supreme Court decision saying baseball was exempt from antitrust law. In the short run, though, Federal League owners were in financial difficulty, and as a result, many of them were bought out by NL owners. Two FL owners were permitted to buy major-league teams, and one of those owners was Weeghman, who purchased the Cubs from Charles W. Murphy and began to make plans to move them into his North Side park.

And that is how the Cubs, known in the early years of the 20th century as West Siders, moved to the North Side in 1916, playing their first game at the park we now know as Wrigley Field on Thursday, April 20, 1916. At the time, with Weeghman owning the team, it retained the name Weeghman Park.

Charlie Weeghman brought over a few of his players from his Federal League team to the Cubs, as well as returning Joe Tinker to a Cubs uniform, this time as manager. Tinker would become the fifth different Cubs manager in as many seasons (1912, Frank Chance; 1913, Johnny Evers; 1914, Hank O'Day; 1915, Roger Bresnahan; 1916, Tinker).

There was a considerable amount of optimism when the Cubs, having begun their season with a 2–4 road trip to Cincinnati and St. Louis, returned to Chicago on Thursday, April 20 for that franchise-first North Side game, against the Reds.

The *Chicago Tribune* reported that every ticket for the opener had been sold and "thousands" were turned away. The park did not have an upper deck at that time and capacity was about 20,000.

Quite a bit of hoopla surrounded that Opening Day in 1916. A car parade began at 1 p.m. at Grant Park and arrived at the Clark and Addison ballyard about an hour before the scheduled game time (3 p.m.), with four brass bands greeting their arrival. When the American flag was raised over the park for the first time for a Cubs game, a 21-gun salute was made. A local tailor offered a suit to the first player to hit a home run in the Cubs' new home.

That honor, and presumably the suit, went to Johnny Beall of the Reds, who homered with nobody on in the sixth inning off Cubs starter

Claude Hendrix. Beall played in just six games for the Reds in 1916 and that was his only homer of the season and one of just three he hit in 58 MLB games. The honor for the first Cub to homer at the North Side park would have to wait two more days. Max Flack homered in an 8–7 win over the Reds on April 22.

But the Cubs had the last laugh on their first North Side Opening Day, winning 7–6 in 11 innings on a line-drive single by Vic Saier. The Cubs trailed 6–3 going to the bottom of the eighth but scored two in the eighth and one in the ninth to send it to extra innings.

It was the second of seven straight wins for the Cubs, but that would be the high point of the season. The 1916 Cubs had only one winning month (April, 8–5), and finished fifth with a 67–86 record.

The ballpark at Clark and Addison would be renamed Cubs Park in 1920 after William Wrigley Jr. bought the team from Charlie Weeghman. It was named Wrigley Field, in the team owner's honor, in December 1926.

The triple play is an exciting one in any ballgame, turning a nobody-out situation into the end of an inning in the blink of an eye.

When was the first triple play turned by the Cubs at Wrigley Field, and which players were involved?

It took nearly four years of Cubs play at Wrigley Field—then known as Weeghman Park after the team's owner—for the team to turn a triple play at the ballpark at Clark and Addison.

It happened in the first game of a doubleheader against the Brooklyn Robins on Friday, September 12, 1919.

Interestingly, the game recap in the *Chicago Tribune* did not mention this play at all. The *New York Times* report on the game did, though, and here's how it happened. In the top of the sixth inning with the Cubs leading 2–0, Brooklyn's Hi Myers hit a ground ball toward Cubs shortstop Charlie Hollocher, who booted it for an error, allowing Myers to reach base. Zach Wheat followed with a single, with Myers stopping at second base.

The next batter was Ed Konetchy, who hit a line drive right at Hollocher. The runners had been off with the pitch. Hollocher stepped on second base to double Myers off for the second out and completed the triple play with a throw to first baseman Fred Merkle. Yes, *that* Fred Merkle, the young New York Giant whose "bonehead" baserunning play in 1908 had helped the Cubs to a tie in a game they otherwise might have lost, and eventually the Cubs bested the Giants in the makeup game for that tie to win the pennant. They went on to win the 1908 World Series over the Tigers, their last such win for 108 years.

As for that 1919 game, the Cubs went on to win 3–1, but lost the nightcap to Brooklyn 5–4. The Cubs finished 75–65 in a season that had been shortened to 140 games because of the flu pandemic, a distant third, 21 games behind the pennant-winning Cincinnati Reds.

Hollocher played for the Cubs through 1925, then retired from the game at just 27 due to a stomach ailment that doctors couldn't find a cause for and died in 1940 from what appeared to be a self-inflicted gunshot wound. He was just 44 years old.

Merkle, who played for the Giants in the 1911, 1912, and 1913 World Series and also in the Fall Classic for Brooklyn in 1916, appeared in the Series for the Cubs in 1918, batting .278 (5-for-18) with four walks in a losing cause. He left the major leagues after 1920, played four years in the independent minor leagues, then made a handful of appearances for the Yankees in 1925 and 1926 after which he left baseball and moved to Florida. When Merkle died in 1956 at age 67, his obituary in the *New York Times* said Merkle would likely be "best remembered" for the play that might have cost the Giants the pennant in 1908.

It has now been four decades since the Cubs have turned a triple play at Wrigley Field. Here are the triple plays by the Cubs at Wrigley since that first one in 1919:

August 23, 1924, second inning, vs. Brooklyn Dodgers
June 5, 1925, seventh inning, vs. Brooklyn Dodgers
September 22, 1925, eighth inning, vs. Brooklyn Dodgers
May 11, 1934, first inning, vs. Brooklyn Dodgers
August 22, 1942, 11th inning, vs. Cincinnati Reds
August 8, 1947, eighth inning, vs. Cincinnati Reds
September 1, 1947, fourth inning, vs. Cincinnati Reds
September 30, 1962, eighth inning, vs. New York Mets

July 14, 1965, second inning, vs. Milwaukee Braves

July 25, 1965, fourth inning, vs. Pittsburgh Pirates

June 2, 1983, second inning, vs. Pittsburgh Pirates

These triple plays were turned by the Cubs at home in the modern era before their move to Wrigley Field:

June 14, 1901, third inning, vs. New York Giants

September 23, 1907, fifth inning, vs. Philadelphia Phillies

August 27, 1910, third inning, vs. New York Giants

May 1, 1914, second inning, vs. St. Louis Cardinals

Here are the triple plays turned by the Cubs on the road in the modern era:

August 21, 1905, first inning, at Brooklyn Superbas

October 2, 1910, third inning, at Cincinnati Reds

August 30, 1921, third inning, at New York Giants

May 30, 1927, fourth inning, at Pittsburgh Pirates (unassisted, by Jimmy Cooney)

September 3, 1944, first inning, at Cincinnati Reds

June 12, 1955, seventh inning, at Brooklyn Dodgers

April 27, 1958, first inning, at San Francisco Giants

July 21, 1963, third inning, at Pittsburgh Pirates

October 3, 1965, fifth inning, at Pittsburgh Pirates

July 2, 1972, seventh inning, at Pittsburgh Pirates

August 8, 1985, eighth inning, at St. Louis Cardinals

July 9, 1986, fifth inning, at San Francisco Giants

May 10, 1997, fifth inning, at San Francisco Giants

July 29, 2020, seventh inning, at Cincinnati Reds

The W flag is an iconic part of Wrigley Field and the Cubs, flown over the center field scoreboard when the Cubs win.

When was the first time the W flag flew above the historic Wrigley Field scoreboard to denote a Cubs victory?

The W flag you see flown today at Wrigley Field when the Cubs win, a blue "W" on a white background, has gone through quite a number of iterations over the years.

The Wrigley Field bleachers on September 19, 1937, with the scoreboard not yet complete.
CHICAGO CUBS.

And its existence likely began as something William Wrigley borrowed.

In 1919, Wrigley, who was still a couple of years from consolidating his complete ownership of the Chicago Cubs, bought Catalina Island, off the coast of Southern California. Along with the island, Wrigley purchased a company called Wilmington Transportation, which provided ferry service from the California mainland to Catalina. Michele Bestudik, Santa Catalina Island Co. historian, was quoted in the *Chicago Tribune* in March 2023 as saying that "all of Wilmington's vessels flew the white W on a dark blue background."

This design, almost precisely, was used on an invitation sent out by Wrigley 10 years later upon the opening of a casino on the island.

Several years after that, Wrigley's son Philip K., who had become the Cubs' owner upon William's death in 1932, embarked on a project

A view of the back of the Wrigley Field scoreboard in the winter of 1937–1938.
REMEMBER WRIGLEY FIELD.

to build permanent bleachers at Wrigley Field, the same bleachers (later enlarged) that exist at the ballpark today.

The new bleachers opened on Sunday, September 5, 1937, but were not completely finished on that date. The first date the bleachers were complete and fully open to fans was Sunday, September 19, 1937, as the Cubs defeated the Brooklyn Dodgers 2–1. However, the photo from that date shows the center-field scoreboard incomplete and no "masthead" for flags in the middle of the board, as exists today. Scores were still being posted on the temporary board in left field.

Two flagpoles were later installed on each end of the board, as shown in the photo of the board that was taken from the corner of Waveland and Sheffield during the fall or winter of 1937, most likely during the Chicago Bears football season, as there is visible something below the

The back of the Wrigley Field scoreboard and the entrance to the bleachers in
April 2016.
DAVID SAMESHIMA.

middle of the board, which is where the clock for football games was
installed.

Later, an Art Deco–style "CHICAGO CUBS" flag was painted on
the back of the board, depicted here after the bleacher reconstruction was
complete in 2016.

The masthead for flags was installed on the board for the 1938 season
and remains in place to this day. The Cubs lost their first home game that
year to the Cardinals 6–5 on Friday, April 22.

The next day, Saturday, April 23, 1938, Larry French threw a four-hit
shutout and the Cubs beat St. Louis 4–0.

That's the day the W flag first flew over Wrigley Field to denote
a win.

Bill Veeck Jr., later owner of the Chicago White Sox and the son
of William Veeck, who had previously been Cubs team president, was
given the task of leading the project to "beautify" Wrigley Field. In

Veeck's 1962 autobiography, he wrote: "There was only one promotional gimmick I ever got away with. Mr. Wrigley permitted me to install lights on top of the flagpole to let homeward-bound Elevated passengers know whether we had won or lost that day. The flagpole was on top of the new scoreboard, and at its summit I put a crossbar with a green light on one side and a red light on the other. The green light told the El passengers we had won, the red that we had lost."

In addition to the lights, the Cubs also decided that they would take the "W" flag—which they had likely previously used simply to denote the initial of the owner—and fly it over the scoreboard every day that the team won, with a corresponding "L" flag if the Cubs lost.

Over time, the colors of both the flags and the lights have changed. When the Cubs retired Ernie Banks' jersey in 1982 and began to fly that retired number flag on a foul pole, the "W" flag flipped from white-on-blue to blue-on-white, and the "L" flag for losses became the reverse—although the Cubs failed to note this change in their media guide until team staffers were revamping the guide for the 1990 All-Star Game. The lights indicating whether the Cubs won or lost that day were eliminated for a time but were restored in 1978 in what the team's media guide termed an "innovation" and were blue for a win and white for a loss. At that time that matched the flag colors, but when the colors were inverted in 1982, the light colors did not flip.

The popularity of the "W" flag among fans began during the team's run to the NL Central title in 2003. Fans came to Wrigley Field that year with homemade "W" flags and unfurled them after the team won, eventually prompting the ballclub to begin selling "W" flags. In 2007, when "Go Cubs Go" was played after home wins, "W" flags began to proliferate at the ballpark. For a time, the team even used #FlyTheW as its official marketing slogan.

Today, many fans bring "W" flags to Cubs games both home and road and unfurl them after the team wins. And the flag still flies over Wrigley Field when the Cubs win—but just once. Each W flag is atop the scoreboard until the morning following a Cubs win, after which it is lowered, authenticated, and auctioned, with proceeds benefiting Cubs Charities.

The W flag flying atop the Wrigley scoreboard for the first time after the Cubs defeated the Cardinals on April 23, 1938.
CHICAGO TRIBUNE HISTORICAL IMAGE / TCA.

Organ music has been a staple at Wrigley Field, as well as many other major-league ballparks, for many years.

When was the first time organ music was heard at the Cubs' North Side home?

Saturday, April 26, 1941, was a perfectly ordinary day at Wrigley Field. The Cubs lost to the Cardinals 6–2 on a pleasant, sunny day with seasonable temperatures in the mid-60s.

Just 8,499 showed up for that contest, as the Cubs had been heading down the National League standings through the previous two seasons. Those who did attend on that weekend date were treated to a baseball first: music from a pipe organ, played live by Ray Nelson.

Not only was that the first day organ music was heard at Wrigley Field, it was the first time for that sort of thing in any major-league ballpark.

189

It wasn't played the way you might think of organ entertainment at the ballpark today, with the organist playing "Charge!" or another little ditty to exhort the home team to play well. Instead, the music was limited to pregame entertainment because of music industry regulations.

Then as now, music played for public performance, whether recorded or live, has rights owned by two organizations: Broadcast Music Inc. (BMI) or the American Society of Composers, Authors and Publishers (ASCAP). Because the Cubs did not at the time hold rights to play ASCAP music publicly, Nelson had to end his playing at 2:30 p.m., when the radio pregame show began, in order to not violate ASCAP rights by potentially having his music playing heard over the radio, similar to the way you might have your personal YouTube video have a copyright notice issued because it contains incidental music that doesn't have anything to do with your video.

Among the songs played by Nelson on that first day was "When the Midnight Choo Choo Leaves for T-U-L-S-A," which was a Cubs-themed song based on a popular Irving Berlin ditty "When the Midnight Choo-Choo Leaves for Alabam'." The title came from the fact that Tulsa was a Cubs minor-league affiliate in the early 1940s.

The *Chicago Tribune* reported that Nelson would "sort his album before the Cubs come home on May 13" and play exclusively BMI selections, so it wouldn't matter if they were heard on the radio, as the Cubs had the rights to play BMI music. Nevertheless, organ music would soon vanish from Wrigley Field. It did not return until 1967, when the first Lowrey organ was installed and Jack Kearney began to entertain fans pregame and eventually during games. Other organists who played at Wrigley in the 1960s, 1970s, and early 1980s: Frank Pellico (who has played the organ at Chicago Blackhawks games since 1991), Vance Fothergill, John Henzl, Ed Vodicka, and Bruce Miles, the latter no relation to a longtime Cubs writer by the same name for the suburban *Daily Herald*.

In 1987, the Cubs hired Gary Pressy to play organ music at Wrigley Field, and he worked in that capacity for 2,687 consecutive home games before his retirement at the end of the 2019 season.

Today, John Benedeck and Josh Langhoff share organist duties at Wrigley, continuing a tradition that dates back more than 80 years.

The Cubs installed lights at Wrigley Field in 1988, the last of the "Original 16" teams to do so.
They've been playing night games at the park since then, but based on the generally accepted understanding of what is a "night game," when was the actual first night game at Wrigley?

As you might have surmised, this is a trick question. The Cubs had finished installing permanent lights in Wrigley Field in July 1988. The ballclub held a charity event "under the lights" later that month with that evening's events featuring a home-run derby with Cubs stars Ryne Sandberg, Andre Dawson, Ernie Banks, and Billy Williams. They then scheduled the first Wrigley night game for Monday, August 8. The Cubs played 3 1/2 innings against the Philadelphia Phillies that night and then a torrential rainstorm postponed that game before it was official. (It was made up as part of a doubleheader in September.) The next night, Tuesday, August 9, the Cubs defeated the New York Mets under the lights 6–4.

That goes into the books as the first official night game at Wrigley Field, but that's not the question you were asked. The generally accepted definition of a "night game" is any game that begins at 6 p.m. local time or later.

Based on that, the Cubs' first night game at Wrigley took place Friday, June 25, 1943.

"But wait," you're saying, "how could they have done that without lights?"

Here's the explanation.

During World War II, when the country was focused on winning the war and many people worked long hours at war plants, there wasn't a lot of free time for fans to attend baseball games.

So in the summer of 1943, the Cubs decided to experiment with a game that began at 6 p.m.—thus, by the generally accepted definition, a night game. The Cubs had hoped to draw more people to Wrigley Field, even without artificial light, by playing in the evening after working hours.

The game was billed by the team as a "twilight" game, and the concept seemed worthwhile. Because it was Friday, the Cubs continued their usual "Ladies Day" concept for that day of the week and 10,070 attended, 3,450 of whom were women admitted free.

The Cubs shut out the first-place Cardinals 6–0 that evening, and the game ran two hours, 17 minutes, thus ending before the clock sunset time of 8:30 p.m. that day.

Hi Bithorn, the first Puerto Rican native to play in Major League Baseball, threw a two-hit shutout. He would go on to lead the National League in shutouts that year with seven. He also had a single and double that evening and drove in one of the Cubs' six runs.

Bithorn had a fine year in 1943, going 18–12 with a 2.60 ERA, 1.170 WHIP, and leading the National League with seven shutouts on a team that went 74–79. He got some MVP consideration (finishing 32nd), and had there been a Cy Young Award then, he would probably have finished high in the voting. But Bithorn missed 1944 and 1945 in military service, and when he returned in 1946, at age 30, wasn't nearly as dominant. After a couple of games with the White Sox in 1947, he returned to his native Puerto Rico, and, per his SABR biography, he was shot and killed by a policeman in Mexico in 1951, after a financial dispute. Bithorn was just 35. A baseball stadium in San Juan, Puerto Rico, was named after him in 1962, and the Cubs played a three-game series against the Montreal Expos there in 2003.

The Cubs, who were by 1943 five years removed from their most recent pennant in 1938, went just 22–36 after that "twilight" win and sat in last place in the National League, 13 games behind the first-place Cardinals. They would play better for the rest of the year, going 52–43 to finish with a 74–79 record, but that was good only for a fifth-place finish, 30 1/2 games behind the pennant-winning, 105-win Cardinals.

Meanwhile, even though the 10,000-plus ranked in the top 20 for Cubs attendance in 1943, they never again tried a "twilight" game. It really would have worked only from about the middle of June to the middle of July, as before or after those dates sunset times would have been too early, even with most games back then taking only a bit more than two hours. Team owner P. K. Wrigley called night baseball "just a passing fad" and after having donated steel that had been earmarked for light towers in 1941 to the effort to win World War II never again seriously contemplated installing lights at Wrigley. That would have to wait until after the Tribune Company bought the team from the Wrigleys.

And so the Cubs didn't have another home game scheduled to start at 6 p.m. or later until that fateful evening, Monday, August 8, 1988, when they tried to play at night but storms postponed that for an extra day. It was as if baseball gods were saying, "You may play at night here . . . but not tonight." Thus, the first actual Cubs game played under artificial light at Wrigley Field didn't happen until the next night, Tuesday, August 9, 1988, a 6–4 win over the Mets.

Tie games used to be a regular occurrence at Wrigley Field because of its lack of lights pre-1988.

When was the first Opening Day game at Wrigley Field that ended in a tie?

Besides the tie games at lightless Wrigley Field, baseball teams used to register tie contests under quite a number of scenarios. Among them: local curfews, teams having to catch trains so they agreed on a predetermined stopping time, and after other ballparks got artificial light, occasional failure of said lights.

Today, a tie game can occur only in a very specific circumstance—if weather stops the last game between two teams in a season, there's no possible makeup date, the game doesn't have postseason implications, and the score is tied when the game is halted. This happened to the 2016 Cubs, in fact, in the final game they played in Pittsburgh that year. The game was tied 1–1 when a steady rain began. Play was stopped, and as the previous conditions were satisfied, the game was declared a tie, so the Cubs' official 2016 regular season record was 103–58–1. This game is the most recent tie game for any major-league team.

Before a rule allowing games halted by darkness at Wrigley Field to be suspended was enacted in June 1969, though, any game that could not be completed at the corner of Clark and Addison because the sun went down and where the score was tied when the game was stopped was declared a tie.

From the time the Cubs moved into Weeghman Park (later renamed Wrigley Field) in 1916, 30 games were halted for darkness with the score tied. Of those 30, 18 were the second games of doubleheaders, where it's understandable that play could have gone on until too late in the afternoon (or early evening) to continue.

Just one such game occurred on Opening Day. That happened on Monday, April 12, 1965, against the St. Louis Cardinals, and it was quite a game, attended by 19,751 on a cloudy and very windy 47-degree afternoon. The Cardinals blew a 5–0 first-inning lead, the Cubs had to come from three runs down in the bottom of the ninth to send the game to extra innings, and also had to come from behind in the 11th inning to tie the game—after which they loaded the bases with two out, but could not score.

After the five-run St. Louis first inning, the Cubs plated two in the bottom of the second on RBI doubles by George Altman and Doug Clemens. Two more came home in the next inning on a home run by Roberto Pena—who was playing in his first MLB game—and a single by Ernie Banks.

The Cardinals then scored two in the top of the fourth to go up 7–4, but Pena doubled in two runs in the bottom of the inning to bring the Cubs back to within one run. St. Louis made it 8–6 in the sixth when former Cub Lou Brock stole third and scored on a throwing error and added a run to that lead in the top of the ninth on an RBI single by Curt Flood.

And so it was that the Cubs trailed by three heading to the last of the ninth. The first two Cubs in that inning were routine outs, but Ron Santo walked and George Altman singled. Banks, down to his final strike, followed with a game-tying three-run homer that resulted in a "tumultuous response from those hardy fans still in the old ball park," according to Edward Prell's *Chicago Tribune* recap of the game.

Neither team scored in the 10th inning, and in the 11th, Brock continued to torment his erstwhile team with a one-out RBI single to give the Cardinals a 10–9 lead.

The Cubs did not give up, though. Pena had the game of his life at the plate that day, going 3-for-6 with three RBI and three runs scored, but he also made three errors that resulted in two unearned runs for the Cardinals. The Cubs' rookie shortstop led off the last of the 11th with a single and advanced to second on a passed ball and took third on a ground out. Santo doubled deep to left-center and Pena scored the tying run.

With one out, a single could have won the game for the Cubs. Altman, the next batter, was issued a walk by future Hall of Famer Steve Carlton, another player making his MLB debut that chilly day at Wrigley Field. Carlton was then removed for veteran right-hander Bob Purkey, who retired Banks on a fly to center, with Santo taking third. Purkey threw two balls to Clemens, at which time the Cardinals elected to intentionally walk him to load the bases and pitch instead to Cubs catcher Vic Roznovsky, who flied to center to end the inning.

At that point it was about five minutes to six o'clock. Sunset in Chicago on April 12, 1965, was 6:28 p.m.—this was long before Daylight Saving time was moved back into March—and so the umpires called the game at that point, and by the rules of the day it was a tie.

Also by baseball rules of the time, any tie game had all its statistics counted but had to be replayed from the beginning. And so this game was eventually made up as part of a doubleheader on Sunday, July 11, which the Cubs swept by identical 6–0 scores. After that sweep, the Cubs were in eighth place but "only" nine games behind the first-place Reds. They went 32–45 the rest of the way and finished 72–90, the 10th time in the 18 seasons between 1948 and 1965 that a Cubs team lost at least 90 games.

As for Pena, he batted just .207 the rest of the year, made 17 errors, and spent a couple of months in the minor leagues. At one time thought of as the Cubs' "shortstop of the future," he lost his position to Don Kessinger and was selected by the Phillies in the minor-league draft after the 1966 season. He played briefly for Philadelphia, San Diego, Oakland, and Milwaukee through 1971.

The Cubs have played one tie game at home since lights were installed in Wrigley Field. That happened on Friday, May 28, 1993, and since that game was stopped because of rain, not darkness, it could not be suspended. The game had already been delayed 37 minutes in the third inning when the Cubs and Montreal Expos each scored two in the fifth. Rain came again and a one hour, 14 minute delay ensued, after which the game was declared a tie. It was made up as part of a doubleheader at Wrigley Field on Tuesday, August 17, which the teams split.

In all of major-league history, there have been just 18 documented games where the game time temperature was below freezing (32 degrees Fahrenheit).

When was the first Cubs game at Wrigley Field played in subfreezing temperatures?

The first—and to date only—documented game at Wrigley Field to be played where the game time temperature was reported as below freezing happened on Tuesday, April 8, 1997, against the Florida Marlins. It was that year's home opener and at game time, it was 29 degrees with a reported wind speed of 22 miles per hour, and by the wind chill calculations used at the time, the wind chill was 1 degree (though by a new wind chill calculator introduced in 2001, those conditions now would produce a wind chill of 15, still quite cold). A *Chicago Tribune* article called the conditions "Arctic-like baseball" and noted that the White Sox, also scheduled for a home game that day, postponed it and moved the next day's game from 7:05 p.m. to 1 p.m. Marlins manager Jim Leyland was quoted in the *Tribune* as saying, "This is one day even Ernie Banks wouldn't say 'Let's play two.'"

The boxscore for this game at baseball-reference.com says it was sunny at game time, but this author attended that game and remembers it as eventually turning into a mostly cloudy afternoon during which it was impossible to get warm, no matter how well you were dressed for the weather.

The Cubs, meanwhile, were even colder than the climate. They had lost their first six games on a road trip to warm Miami and Atlanta, and so there wasn't much optimism among Cubs fans when the team took the field on that frigid day. The Marlins scored a run off Steve Trachsel in the first inning, but the Cubs tied it up on a Sammy Sosa homer in the second and took a 2–1 lead in the third. The Marlins tied the game in the fourth, but the Cubs again took the lead 3–2 when Sosa drew a bases-loaded walk in the fifth.

That tenuous lead held into the top of the seventh, when Charles Johnson doubled in two runs off Trachsel to take a 4–3 lead, and the Marlins added a run in the ninth and held on for a 5–3 win.

Two days later, on an afternoon nearly as cold (37 degrees), Marlins right-hander Alex Fernandez nearly no-hit the Cubs until Dave Hansen beat out an infield grounder with one out in the ninth. Trailing 1–0, the next two Cubs hitters reached base on errors, but Jose Hernandez, who had run for Hansen, was thrown out overrunning third base. Fernandez then struck out Ryne Sandberg to end the game, the Cubs' eighth straight loss. The losing streak eventually stretched to 14, which set not only a Cubs franchise record but a National League record for the most losses to begin a season. The April 8, 1997, game is the only one the Cubs have ever played where the game time temperature was below freezing.

The streak finally ended when the Cubs defeated the Mets 4–3 in the second game of a doubleheader at Shea Stadium on Sunday, April 20.

Of the 18 games that have been played when the game-time temperature was confirmed to be below freezing, five have been in Coors Field in Denver, where the coldest-ever game-time temperature of 23 degrees was recorded for the first game of a doubleheader on Tuesday, April 20, 2013. That was a twin bill played because the previous day's game had been snowed out. It warmed up a bit for Game 2 of that doubleheader—30 degrees at game time.

ROAD GAME FIRSTS

The Cubs were the last of the "Original 16" teams to install lights in their home ballpark, so no official night games were played at Wrigley Field until August 9, 1988.

But night games had been played in the major leagues since the Cincinnati Reds installed lights at Crosley Field in 1935.

When was the Cubs' first night game?

During the Great Depression, teams were looking for anything they could dream up that would increase attendance, given that people didn't have a lot of disposable income. Several minor-league teams had tried games under artificial light in the early 1930s, and major-league clubs were considering it. But Hall of Famer Clark Griffith was once quoted as saying, "There is no chance of night baseball ever becoming popular in the bigger cities. People there are educated to see the best there is and will only stand for the best. High class baseball cannot be played at night." Commissioner K. M. Landis reportedly told Cincinnati Reds general manager Larry MacPhail, "Young man . . . not in my lifetime or yours will you ever see a baseball game played at night in the majors."

But MacPhail and Reds owner Powel Crosley felt that they needed to try night games, as their team was having financial troubles, and they were able to convince Landis to allow them to do it. In 1935, the Reds installed lights and were permitted seven night games. The first of those took place on Friday, May 24, 1935, against the Phillies, with a ceremonial light switch pushed in the White House by President Franklin D. Roosevelt. Attendance immediately took a big jump, as 20,422 paid to see the Reds win 2–1. It wound up being the sixth-largest crowd of the season at Crosley Field. Newspapers of the time reported about the baseballs standing out against the night sky and the grass looking "far greener" at night than during the day.

Just a few weeks later, the Cubs would visit Crosley Field and play their very first game under artificial light. It happened on Monday, July 1, 1935. The Cubs entered this day of play in third place in the National League, nine games behind the league-leading Giants.

The first Cub to bat in a night game was Augie Galan, who grounded out. But the Cubs got RBI hits from Phil Cavarretta, Ken O'Dea, and Chuck Klein and led 3–1 after the first inning and 4–3 after two. Three more Cubs runs crossed the plate in the top of the fifth, driven in by O'Dea, Frank Demaree, and Woody English. Each team scored once more and the Cubs won 8–4, taking their first game under the lights. The team would eventually run off 21 wins in a row in September and win the National League pennant with a record of 100–54, the last time any Cubs team would win 100 games until 2016.

The Cubs would go on to play another single night game at Cincinnati in 1936 and 1937, then the Brooklyn Dodgers added lights in 1938 and the Cubs played one game under the lights there in 1938 in addition to one in Cincinnati. Baseball officials still didn't think night games were here to stay, and most teams were extremely limited in the number of night games they were permitted to schedule until the World War II years, to try to give entertainment after work hours for workers mobilized for war production. The Cubs played 18 night games in 1944 and 16 in 1945, and then would play regularly at night on the road until lights finally came to Wrigley Field in 1988.

Interestingly, with lights in the early years of night games not being as efficient as they are now, they often wouldn't work well at dusk, and so many night games in the 1930s and 1940s were scheduled to begin at 8:30 p.m. or even 9 p.m. It was often expected that people would have dinner at home or at a restaurant, then come to the game for entertainment, much as they might do dinner and a movie or live theater. Last, it wasn't until the 1960s in many major-league cities that the concept of turning the lights on to complete a day game became common.

For more than 50 years, the National and American Leagues consisted of eight teams each, with none located south or west of St. Louis. Then the Dodgers and Giants pulled up stakes in New York and moved to Los Angeles and San Francisco, respectively.

When was the first Cubs game on the West Coast?
The Giants and Dodgers, New York fixtures dating back to the late 19th century, moved to California in 1958. The Dodgers were wooed first from their longtime Brooklyn home with promises of land for a new stadium, and owner Walter O'Malley was able to convince Giants owner Horace Stoneham to follow him West to keep their rivalry going—and have at least one team fairly close by. The widespread use of commercial air travel was relatively new at the time and most teams still traveled short distances by train.

But air travel had become safe and fast enough that teams could travel from the Midwest and East Coast to California, and that's exactly what the Cubs did in early 1958.

In fact, they became the first team other than the Giants to play the Dodgers in California. The Dodgers and Giants had opened the 1958 season with six games against each other, three in San Francisco and three in Los Angeles.

The Cubs, after opening the season with two in St. Louis and then three against the Cardinals at Wrigley Field from April 15 to 20, traveled to Los Angeles on Monday, April 21, an off day, and played their first West Coast game on Tuesday, April 22, 1958, at the Los Angeles Coliseum against the Dodgers. In addition to being the Cubs' first West Coast game, it was the first major-league night game played in the Dodgers' temporary home, which was being criticized by players, fans, and writers around baseball for its odd configuration, something *Chicago Tribune* writer Edward Prell noted as "unanimous blasting of the Coliseum as unfit for playing baseball."

The LA Coliseum was a football stadium in which they had squished a baseball diamond into one corner. A fence of sorts was put in right and center field (though far from home plate), but in left field, the outfield wall was just 250 feet from the plate, so a 42-foot-high screen was erected and balls had to go over the screen to be home runs. If baseballs bounced off the screen, they were in play.

As for that first Cubs game in LA, they might as well have not bothered. The Dodgers scored two in the first inning on a home run by Gino Cimoli with a man on base off 22-year-old Cubs rookie Glen Hobbie. They added another in the second. Ernie Banks homered with a runner on in the sixth for the only Cubs runs of the night in a 4–2 loss. A crowd of 39,459 attended the game, which sounds like a large gathering but really wasn't, as the Coliseum held over 92,000 fans for baseball.

The Cubs actually got off to a good start in 1958, led by Banks, who would win the first of two straight National League MVP Awards that year when he batted .313/.366/.614 with career highs of 47 home runs, 129 RBI, and 379 total bases, all of which led both major leagues. The team was in first place May 8 with a 13–8 record, then floundered for most of May and June before winning 11 of 15 in early July to come within 2 1/2 games of first place July 18 with a 46–42 record. Despite Banks' heroics, the pitching did not hold up and the Cubs finished fifth with a 72–82 record. It was their most wins and best finish in five years, since a 77–77 mark in 1952.

In the early 1960s, two teams were added to both the National and American Leagues in the first of several expansions of the major leagues.

When was the Cubs' first game against an expansion team?

The American League added two teams in 1961, the Los Angeles Angels and Washington Senators, the latter replacing the "original" Senators, who moved to Minnesota and became the Twins.

The National League waited another year, until 1962, to add two ballclubs and match the AL's 10-team league. The New York Mets and Houston Colt .45s became NL teams that season, and the Cubs didn't have to wait very long to play one of them, as they played their first game of the 1962 season in Houston on Tuesday, April 10.

Still enmeshed in the College of Coaches experiment (which, of course, eventually failed spectacularly), "head coach" El Tappe sent right-hander Don Cardwell out to face Houston. Cardwell had made a splash by throwing a no-hitter in his first Cubs appearance in May 1960 but hadn't pitched anywhere near that well since. Opposing him was Bobby Shantz, an expansion draft pick who had been a star for the Philadelphia Athletics more than a decade earlier (and who would later pitch for the Cubs, briefly, in 1964).

It did not go well for the North Siders. They trailed 1–0 in the bottom of the third when Cardwell issued two walks leading off the inning. Roman Mejias followed with a three-run homer into what were described as "shocking pink" bleachers by *Chicago Tribune* writer Richard Dozer, and another homer two outs later by Hal Smith gave Houston a 5–0 lead. At that point, Cardwell was pulled for Dave Gerard, a right-hander who was making the very first appearance of his only major-league season.

The Cubs made it 5–1 on a solo homer by Ernie Banks in the top of the seventh, but Houston came back with three runs off Barney Schultz in the bottom of the inning. Another single run was posted on a sacrifice fly by Lou Brock in the top of the eighth, but Houston put up another three-spot in the bottom of the inning off Al Lary, whose biggest claim to fame was that he was the brother of Frank Lary, a longtime pitcher with the Tigers. On this day Al Lary was appearing in his first MLB game in eight years. He would pitch in just 14 more that season, spend two more years in the Cubs minor-league system, then hang up his spikes.

The Cubs lost the game 11–2, but that wasn't the worst thing about their first trip to Colt Stadium, which one preseason publication referred to as "a barn-like thing" that became best known for oppressive humidity and mosquitoes before Houston's major-league team rebranded as Astros and moved to the new Astrodome in 1965.

No, the worst thing was that the Cubs got swept in a three-game series by the brand-new team in Houston. In fact, the Cubs lost their first seven games in 1962 and nine of their first ten. By May 1, they were 4–17 and already 11 games out of first place. The Cubs did manage to win the season series from Houston with 11 wins in 18 games, but the Colt .45s had the last laugh, finishing in eighth place in the new 10-team National League with a 64–96 record, while the Cubs set a franchise record for losses with 103 and finished ninth, saved from a last-place finish only by the horrendous 40–120 expansion New York Mets. The Cubs, though, went just 9–9 against the Mets, the only team against whom the 1962 Mets did not have a losing record.

The league overall might have celebrated when the Astros moved into the Astrodome from Colt Stadium, but the new domed edifice became a house of horrors for the Cubs. In 1966, Cubs manager Leo Durocher became incensed at mocking videos put on the new electronic scoreboard when the Cubs were in town and he ripped a bullpen phone out of the dugout wall. The Astros sent Durocher a bill for the damage, though it's unclear whether Leo or the Cubs ever paid it.

The Astrodome was home to Houston's team from 1965 through 1999. During those years the Cubs went 83–137 in the Astros' domed ballpark, a .377 winning percentage that was their second worst in any road city in that time frame (only a .343 mark posted in Pittsburgh was worse). But it was even more awful for the Cubs in that indoor stadium through 1980—they were 34–74 (.288) there during that span.

The Astros moved to the American League in 2013, so the Cubs don't play them in Houston that often anymore—but since Minute Maid Park became their home in 2000, the Cubs actually had a winning record in Houston at 56–55, until they were swept there in May 2023 to drop that mark under .500 at 56–58.

NO-HITTER FIRSTS

Through the end of the 2023 season, there have been 322 recognized no-hitters thrown in the major leagues.

Who threw the first no-hitter for the Cubs after the pitching distance was standardized at 60 feet, six inches?

The Cubs weren't known as "Cubs" when Walter Thornton didn't allow a hit to the Brooklyn Bridegrooms (an early nickname given to the Dodgers when several of their players had been recently married). This game happened on Sunday, August 21, 1898, at the team's then-home of West Side Grounds and the team's unofficial nickname was "Orphans" because longtime leader and manager Adrian "Cap" Anson had retired the year before.

Thornton wasn't a pitcher one might have expected to do this. The *Chicago Tribune* recap of the game noted that he threw with "weird wild speed," and Thornton had limited success from 1895 to 1897 with the Chicago NL team, posting a 5.10 ERA in 28 games (23 starts), also playing the outfield 59 times in 1897 and 34 games worth in 1898. He'd thrown a bit better in 1898, though, and in this doubleheader nightcap it all came together for Thornton. He issued three walks, and when the final out was recorded on a ground ball to third base, the *Tribune* reported the crowd of about 10,000 "went into paroxysms of applause, under which Thornton escaped to the clubhouse."

After 1898, though, Thornton left baseball. This wasn't uncommon in those days, as many professions paid more than baseball teams did, and per Thornton's SABR biography, he wound up living in both the Pacific

Northwest and California but eventually died destitute in Los Angeles in 1960. Nevertheless, he'll always have his line in the Cubs and MLB's record books as having thrown a no-hitter, and the first for the Cubs from the pitching distance of 60 feet, six inches that had been established in 1893.

Four no-hitters were recorded by Chicago NL pitchers before the 60 feet, six inch pitching distance was established in 1893. Larry Corcoran, a star for the team in the 1880s, had three of them, thrown on August 19, 1880 (against Boston); September 20, 1882 (against Worcester); and June 27, 1884 (against Providence). The following year, future Hall of Famer John Clarkson pitched a no-hitter, also against the Providence Grays, on July 27, 1885. Clarkson's was the first for the franchise thrown on the road.

In the modern era, there have been 12 no-hitters by Cubs pitchers:

August 31, 1915: Jimmy Lavender, 2–0 over the Giants at New York

May 12, 1955: Sam Jones, 4–0 over the Pittsburgh Pirates at Wrigley Field

May 15, 1960: Don Cardwell, 4–0 over the St. Louis Cardinals at Wrigley Field

August 19, 1969: Ken Holtzman, 3–0 over the Atlanta Braves at Wrigley Field

June 3, 1971: Ken Holtzman, 1–0 over the Reds at Cincinnati

April 16, 1972: Burt Hooton, 4–0 over the Philadelphia Phillies at Wrigley Field

September 2, 1972: Milt Pappas, 8–0 over the San Diego Padres at Wrigley Field

September 14, 2008: Carlos Zambrano, 5–0 over the Houston Astros at Miller Park in Milwaukee

August 30, 2015: Jake Arrieta, 2–0 over the Dodgers at Los Angeles

Sunday, April 21, 2016: Jake Arrieta, 16–0 over the Reds at Cincinnati

September 13, 2020: Alec Mills, 12–0 over the Brewers at Milwaukee

June 24, 2021: Zach Davies, Ryan Tepera, Andrew Chafin, and Craig Kimbrel, 4–0 over the Dodgers at Los Angeles

The Cubs have been no-hit just seven times in their history. That's the fewest times being no-hit for any of the "Original 16" major-league teams. In fact, the Cubs hold the major-league record for the longest stretch between games in which they were no-hit (7,920 consecutive games of at least nine innings between September 10, 1965, and July 24, 2015).

When was the first time the Cubs were no-hit?

After three straight losing seasons, the Cubs, under manager Frank Selee, returned to contention in 1903. This was led by many of the men who would eventually become four-time NL champions and two-time World Series champions, Frank Chance, Joe Tinker, Johnny Evers, and Johnny Kling, along with pitcher Jack Taylor, who would complete all 33 of his starts that year.

The team had a pair of eight-game winning streaks in May sandwiched around a single loss, roaring into first place and remaining there until early June, when they were overtaken by the Giants and the eventual league champion Pirates.

By September, the Cubs had fallen into third place, though a five-game winning streak had brought them to a very good 78–52 record.

It was the game that ended that winning streak that became the first no-hitter thrown against the Cubs, the second game of a doubleheader against the Phillies at West Side Grounds.

Chick Fraser of the Phillies threw that no-no against the Cubs on Friday, September 18, 1903, in the second game of a doubleheader, in front of an estimated 2,500 fans at the Cubs ballpark.

Fraser was a middling sort of pitcher who had allowed 58 runs in 99 innings in his previous 13 appearances (11 starts) coming into that game. That probably would not produce as bad an ERA as it might seem, as errors were common in those days and many of those runs were likely unearned, though specifics on earned/unearned runs from that long-ago time are not available.

Fraser walked five and struck out four in his no-hit game, and the *Chicago Tribune* headlined its unbylined recap of the game with "PITCHING FEAT OF THE SEASON" and said: "'Chick' Fraser of the Zimmerites shut the Colts out without a run or hit in the second of the two games played on the west side yesterday, pitching the first full game without a hit in either big league this season, and incidentally putting a big crimp in the second place hopes of the Seleeites."

Back then, teams were often referred to in newspaper reports by the identity of their manager. Charles Zimmer was the manager of the Phillies, who were absolutely terrible in 1903, finishing seventh with a 49–86 record. The no-hitter was one of just six Phillies wins over the Cubs that year in 18 tries.

The name "Colts" should also be noted. In the early part of the 20th century, team nicknames were often given by newspaper headline writers and weren't official team brands as they are today. Some papers used "Colts" in 1903; others had switched to "Cubs" and historical references refer to the team as "Cubs" beginning that year.

The loss did hurt the Cubs in striving for second place. It happened with just seven games remaining in the season, and the team's 4–3 mark in those seven contests wasn't enough to overtake the Giants, who finished second, 6 1/2 games behind Pittsburgh. The Cubs finished third, eight games back.

As for Fraser, he would eventually be acquired by the Cubs in January 1907 from the Reds, and he pitched reasonably well in a part-time role for the 1907 and 1908 Cubs pennant winners, though he didn't pitch in either World Series.

After Fraser's playing career ended, he became a coach and scout for the Pirates, who were at the time run by his brother-in-law, Fred Clarke (Clarke's wife was Fraser's wife's sister). Later, he also managed in the minor leagues and scouted for the Yankees before he died in 1940, aged 66.

In 1923, Sam Jones threw a no-hitter for the Yankees over the Athletics, becoming the first pitcher to accomplish that feat with no strikeouts. (Oddly enough, a different pitcher named Sam Jones threw a no-hitter for the Cubs in 1955.)

Name the pitcher who was the first Cub to throw a no-hitter with no strikeouts.

The Cubs left-hander who threw a no-hitter without striking out any hitters is Ken Holtzman, who did it at Wrigley Field on Tuesday, August 19, 1969, against the Braves. That was one of the highlights of that season for that star-crossed team that collapsed in September.

Holtzman had burst on the scene for the Cubs just three months after he was drafted in the fourth round in 1965 out of the University of Illinois, pitching three games in the major leagues at age 19 that September.

Making the Cubs rotation the following year at age 20, Holtzman had the normal ups and downs you might expect from a pitcher of that age. On September 25, 1966, he showed the form that hinted that he might have a no-hitter in his future.

The Dodgers, still in a tight race with the Giants for the NL pennant, came to Wrigley Field for a four-game series. LA took two of the first three games of the series, and that set up a highly anticipated matchup in the finale between Holtzman and Sandy Koufax—billed as "The Battle of the Jewish Left-handers." A crowd of 21,259 attended the game that Sunday afternoon at Wrigley Field—the fourth-largest Cubs home crowd that year.

The Cubs scored a pair in the first inning off Koufax. That in itself was unusual—the Cubs had scored two runs off Koufax in an entire game just one other time in his nine previous starts against them dating to 1964.

Meanwhile, Holtzman started mowing down Dodgers. He issued a leadoff walk to Dick Schofield in the third, but the next batter hit into a double play. That was the only LA baserunner through eight innings—Holtzman had faced the minimum 24 batters through eight.

Schofield led off the ninth with a single that, according to Richard Dozer of the *Chicago Tribune*, "bounced over Kenny's reach and past second base." That broke up Holtzman's no-hit bid.

Holtzman walked Al Ferrara, then struck out Jim Gilliam. Maury Wills singled in Schofield to make it 2–1. Willie Davis then hit a line drive—but right at Glenn Beckert, who turned it into a game-ending double play.

So when the Cubs were high flying for most of the 1969 season, there were hints that Holtzman might actually throw a no-no. He threw a three-hit shutout against the Astros in May, then a two-hitter against the Padres in early August.

There wasn't any real anticipation he could do it against a good-hitting Braves team when they came to Wrigley Field on August 19. But one thing that happened before that day's game turned out to be a big help for Holtzman—the weather. A strong cold front had roared through Chicago the previous evening, and while the August temperature was still a pleasant 76 degrees at game time, a strong wind was blowing in from left field.

With the Cubs leading 3–0 in the top of the seventh and Henry Aaron at bat, the no-hitter appeared to be lost when the Atlanta superstar sent a Holtzman offering deep to left. It appeared headed for Waveland Avenue, a home run. But the wind blew it back into the ballpark and Billy Williams caught it at the curve of the well just in front of the left-field bleacher wall.

Perhaps rattled a bit, Holtzman walked the next hitter, Rico Carty, but that was the last Atlanta Brave he let reach base. He retired the final seven Braves batters, getting Aaron to ground to Beckert for the final out. In so doing, Holtzman became the first Cub to throw a no-hitter since Don Cardwell in 1960. Holtzman walked three in his gem but recorded no strikeouts. Through the end of the 2023 season, he is the only National League pitcher to do so.

Holtzman went on to throw a second no-hitter for the Cubs, matching his 1969 feat on June 1, 1971, against the Reds in Cincinnati—and then lost *another* no-no in the ninth on June 8, 1975, while with the A's, against the Detroit Tigers. Future Cub Tom Veryzer doubled off Holtzman with two out in the ninth, but he struck out Ron LeFlore to complete a one-hit shutout.

With just a bit of luck, Ken Holtzman might have thrown *four* no-hitters.

Ken Holtzman, who threw two no-hitters for the Cubs, at Wrigley Field.
JEWEL TEA VIA TRADINGCARDDB.COM, PUBLIC DOMAIN, VIA WIKIMEDIA COMMONS.

Holtzman returned to the Cubs in a deal with the Yankees for Ron Davis on June 10, 1978. He was still just 32 years old, and Cubs management hoped he could provide some pitching help for a team that had trouble preventing runs. But Holtzman was done—in 46 appearances (26 starts) for the Cubs in 1978 and 1979, he posted a 5.06 ERA and allowed 25 home runs in 170 2/3 innings. He did have one last solid game for the Cubs, a three-hit shutout of the Astros in the first game of a doubleheader on July 7, 1979, one last memory for Cubs fans of a potentially great career.

After his career, Holtzman settled in the Chicago suburbs for many years and worked as an investment banker. He returned to baseball briefly in 2007 as a manager in a baseball league created in Israel, which went under before the season ended. Holtzman is now retired and living in his hometown of St. Louis.

Combined no-hitters, with more than one pitcher accomplishing the feat, used to be rare in major-league history. Through 2002 there had been just eight such games. But with relief use becoming more common in recent years, 12 more were thrown between 2003 and 2023.

When was the first time Cubs pitchers combined on a no-hitter?

The first time more than one Cubs pitcher allowed no hits to the team's opponent happened on Thursday, June 24, 2021, when Zach Davies, Ryan Tepera, Andrew Chafin, and Craig Kimbrel combined to do it against the Dodgers in Los Angeles.

It was perhaps the last thing expected from Davies, who had struggled early in his only Cubs season and entered this start with a 4.66 ERA. In fact, Davies had been hit hard in his previous start, allowing seven hits and eight runs in six innings in a 10–2 Cubs loss to the Marlins at Wrigley Field.

But he pitched well—well, sort of—against the powerful Dodgers. The phrase *effectively wild* comes to mind, as Davies walked five in his six-inning stint in this game and threw just 58 strikes in 94 pitches.

When Davies departed the game for pinch-hitter Jake Marisnick in the top of the seventh, the Cubs already had a 3–0 lead, in part courtesy of a two-run homer hit by Willson Contreras in the sixth. Marisnick, batting with two runners on base and no one out, singled in the Cubs' fourth run of the evening.

Tepera entered in relief and issued a two-out walk but got Austin Barnes to hit a line drive at Eric Sogard at second base to end the inning.

Chafin, who had quite a bit of success as a setup man that year for the Cubs, came in to throw the eighth inning and also issued a walk, this one with one out, but then induced Max Muncy to hit into an inning-ending double play.

The Cubs didn't score in the ninth and though it was not a save situation, manager David Ross called on closer Craig Kimbrel to close things out. Kimbrel walked the first man he faced, Chris Taylor, running the Cubs' walk count on the evening to eight. That's the fourth-most walks in any no-hitter. But Kimbrel recovered quickly and struck out Cody Bellinger, Albert Pujols, and Will Smith to end the game. It was the

Cubs' 17th no-hitter and 13th since the pitching distance was established at 60 feet, six inches in 1893.

As for Kimbrel, he didn't even know there was a no-hitter going when he entered the game. Interviewed on the Cubs' Marquee Sports Network after the game, Kimbrel said, "I'm not gonna lie. I had no idea until the last out and everybody came running out. I was just locked into the game and going out there to do my job."

The Cubs have been no-hit seven times in their history, last in 2015. None of those were combined no-hitters.

There have been five combined no-hitters since the Cubs' multi-pitcher effort in 2021:

September 11, 2021: Corbin Burnes and Josh Hader for the Brewers over Cleveland

April 29, 2022: Tylor Megill, Drew Smith, Joely Rodríguez, Seth Lugo, and Edwin Díaz for the Mets over the Phillies

June 25, 2022: Cristian Javier, Hector Neris, and Ryan Pressly for the Astros over the Yankees

November 2, 2022: Cristian Javier, Bryan Abreu, Rafael Montero, and Ryan Pressly for the Astros over the Phillies in the World Series, the second World Series no-hitter

July 8, 2023: Matt Manning, Jason Foley, and Alex Lange for the Tigers over the Blue Jays

During spring training 2023, the Cubs accomplished something they had never done previously in any spring game in franchise history. What was this first?

No-hitters are rare enough during the regular season—through the end of 2023 there had been 322 in the major leagues in the 148 seasons since the National League was founded in 1876, averaging a bit more than two per season.

They're even rarer in spring training, largely because of the number of minor leaguers who play in games, frequent changes of pitchers, and a much more casual attitude to whether the team wins or loses.

On Friday, March 3, 2023, seven Cubs pitchers combined on the first spring training no-hitter in franchise history. Let's give each one of those

Cubs hurlers a shout-out: Justin Steele (two innings), Javier Assad (two), Brad Boxberger (one), Adbert Alzolay (one), Jeremiah Estrada (one), Cam Sanders (one), and Nick Burdi (one) held the San Diego Padres hitless in a 4–0 win in the Padres' spring ballpark in Peoria, Arizona, in front of 7,300 fans.

The seven hurlers issued five walks, including two by Burdi in the ninth before he ended the game on a double-play ball, and combined to strike out seven Padres hitters.

As is the case many times in no-hitters, a good defensive play helped keep it intact. Yonathan Perlaza made a running, diving catch of a fly ball to right field to end the sixth inning.

Among the Cubs' four runs in the game was a long home run by Edwin Rios to right field that traveled an estimated 430 feet.

The no-hitter was the 43rd documented spring training no-hitter, per the website nonohitters.com, which keeps track of such things, and the first since Friday, March 24, 2017, when eight Angels pitchers no-hit the Mariners at Tempe Diablo Stadium in Arizona. Thanks to Major League Baseball's new pitch timer, the Cubs' gem over the Padres took just two hours and 14 minutes to complete.

The Cubs have been involved in one other spring training no-hitter, when they were held hitless by two New York Giants pitchers, Jim Hearn and Monty Kennedy, on Monday, March 17, 1952, at Wrigley Field. Not in Chicago, though; that game was played at Wrigley Field in Los Angeles, where the Cubs had traveled from their then–spring headquarters on Catalina Island off the California coast to play an exhibition game. The Giants won the game 10–0, with the attendance a smallish 2,139. The 1952 Cubs matched the 2023 Padres in a losing no-hitter by drawing five walks.

ACKNOWLEDGMENTS

I begin by expressing my gratitude to Niels Aaboe, who was my editor for my Cubs World Series book *A Season for the Ages*, for thinking of me to write this book for Lyons Press.

Niels passed away in April 2023. I'll always be grateful for his help and guidance.

Ken Samelson, who also assisted with *A Season for the Ages*, became the editor for *Chicago Cubs Firsts*, and this book would not have been completed without his help. Many thanks to Ken for stepping in, and also thanks to Rick Rinehart, Chris Fischer, and Justine Connelly at Lyons Press for making the writing process so smooth and easy. Thanks also to Jason Rossi for his help in promoting the book.

There are some other teams covered in Lyons Press's Firsts Series, and I want to particularly thank Howie Karpin (Yankees) and Bill Nowlin (Red Sox) for sharing insights on how they put together their books, which was of great help to me in organizing *Chicago Cubs Firsts*.

One of the most important parts of this book was finding the first day that the famous "W" flag flew over Wrigley Field. In order to do that I needed several photos that showed how that came to be, photos that grace the pages of this book. From the Cubs, thanks to Julian Green, Pat Manaher, and Taylor Riskin; from Tribune Content, thanks to Rick DeChantal and Elaine Varvatos; and to the site *Remembering Wrigley Field*, thanks to Steven Shundich.

Thanks also to my friend David Sameshima for helping me find one specific image from his large library of Wrigley Field photos, as well as to my *Cubs by the Numbers* coauthor, Kasey Ignarski, for his photo of Shawon Dunston.

It is not possible to put together a book of facts like this one without considerable research, which wound up being fun, diving down many Cubs and baseball historical rabbit holes. This sort of task, though, cannot be done without assistance, which I received from Mike Bojanowski and John Wilheim, both of whose knowledge of Cubs history and lore is unparalleled.

A big thank you to Pat Hughes for graciously agreeing to write the foreword for this book. Pat is not only a great Cubs broadcaster, he is also one of the nicest human beings I have ever met.

I am eternally grateful to have been a colleague of the great baseball writer Rob Neyer, whose patient guidance made me a better writer.

Last and as always, to my partner Miriam Romain, who shares life and Cubs baseball with me every single day, and who was helpful in reading over parts of *Chicago Cubs Firsts*. To you and me always.